CONTEMPORARY FRENCH AND FRANCOPHONE NARRATOLOGY

THEORY AND INTERPRETATION OF NARRATIVE
James Phelan and Katra Byram, Series Editors

Contemporary French and Francophone Narratology

EDITED BY JOHN PIER

THE OHIO STATE UNIVERSITY PRESS
COLUMBUS

Copyright © 2020 by The Ohio State University.
All rights reserved.

Library of Congress Cataloging-in-Publication Data
Names: Pier, John, editor.
Title: Contemporary French and francophone narratology / edited by John Pier.
Other titles: Theory and interpretation of narrative series.
Description: Columbus : The Ohio State University Press, [2020] | Series: Theory and interpretation of narrative | Includes bibliographical references and index. | Summary: "Takes the pulse of recent developments in narratological research in the French-speaking countries. We see French narrative theory applied to a wide range of texts, from classical Greek myths to early modern English novels to comics and films"— Provided by publisher.
Identifiers: LCCN 2020010855 | ISBN 9780814214497 (cloth) | ISBN 0814214495 (cloth) | ISBN 9780814278451 (ebook) | ISBN 0814278450 (ebook)
Subjects: LCSH: Narration (Rhetoric) | Discourse analysis, Narrative—French-speaking countries—History and criticism. | French language—Discourse analysis.
Classification: LCC PN212 .C645 2020 | DDC 808/.0360917541—dc23
LC record available at https://lccn.loc.gov/2020010855

Other identifiers: ISBN 9780814256046 (paper) | ISBN 081425604X (paper)

Funding for this publication has been provided by the Center for Research in the Arts and Language (CNRS/EHESS), Paris.

Cover design by Laurence J. Nozik
Text design by Juliet Williams
Type set in Adobe Minion Pro

CONTENTS

Introduction
                JOHN PIER   1

CHAPTER 1   Pragmatics in Classical French Narratology and Beyond
                RAPHAËL BARONI   11

CHAPTER 2   No-Narrator Theories/Optional-Narrator Theories: Recent Proposals and Continuing Problems
                SYLVIE PATRON   31

CHAPTER 3   Narration outside Narrative
                RICHARD SAINT-GELAIS   54

CHAPTER 4   Narrator on Stage: Not a Condition but a Component for a Postdramatic Narrative Discourse
                BENOÎT HENNAUT   70

CHAPTER 5   The Poetics of Suspended Narrative
                FRANÇOISE REVAZ   92

CHAPTER 6   Discourse Analysis and Narrative Theory: A French Perspective
                JOHN PIER   110

CHAPTER 7	Regimes of Immanence, between Narratology and Narrativity	
	DENIS BERTRAND	136
CHAPTER 8	Fiction, Expanded and Updated	
	OLIVIER CAÏRA	155
CHAPTER 9	Narratology and the Test of Greek Myths: The Poetic Birth of a Colonial City	
	CLAUDE CALAME	172
CHAPTER 10	Policing Literary Theory: Toward a Collaborative Ethics of Research?	
	FRANÇOISE LAVOCAT	201

List of Contributors   223
Index   227

INTRODUCTION

JOHN PIER

The essays included in this collection seek to take the pulse of recent developments in narratological research in the French-speaking countries. An outgrowth of the structuralist movement during the 1960s and '70s, narratology in France faded into the background during the following decades for a variety of reasons as its principal actors took up other pursuits and its contributions to the understanding of narrative were either assimilated into new developments or contested by new intellectual and scholarly orientations. The interest of French researchers in narrative did not disappear, however, but tended to be assimilated into or marginalized by other concerns (Paul Ricoeur's phenomenological hermeneutics, Roland Barthes's "text theory," enunciative linguistics, etc.); few of these researchers considered themselves narratologists, even though some of their work had implications for narratology. During this period, a number of English-speaking scholars, well versed in French research, continued to work in this area (e.g., Gerald Prince, Seymour Chatman, Shlomith Rimmon-Kenan, Dorrit Cohn) while the rhetoric of fiction, closer in its origins to the Jamesian tradition than to Russian formalism and structuralism, evolved into rhetorical narratology.

The new directions in research taken during the 1990s in the US and Germany and somewhat later in the Scandinavian countries with the rise of postclassical narratology had little effect in France where, at the time, narratology continued to be associated with structuralism rather than with the paradigm changes that marked the new currents of narrative research. Nevertheless, there arose with the turn of the century a new interest in narratological issues among French researchers, and activity in the field has since intensified, spurred on, in part, by the realization that narratology cannot be summed up by its formalist and structuralist origins. It is notable that while some convergences between English-language and francophone research in the field exist, it is not the case that the classical/postclassical paradigm of narratology fully describes the situation in the French-speaking countries (see Pier 2011). This is a complex topic whose many dimensions have yet to be fully investigated. One consideration to be taken into account is that structural narratology was a less codified and decontextualized undertaking than it is sometimes made out to be: Early on, the transmedial, transcultural, and transhistorical dimensions of narrative were firmly inscribed in the structural approach to narrative, thus calling on the resources of transdisciplinarity, as can be seen in one of the founding documents, volume 8 of the journal *Communications* (1966) (see Pier 2017). Although these questions were somewhat attenuated by French scholars at the time, structural narratology was from the outset open to inquiry into the contextual aspects of narrative that postclassical narratology was later to lay claim to.[1] In any case, it would be overstating the case, as the essays included in this volume will show, to consider that recent French-language narratology reflects "the established dichotomy of text or textual vs. context or contextual" (Sommer 2012: § 4) commonly spoken of with reference to postclassical narratology.

One factor that was to have an impact on narrative theory in French-speaking countries was narrative and identity (individual, collective, cultural), as foregrounded in particular by Ricoeur in his hermeneutic philosophy, which incorporated the structural narratology of Greimas and Genette. Another is the expansion of the objects of research beyond the literary corpus to embrace narrative in the social and human sciences as a whole. It is this development, the narrative turn, which, as argued by Raphaël Baroni (2016) in an informative and insightful overview of the current state and prospects of research in narrative theory, has alerted researchers in the French-speaking countries to the renewal of narratology.[2] More recently, Baroni points out,

---

1. Marie-Laure Ryan observes that "the founding fathers of narratology recognized from the very beginning the medium transcending nature of narrative. . . . Barthes' and Bremond's wish to open up narratology to media other than literature went unfulfilled for years." She adds that "were [Barthes] alive today, he would add blogs, hypertext, and video games" (2014 [2009]: 471).

2. Appearing in volume 30 of the review *Questions de communication*, this article inspired a number of responses in the following issue that debated questions such as the pertinence of the return to the sources, whether the crisis in narratology reveals a cultural crisis, and whether

Christian Salmon's *Storytelling. La machine à fabriquer des histoires et à formater des esprits* (2007; English translation 2010) has stimulated debate over the rhetorically driven "narrativist drift" (*dérive narrativiste*), that is, the radical expansion of narrative itself (and not of narrative theory) and the unsettling impact of storytelling on all areas of social, political, and economic life.[3] At the same time, there is a certain amount of work going on in these countries that bears on transmedial, transhistorical, and transcultural phenomena, which, in a sometimes piecemeal way, draws on the narratological "toolkit" without laying claim to being properly narratological research, and this even though in a number of cases this work may be narratologically relevant. This is but one of the obstacles to mapping out and assessing narratology in these countries. Another factor to be taken into account is that few French-speaking researchers would describe themselves as feminist, postcolonial, rhetorical, cognitivist, or unnatural narratologists, although individual researchers may very well glean insights from these and various other such orientations. All in all, it would be difficult to conclude that the postclassical narratologies have decisively taken root in francophone narrative theory. But this is not to say that these developments have failed to have any echo in French-language research. An anthology of writings edited by Sylvie Patron, *Introduction à la narratologie postclassique*, published in 2018, attests to a growing interest among French speakers in the issues raised and the advances offered by this branch of research.[4] A more diverse collection of essays that nonetheless gives a fair idea of the current tendencies in French-language scholarship, "Le récit en questions," has appeared in the journal *Pratiques* under the editorship of André Petitjean (2019).

One of the main challenges faced by the narratologist is to further the understanding of narrativity in its diverse and ever-changing manifestations and to do so through the lens of perpetually evolving disciplinary, methodological, and epistemological developments without falling victim to narratological imperialism or to a blurring of the boundaries that define the specificity of narrative. Emblematic of the open-ended environment of narratological inquiry is the rise of digitally based and other interactive forms of

---

narratology can be absorbed into the information and communication sciences (Fleury and Walter 2017).

3. Salmon expresses some hostility to narratology, but ironically the reception of his book has proved the positions he stakes out to be germane to a number of issues that are now regarded as critical.

4. Included are contributions by Susan S. Lanser, James Phelan, Monika Fludernik, David Herman, Ansgar Nünning, Marie-Laure Ryan, and Brian Richardson. Also to be mentioned is Baroni's *Les Rouages de l'intrigue* (2017), which incorporates a number of principles of postclassical narratology.

storytelling, resulting in a rethinking and reconfiguration of narrative categories as they have been handed down from the study of text-based narratives.[5] Other examples can be brought to bear on this point, of course, but what is important here is that the use of narrative theories as ready-made props serving some purpose other than the exploration and understanding of narratives per se risks falling short of the heuristic potential of the narratological enterprise. What sets narratology off from other forms of theorizing about narrative is that it proceeds by critical examination of its premises, including those of its predecessors, and, where called for, by reformulating and adapting its own modus operandi appropriately.

It is this objective that the essays assembled in the present volume seek to fulfill. Well versed in French narrative theory, both classical and more recent, the authors also draw on scholarship coming from other research traditions. The result is that these contributions offer a number of syntheses and perspectives representative of recent French-language scholarship in the field that readers from other horizons may not be familiar with or that provide them with further insight into subjects they may have encountered in other contexts. Needless to say, the topics dealt with and the approaches adopted do not cover the full range of research being carried out (an undertaking that exceeds the ambition of this book), but they will, it is hoped, leave readers with a greater awareness of the directions taken by present-day French-language narratology, not to speak of new and developing themes in narrative theory generally.

•

The overall tone of the essays is set by Raphaël Baroni's "Pragmatics in Classical French Narratology and Beyond." Noting that his work on narrative tension, devoted to describing a dynamics of plot, was originally inspired by the functionally oriented approaches of Sternberg, Eco, Brooks, Phelan, and Ryan (authors critical of the formalist-structuralist framework of French narratology) as well as by Tomashevsky, Baroni proposes to take a fresh look at francophone sources of the "classical" period where, in fact, a narrative dynamics did exist, albeit in a latent and muted form. Much emphasis was laid by

---

5. The question is raised as to "how classical narratology, whose main concern has been so far texts that represent a certain combination of modes—diegetic, representational, retrospective, scripted, receptive, autonomous, determinate, and literal—can be extended to digital narratives, which are simulative rather than representational, emergent rather than scripted, participatory rather than receptive, and simultaneous rather than retrospective" (Ryan 2006: xxi).

French-speaking theoreticians on the logical structure of the *fabula*, but interaction between the text and the reader and the problems of narrative interest were not ignored, even by an author such as Greimas. For various aesthetic and ideological reasons, these questions tend, in francophone scholarship, to be relegated to popular literature even today, although their pragmatic and epistemological dimensions, Baroni concludes, have much in common with anglophone research.

In her chapter "No-Narrator Theories/Optional-Narrator Theories: A Survey of Recent Proposals and Continuing Problems," Sylvie Patron offers a critique of "pan-narrator" theories that posit a narrator for all fictional narratives, theories that, she maintains, are fundamental to classical and postclassical narratology alike. Through a systematic survey of the relevant literature, Patron sets out an argument in favor of "optional narrator" theories, dividing these theories into first and second generation, the latter encompassing a variety of analytical, ontological, inferential, and other arguments. She points, however, to the lack of historical perspective among both "optionalist" and "panist" theoreticians. To remedy this shortcoming, she calls for a scientifically conceived history of narrative theories based on the model of the history of linguistic theories as developed by the French school, an approach linked not only to historiography but also to epistemology.

"A novel is a narrative; it is also a book." So begins Richard Saint-Gelais's "Narration outside Narrative." In narratives, it is argued, there is an "inside" of the text produced by the narrator and an "outside" produced by the writer, publisher, graphic artist, and others, one being the subject of narratology, the other of paratextual studies. But the lines between the two dimensions are not impermeable, and Saint-Gelais provides a variety of examples of leakage between them: segmentation of the book into chapters, titles that are actually the words of a character, dubious attribution of epigraphs, characters' names written in colored ink, metaleptic permutations between author and narrator, and so on. Such operations suggest that reading a text as narrative involves a negotiation between text and fiction, a process that Saint-Gelais proposes to call *parafictionalization*: treating "a textual feature as *representing* a diegetic element." Among other things, this process arises out of a more general interpretive strategy through which a narratorial figure may or may not be attributed to the discourse.

The problem of the narrator is also examined by Benoît Hennaut, but in this case in the theater according to the dramaturgical approach to narration. In "Narrator on Stage: Not a Condition but a Component for a Postdramatic Narrative Discourse," Hennaut points out that narratologists (at least those who consider theater to be a narrative genre) generally focus on narratorial figures on the stage and/or in the playscript, effectively adopting the categories of textual narrative analysis. He takes exception to the condition of narratoriality based on a theoretical analogy of textual function applied to the theater, however, and adopts the principle developed by performance studies according to which performance takes precedence over text: In this view, narrative discourse is inscribed within the performance, and it is at this level that events, actionality, and other elements of narrativity are generated. Going a step farther (based on his analysis of postdramatic theatrical productions), Hennaut rules out any necessity for a narrator as a disembodied super-agent and considers performance itself to be the narrative function as expressed through the use of gesture, choreography, sound, lighting, décor, verbal language. "It is on the basis of the eventfulness engendered by performance discourse that a given performance contains narrativity."

A related problem, though in a very different genre, is addressed by Françoise Revaz in "The Poetics of Suspended Narrative": the suspensive effects of the fragmentation of narrative. By suspended narrative is understood "the sequential release of a narrative in installments, with a frequency of publication dictated by the type of publication." This type of narrative, characterized by the rhetoric of seriality and discontinuous reading, is illustrated by a corpus of two kinds: media sagas in the press such as ongoing political or economic affairs in which the writer has no control over the episodes to come, and to-be-continued stories in comics magazines, where the writer is free to determine future episodes. Such narratives challenge the Aristotelian principle of wholeness based on unity and closure, and they do so in instructively contrasting ways that Revaz spells out in detail. This can be seen, for instance, in the boundary lines between the end and the beginning of successive episodes in media sagas as compared to those found in to-be-continued stories, but also in the fact that the former, unlike the latter, defy macro-narrative ordering. Moreover, the fragmentary mode of production (found also in TV series) generates a type of narrative tension in the reading experience that tests the usual norms of works completed prior to their publication.

One of the influential developments in francophone narrative theory has been discourse analysis, the subject of John Pier's "Discourse Analysis and Narrative Theory: A French Perspective." Discourse analysis, which got underway in the late 1960s, was generated partly out of a critique of structuralism, for it prioritizes discourse in context over structure by stressing the inextricable relations between textual organization and enunciation. Most important, however, is that discourse analysis, unlike narratology, takes an interest in discourse in all its forms and in all social and disciplinary domains; in this way, narrative, though undeniably pervasive, must be situated among other forms of discourse. Pier examines the various dimensions of discourse analysis, which include text linguistics (where the relevant division is text and discourse rather than story and discourse), the theory of enunciation (Émile Benveniste), speech genres (Mikhail Bakhtin), and the scene of enunciation (Dominique Maingueneau). The latter two categories in particular provide a set of generic distinctions that make it possible to situate narrative within the vast variety of discourses without the risk of overexpansion of the categories peculiar to narrative.

For some years now, it has been considered that narrativity constitutes a release from the constraints of immanence, a formal and closed concept that cuts structures off from context. However, it is sometimes forgotten that in the earliest full treatment of the subject, in the semiotics of A. J. Greimas, the two principles, narrativity and immanence, were closely interconnected. The evolution of the relations between these principles is examined by Denis Bertrand in "Regimes of Immanence, between Narratology and Narrativity." Narrativity, regarded as central to the semiotic conception of meaning, permeates the categories of Greimassian semiotics. Later, the concept of immanence was radicalized by the members of this school at the expense of narrativity, and narratological pursuits were largely abandoned. Bertrand proposes to renew the connection between the two concepts by adopting a notion put forth by Gilles Deleuze and Félix Guattari: *regimes of immanence*. A narrative discourse consists of at least two such regimes, one structured by the narrative "said" (the enunciated) and forming the subject of narratology, the other bearing on the narrative "saying" (enunciation) and forming the subject of narrativity. The highly metadiscursive interactions between these two regimes are examined in a few passages from Cervantes's *Don Quixote*.

Fiction has long been equated with narrative mimetic fiction. However, the upsurge in the study of fiction as a general phenomenon in recent decades has altered the landscape considerably as new objects of fiction have entered the debate, rendering the distinction between fiction and nonfiction unclear. Olivier Caïra takes stock of this situation in "Fiction, Expanded and Updated." Among the many examples he mentions are, for instance, board and video games, which have a narrative content but are meant to be played rather than told or shown. Another example is interactive digital media, where improvisation is a major feature. Caïra points in particular to nonmimetic forms of fiction and simulation games in which perception and action are simulated rather than represented, another example being abstract nonmimetic games such as checkers or Tetris. To account for these and other varieties of fiction, he rehabilitates the old but neglected distinction between mimetic and mathematical or axiomatic fictions, made salient thanks in part to the rise of the digital technologies. A number of consequences of the expansion and redefinition of fiction are discussed (there is no "language" or "distinction" of fiction, the opposition of fiction and reality is irrelevant, etc.). The importance of fictional framing is stressed (see the works of Erving Goffman), and in place of the so-called fictional contract (to be entered into or not) is fiction as a social institution, establishing authority to be accepted or contested.

One of the major challenges for narratology has long been the treatment of narratives from different epochs and cultures. Claude Calame's "Narratology and the Test of Greek Myths: The Poetic Birth of a Colonial City" is a case study bearing precisely on this problem. Calame argues that "myths" in ancient Greece did not exist as such but were compiled in modern times out of heterogeneous and fragmentary stories in verse devoted to heroic characters, local events, the founding of cities, and so on that were originally performed in ritual and song, particularly during the preclassical period.[6] In his close analysis of Pindar's Fourth *Pythian Ode,* which recounts the foundation of the colonial city of Cyrene in Libya, Calame adopts the semio-narrative approach, an approach that passes from structural narratology to a pragmatically oriented narratology with a focus on the enunciative dimension of the individual narrative. In this way, it is possible to reconstruct the work's narrative syntax and semantic organization within the pragmatic framework of the production and reception of meaning. Thanks to this method, the author is able to highlight, inter alia, how elements from the natural world are integrated into a narrative program of anthropomorphic actions around themes such as autochthony.

The disciplinary status of narratology, once regarded as a method or technique of analysis, has long been a subject of debate but has gained in stature since the advent of the narrative turn and intensified transdisciplinary research by narratologists. In "Policing Literary Theory: Toward a Collaborative Ethics of Research?" Françoise Lavocat argues that in the current state of academic research, narratology offers a number of valuable prospects for the furtherance of literary studies and research in literary theory. In this well-documented study, whose aim is to consider the place of narratology in the current research environment, Lavocat discusses the rise and fall of French Theory from the 1970s to the 1990s, followed by the return, in French academia, to "common sense" and literary history. However, narratology, which maintains a scientific ambition that allows it to span disciplines as well as epochs and cultures, constitutes a collaborative undertaking with an attrac-

---

6. For a major study on Greek mythology, see Calame (2015).

tive potential in the present-day academy. Indeed, concludes Lavocat, it is a disciplinary pursuit that might serve as a model for literary theory.

•

A number of seminars, research centers, and websites exist in France and in Switzerland that will allow scholars to keep abreast of narratological research in the French-speaking countries. These include the research seminar "Recherches contemporaines en narratologie," organized under the auspices of the Centre de recherches sur les arts et le langage (Cral), a research unit at the Centre National de Recherche Scientifique (CNRS) and the Ecole des Hautes Etudes en Sciences Sociales (EHESS) in Paris, created in 2003.[7] Another center in France is the Laboratoire Interdisciplinaire Récits Cultures Sociétés (LIRCES) (formerly the Centre de Narratologie Appliquée, founded in 1984) at the Université Nice Sophia Antipolis.[8] The online review *Cahiers de narratologie*, the oldest review in the field in France, is hosted by LIRCES.[9] The Centre de recherche sur les médiations (CREM) is located at the Université de Lorraine.[10] Also to be mentioned is the Paris Center for Narrative Matters (Université Paris Diderot and The American University of Paris). Finally, in 2018 two dedicated websites, Réseau des Narratologues Francophones (RéNaF)[11] and Pôle de Narratologie Transmédiale (NaTrans), were launched at the Université de Lausanne.[12]

While there is a growing interest in new approaches to narrative theory in France and in other French-speaking countries, it cannot be said that a "school" of narratology has coalesced or that any particular method or theory prevails. It is the case, rather, that French-speaking narrative theorists are attached to addressing specific problems of narrative with appropriately adapted concepts and methods of analysis. Such is the spirit in which the contributions to this volume have been written and are now presented for public debate.

---

7. The website of the seminar, which also lists its annual program of lectures, is http://narratologie.ehess.fr/.

8. Website: http://unice.fr/laboratoires/lirces/fr/accueil. The journal *Cahiers de Narratologie* has been appearing at this center since 1987. It can be consulted online at: https://journals.openedition.org/narratologie/.

9. Website: https://journals.openedition.org/narratologie/.

10. Website: https://crem.univ-lorraine.fr/.

11. Website: https://wp.unil.ch/narratologie/renaf/.

12. Website: https://wp.unil.ch/narratologie/natrans/.

WORKS CITED

Baroni, Raphaël. 2016. "L'empire de la narratologie, ses défis et ses faiblesses." *Questions de communication* 30: 219–38.

———. 2017. *Les Rouages de l'intrigue*. Geneva: Slatkine.

Calame, Claude. 2015. *Qu'est-ce que la mythologie grecque?* Paris: Gallimard.

Fleury, Béatrice, and Jacques Walter, eds. 2017. "La narratologie dans tous ses états." Special issue, *Questions de communication* 31: 183–313.

Patron, Sylvie. 2018. *Introduction à la narratologie post-classique. Les nouvelles directions de la recherche sur le récit*. Villeneuve d'Ascq: Presses universitaires du Septentrion.

Petitjean, André, ed. 2019. "Le récit en questions." Special issue, *Pratiques*, 181–82. https://journals.openedition.org/pratiques/5593.

Pier, John. 2011. "Is There a French Postclassical Narratology?" In *Current Trends in Narratology*, edited by Gretta Olson, 336–67. Berlin: De Gruyter.

———. 2017. "Von der französischen strukturalistischen Erzähltheorie zur nordamerikanischen postklassischen Narratologie." In *Grundthemen der Literaturwissenschaft: Erzählen*, edited by Martin Huber and Wolf Schmid, 59–87. Berlin: De Gruyter.

Ryan, Marie-Laure. 2006. *Avatars of Story*. Minneapolis: University of Minnesota Press.

———. 2014. [2009]. "Narration in Various Media." In *Handbook of Narratology*, 2nd ed., edited by Peter Hühn, Jan Christoph Meister, John Pier, and Wolf Schmid, vol. 1: 468–88. Berlin: De Gruyter.

Salmon, Christian. 2010. [2007]. *Storytelling: Bewitching the Modern Mind*. Translated by David Macey. London: Verso.

Sommer, Roy. 2012. "The Merger of Classical and Postclassical Narratologies and the Consolidated Future of Narrative Theory." *DIEGESIS* 1, no. 1. https://www.diegesis.uni-wuppertal.de/index.php/diegesis/article/view/96/93#sdendnote5sym.

CHAPTER 1

Pragmatics in Classical French Narratology and Beyond

RAPHAËL BARONI

Over the past decades, many narratologists have criticized the limits of formalism and proposed new models for exploring the dynamics of narratives. From this perspective, which places more emphasis on pragmatics, but also on the new rhetoric, reception theory, cognitive science, and so on, what is at issue is not only the *form* of narrative but also its progressive *formation* in the reader's mind and its *emotional impact* (see, among others, Sternberg 1978; Eco 1979; Brooks 1992 [1984]; Phelan 1989; Ryan 1991; Herman 2002; Kafalenos 2006; Baroni 2007; Keen 2007; Dannenberg 2008). With the rise of these approaches, the focus of attention has shifted from the text-based description of narrative structures to an exploration of the interaction between narrative representation and its audience. As Dan Shen (2013) has argued, this evolution can be regarded as a recontextualization of narrative phenomena, the text being considered through the interaction between authors and readers.

The main idea I want to challenge in this chapter is the opinion that, in this debate, French narratology can only offer outdated conceptions because it was—and in some ways still is—a prisoner of a formalist paradigm. I have a personal reason to challenge this idea because in *La Tension narrative* (2007), I developed a functionalist theory of narrative sequence aimed at describing the dynamics of plot. At the time, my thinking was mostly based on French narratologists, while Anglo-American narrative theory played only a marginal role. Later, I had the feeling that I had become a member of a mostly English-speaking family. On looking more closely at my origins, however, I still have the conviction that a functionalist conception of narrative dynamics existed in the French tradition, at least in a latent form, and that my book represents only the tip of an iceberg. My aim is also to explain why this pragmatic approach remained latent for such a long time in French theory, and how this theory has evolved since its "classical" period.

1. OBJECTIVIST VERSUS FUNCTIONALIST PERSPECTIVES

An example might help to clarify the nature of the epistemological difference. This example risks oversimplifying some important issues, but it is useful, at least heuristically and tentatively, to divide narrative theorists into two distinctive communities: "Narratologists A" and "Narratologists B."[1] The following text will be used to differentiate the two paradigms:

> Senate Leader Takes Risk Pushing Public Insurance Plan
> WASHINGTON—In pushing to include a government-run health insurance plan in the health care bill, the Senate majority leader, Harry Reid, is taking a calculated gamble that the 60 members of his caucus could support the plan if it included a way for states to opt out.[2]

Now, the difference between Narratologists A and B will become obvious if we ask the following question: "Is there a plot in this text?" Of course, this question differs sharply from the following question: "Is this text a narrative?" The text might not be a good narrative, since we don't find here a complete *fabula*. Nevertheless, it must be admitted that some (perhaps most) readers will easily "*narrativize*" the text by imagining a storyworld where causality and temporality are present and where a complication would entail a possible, yet uncertain, resolution. In fact, the way one defines the dependence of narrativity and plot on textual structures or, alternatively, on the reader's cooperation is a good way to distinguish between different paradigms in narrative theory.

1. For Narratologist A, there's no plot in this text because a plot must be inherent in the representation and correspond to the logical structure of the *fabula*. Because of this incompleteness, the text should not be consid-

---

1. The "classical" versus "postclassical" paradigm does not pertain here for various reasons that cannot be discussed in this chapter, but it is clear that those using these labels are dealing with closely related issues. For a critique of "classical" versus "postclassical" narratology, see Sternberg (2011).

2. *New York Times*, October 23, 2009, A1, by Robert Pear and David M. Herszenhorn.

ered a narrative in the full sense. Following the idea that there is a homology between the grammar of sentences and the grammar of stories, Narratologist A postulates that, just as a complete sentence contains at least two parts, a subject and a predicate, so a narrative must contain at least two "macropropositions," usually defined as the "complication" and the "resolution" of the plot (van Dijk 1972; Adam 1985). In this definition, plot is related to the sequential logic of an action located at the level of the *fabula*, and it *also* corresponds to the superstructure of the narrative because the semantic logic of the *fabula* structures the text through a process of "emplotment." In this case, plot is incomplete, since only a complication can be found. And even this complication is incomplete, since what is defined as "*the* health care bill" might be quite obscure for someone who doesn't know what the political agenda of the US was at the end of 2009.

2. For Narratologist B, the perspective is quite different. The interaction between the text and the reader in a specific context becomes essential, while textual structures remain secondary. Or, more precisely, the narrative structures are important *only if* they are considered as devices aimed at triggering cognitive activities, impelling the reader to build up a mental representation of a plot "in its unresolved aspect."[3] Rhetorically and cognitively speaking, emplotment could be defined as a way to orient the reader's attention toward a possible resolution. For a functionalist like Meir Sternberg, even the narrativity of the representation relies on its capacity to arouse narrative interests such as suspense, curiosity, or surprise. As stated by Eyal Segal:

> Unlike most narratological approaches, Sternberg's defines [the] essence of narrative not in the mimetic terms of represented or narrated *action*, but rather in the rhetorical-communicative terms of narrative *interest*. This interest is aroused in the reader by the creation of informational gaps regarding any aspect of the represented world of the story—be it an event, a motive for action, a character-trait, a relationship, a viewpoint, a picture of society, or even an entire reality-model. Most basically, such gaps result from the interplay between two temporalities: that of the lifelike sequence of represented events, and that of its artful disclosure along the telling/reading sequence; or, in short, the mimetic and the textual. (2011: 302)

---

3. Hilary Dannenberg has stressed this aspect of plot: "The reading of a narrative is fuelled by two different aspects of plot. First, there is the intranarrative configuration of events and characters, which is an ontologically unstable matrix of possibilities created by plot in its still unresolved aspect. This in turn fuels the reader's *cognitive desire* to be in possession of the second aspect of plot—the final configuration achieved at narrative closure when (the reader hopes) a coherent and definitive constellation of events will have been achieved" (2008: 13).

It must be added that for Sternberg, forms "do not exist anywhere, except in the mind that makes functional sense of discourse. . . . The forms do not have any independent existence, and that is why my narrative theory is irreconcilable, and cannot be mixed up, with an approach like Genette's and most of the other theories in narratology" (2011: 41–43). In addition, in a functionalist approach like Sternberg's, a representation can be considered as a narrative even when "textual" and "mimetic" sequences remain "latent," opening up a space for the study of narrative dynamics in still pictures[4] as well as in incomplete episodes of serialized narrations. Sternberg is clear on this point: "I define narrativity as the play of suspense/curiosity/surprise between represented and communicative time (in whatever combination, whatever medium, whatever manifest or latent form)" (1992: 529).

Cognitive science has also enriched the description of narrative sequences beyond formalist perspectives. Monika Fludernik's "natural narratology" makes it possible to ground narrativity in "experientiality," namely, human experience that "typically embraces goal-oriented behavior and activity, with its reaction to obstacles encountered on the way" (1996: 29). Here, the open cognitive structure of human goals and plans becomes central, while teleological models insisting on narrative determinisms are called into question. Instead of being focused only on the internal logic of the story, cognitive scientists look into the ways that "storyworlds" are shaped by readers, using textual information coupled with cognitive schemas such as the teleological orientation of intentional actions, scripts of daily routines, generic conventions, and so on. By using the term *storyworld* instead of *story* or *fabula*, David Herman signals the nature of this shift:

> *Storyworld* points to the way interpreters of narrative reconstruct a sequence of states, events, and actions not just additively or incrementally but integratively or "ecologically"; recipients do not just attempt to piece together bits of action into a linear timeline but furthermore try to measure the significance of the timeline that emerges against other possible courses of development in the world in which narrated occurrences take place. . . . Narrative understanding requires determining how the actions and events recounted relate to what might have happened in the past, what could be happening (alternatively) in the present, and what may yet happen as a result of what already has come about. The importance of such processing strategies in narrative contexts is part of what motivates my shift from story to story*world*. (2002: 14)

---

4. The question of musical narrativity is more complex, since it is difficult to consider that instrumental music is able to articulate a mimetic sequence, even latently. See Baroni (2012).

If rhetorical and cognitivist perspectives are combined, the status of our example changes completely: It becomes a suspenseful story told by the journalist in which there are important stakes involving a "risk" and a "calculated gamble" by a protagonist as well as an "informational gap" that triggers the reader's desire to know how the story will end. In addition, the text makes a projection toward a possible resolution with "the 60 members of [the] caucus [that] *could* support the plan." Of course, the story is incomplete because the resolution remains virtual, but in this way it is like many fictions that keep readers hanging in a state of unresolved suspense, since, as a functionalist would put it, "closure" and "completeness" are two different things.[5] Everyone would agree that a suspenseful episode of a feuilleton is a narrative in the full sense of the term, even when it ends with a cliffhanger.[6] Also, we see that, from this perspective, *fabula* is not a property of the text, but rather an ever-evolving representation of a possible course of events shaped in the mind of the reader, a "storyworld" based on textual information, but also on contextual knowledge such as the memory of social events, paratext, scripts, generic conventions, intertextuality, projections, and so on.

Another important distinction between Narratologist A and Narratologist B is the fact that, for the former, the "complication" of a plot[7] (*le noeud de l'intrigue*) is a problem the character must face at an early stage of the *fabula*, while for the latter, complication is a problem confronted by the reader from the outset of the *sjuzhet* on trying to figure out what happened before or what will happen next in the story. This is an important point, because for Narratologist B the "resolution" of a conflict in the *fabula* can easily become the "complication" of a plot if the teller is skillful enough to arouse the curiosity of the reader concerning the origin of the conflict or its unfolding. This is why Sternberg, among others, insists on the fact that narrative interest always involves the interplay between the temporal sequence of the *fabula* and the teleology of the narrative representation, encompassing all possible manipulations of the chronology. Also, it is the reason why I have linked the dynamics

---

5. For a conceptualization of the difference between closure and completeness, see Phelan (1989: 17–18).

6. On cliffhangers, see Terlaak Poot (2016).

7. James Phelan (1989) considers that there is a difference between *plot* (the logical structure of the *fabula*) and *progression* (the dynamic sequence of a reader progressing in the text). In my view (see Baroni 2017: chap. 1), *plot/intrigue* is a highly polysemic notion (see Kukkonen 2014: §§ 2–5). In one of its definitions, *plot* can be equated with the concept of *progression*, while *fabula* designates more directly the logical structure of the story. The connection between *plot* and narrative dynamics is more obvious in French because "active" derivations can be drawn from the substantive *intrigue*: *intriguer* (to intrigue, to plot), *intrigant* (intriguing), *intrigué* (puzzled, intrigued), and so on. For the "meaning" of plot and intrigue, see Villeneuve (2004). Note that Dannenberg (2008: 13) and Brooks (1992 [1984]) share the dynamic definition of plot that I use in this chapter.

of plot to the "reluctance" of the "hermeneutic code" and not solely to the logic of the actions, or the "proairetic code" in Roland Barthes's terminology (more on this below).

Federico Pianzola and Franco Passalacqua have highlighted the epistemic and ontological differences between objectivist and constructivist paradigms. In the latter case, which fits perfectly to the profile of our "Narratologist B," they make the following observations:

> 1. Ontological level: the ontological status of being narrative is not a datum of (the perception of) reality, but it rather depends on the occurrence of certain pragmatic conditions. An object is not narrative in itself but becomes narrative in a particular semiotic situation. Hence, narrativity is the result of a process of construction and combination of certain processes and properties whose specificity is also dependent on extra-objectual factors: it is a construction that is the outcome of the audience-discourse relationship.
> 2. Epistemic level: the possibility of knowing/experiencing something as narrative strictly depends on the presence of specific pragmatic conditions. The perceiving subject and the discursive context (information about the author, paratext, genre specific conventions, etc.) play a key role in the constitution of the narrative object. The possibility of knowing/experiencing an object as narrative requires a particular act, a specific disposition on the part of the subject in relation to the object in a particular context. (Passalacqua and Pianzola 2016: 207–8)

To sum up, Narratologist A is mainly interested in all that belongs objectively to the text, independently of its context and pragmatic considerations, while Narratologist B focuses on the *interaction* between what is in the text—including reflections on how the author has decided to disclose narrative information—and what the reader can infer during the progressive actualization of the narrative.

2. FUNCTIONALIST CONCEPTIONS IN FRENCH STRUCTURALIST THEORY AND BEYOND

At first sight, it might be thought that the French tradition is the ideal incarnation of the "A model,"[8] while over the past decades many English-speaking

---

8. For a dissenting view, see Chambers (1984).

narratologists have switched—more or less completely and with more or less reluctance—to different avatars of the "B model." Thus, nearly thirty years ago, Sternberg denounced how narrative sequence had been conceptualized in Russian formalism and French structuralism, arguing that the "logic of action" had been de-poeticized, de-motivated, and even "de-plotted" by Propp, while Genette's theory "undermined the functional calculus of time, as of narrative structure in general" (Sternberg 1992: 485–86). Sternberg might be the most polemical critic of French structuralism, but he is far from being the only one. The need for a reconceptualization of narrative theory is also visible in the works of Peter Brooks, who claimed in 1984 that

> the study of narrative needs to move beyond the various formalist criticisms that have predominated in our time: formalisms that have taught us much, but which ultimately—as the later work of Barthes recognized—cannot deal with the dynamics of texts as actualized in the reading process. (1992 [1984]: 36)

David Herman, among others, also insists on the difference between cognitivist models of storyworlds and older conceptions of the *fabula* developed in the realm of formalism:

> The approach [of Propp] gave an overly deterministic coloration to narrative sequences. . . . Part of the interest and complexity of narrative depends on the merely probabilistic, not deterministic, links between some actions and events. (2002: 94)

Of course, Todorov, Greimas, Bremond, and Larivaille, to name but a few, have built on Propp in order to define what was supposed to be a universal concept of "narrative sequence," supposedly autonomous from the superficial level constituted by the narrative discourse and distinct from other considerations concerning rhetorical strategies and narrative interest, and, more generally, from the interactions between the text and the reader. If the reader played a role, this was only because it was assumed that the reader had the cognitive capacity to decode (and thus understand and remember[9]) what was encoded by the author.

---

9. There is a strong connection between structuralist models of narrative sequence and the first generation of cognitive psychologists who used the "schema theory" in order to figure out how a narrative is reorganized by memory. See, for example, Bartlett (1995 [1932]). The validity of the schema theory has been criticized over the years, but true or false, it was not intended to describe the cognitive dynamics of the reading process.

But things are in fact more complicated. The point I want to defend is that almost all ingredients for developing a "B model" of plot dynamics can be found in French narratology, even in the classical models developed during the late 1960s and '70s. This does not mean that French structuralists developed B models, but that B-model statements were sometimes inserted in A models together with all the consequent problems of the epistemological "commensurability" of the concepts and their subsequent applicability in narrative analysis. Even so, if the argument were based only on these B-model statements, it would be possible to develop a full functionalist model of narrative sequence.

Propp, of course, has been very influential, but he was not the only Russian theorist that French critics were reading at that time. In 1965, Todorov published a French translation of "Thematics," the famous article by Boris Tomashevsky. This article provides the following description of narrative dynamics:

> The situation of conflict creates a dramatic movement because a prolonged coexistence of two opposing principles is not possible and one will prevail. On the contrary, the situation of reconciliation does not lead to a new movement and does not arouse the reader's expectation, which is why such a situation arises at the end and is called a resolution [*dénouement*].[10] (Tomashevsky 1965 [1928]: 273–74)

It is clear that this definition is related to a type B model of plot[11] because it emphasizes the interaction between what is being told, how it is told, and how the progression of the text affects the audience. In the words of Tomashevsky, the "resolution" (*dénouement*) is located at the final part of the discourse only because it "does not awaken the reader's expectation": Thus, form is defined according to its function in the narrative interaction.

Building on Tomashevsky, in his "Introduction to the Structural Analysis of Narrative," Roland Barthes discussed the complementary nature of "catalyst" and "nucleus" (also called "cardinal function"):

---

10. All translations from the French in this essay are my own.

11. Note that, contrary to the English translation by Lemon and Reis, Todorov does not consider "sjuzhet" and "plot" as equivalents. The term "plot" is used only in relation to this definition of a dramatic movement oriented toward an uncertain resolution, thus making room for an intersequential comprehension of plot dynamics. Indeed, Tomashevsky mentions the possibility of nonchronological plots by mentioning "regressive resolutions" ("dénouements régressifs" in Todorov's translation; see Tomashevsky 1965 [1928]: 275–76). I discuss this point in Baroni (2007: 74–90).

> In order to classify a function as cardinal, all we need verify is that the action to which it refers opens (or maintains, or closes) an alternative directly affecting the continuation of the story, in other words, that it either initiates or resolves an uncertainty. If in a fragment of narrative the phone rings, it is equally possible to answer or not answer the call, procedures are bound to carry the story along different paths. On the other hand, between two cardinal functions, it is always possible to bring in subsidiary notations, which cluster around one nucleus or another, without modifying its alternative nature. . . . These catalysts are still functional, insofar as they enter into correlation with a nucleus, but their functionality is toned down, unilateral, parasitic. (Barthes 1975 [1966]: 248)

Here again, the distinction between "catalyst" and "nucleus" (the latter also defined by Barthes as "risk-laden moments of narrative") is based on their value in the discursive interaction: Functions that really matter are those opening alternatives in the reader's mind, like the "gamble" taken by Harry Reid in the example discussed above, which can also be defined as a "conflict situation" that "creates a dramatic movement." Thus, in Barthes, as in Tomashevsky, the description of a narrative form relies directly on its functional interpretation. Todorov adopted a similar view in an essay published in 1967. Close to the functionalist model later developed by Sternberg (1978), Todorov highlights the distinction between two different kinds of narrative interest: suspense and curiosity.

> We realize here that two entirely different forms of interest exist. The first can be called *curiosity*; it proceeds from effect to cause: starting from a certain effect (a corpse and certain clues) we must find its cause (the culprit and his motive). The second form is *suspense*, and here the movement is from cause to effect: we are first shown the causes, the initial *données* (gangsters preparing a heist), and our interest is sustained by the expectation of what will happen, that is, certain effects (corpses, crimes, fights). This type of interest was inconceivable in the whodunit, for its chief characters (the detective and his friend the narrator) were, by definition, immunized: nothing could happen to them. The situation is reversed in the thriller: everything is possible, and the detective risks his health, if not his life. (2013 [1966]: 229)

In the article discussed above, it is clear that the text arouses some kind of suspense, since the exposition of initial data elicits our expectation of "what will happen." In *S/Z*, his study of Balzac's story "Sarrazine," Roland Barthes proposed a deeper analysis of two sequential codes ("hermeneutic" and "proairetic") that can be associated with the two forms of narrative interest described by Todorov.[12] In the description of the "hermeneutic code," we also find a clear connection between a narrative strategy, described as "reluctance" (*réticence*), and the way it affects the reader by arousing what is defined as a "desire for the resolution":

> In fact, the hermeneutic code has a function, the one we (with Jakobson) attribute to the poetic code: just as rhyme (notably) structures the poem according to the expectation and desire for recurrence, so the hermeneutic terms structure the enigma according to the expectation and desire for its solution. The dynamics of the text (since it implies a truth to be deciphered) is thus paradoxical: it is a static dynamics: the problem is to *maintain* the enigma in the initial void of its answer; whereas the sentences quicken the story's "unfolding" and cannot help but move the story along, the hermeneutic code performs an opposite action: it must set up *delays* (obstacles, stoppages, deviations) in the flow of the discourse; its structure is essentially reactive, since it opposes the ineluctable advance of language with an organized set of stoppages: between question and answer there is a whole dilatory area whose emblem might be named "reticence," the rhetorical figure which interrupts the sentence, suspends it, turns it aside (Virgil's *Quos ego*). (Barthes 2002 [1970]: 75)

Here again, we see that the incompleteness of the news article could be interpreted, according to the "hermeneutic code," as a textual "reluctance" (even if, in this case, it is not intentional). It is precisely this reluctance that has the power to arouse in the reader's mind a "desire for resolution."

As stated by Monika Fludernik, in *Logique du récit* Bremond "makes an important contribution by incorporating in his sequential model the crucial experience of unresolved directions" (1996: 21). Thus, Bremond criticizes the determinist conception of the morphology of Propp:

---

12. The distinction between those two codes and the two narrative interests highlighted by Todorov can also be considered as ancestors of the opposition introduced by Phelan between "instabilities" and "tension": "To recognize this difference in kind I reserve the term 'instabilities' for unstable relations within story and introduce the term 'tension' for those in discourse. Some narratives progress primarily through the introduction and complication of instabilities, whereas others progress primarily through tensions, and still others progress by means of both" (Phelan 1989: 15). In my own model, I use the term "narrative tension" as a hypernym for both "suspense" and "curiosity" in order to emphasize that they are both related to the dynamics of the narrative representation.

Even if the hero always wins, and even if the listener knows this outcome in advance and requires it, this victory has dramatic interest only to the extent that the chances of failure, in competition with the strong finality of the story, manage to keep him holding his breath until the end of the fight. (1973: 21)

If we apply this conception to our example, when Harry Reid "takes risk pushing public insurance plan," his actions entail both virtualities of success and failure; the dramatic interest of this situation is directly linked to the alternatives inscribed in the sequence.

An entire book dealing with narrative interest, *Production de l'intérêt romanesque*, was published by Charles Grivel in 1973. Grivel explains that "there can be a narration only from failure—conflict—struggle" because "misfortune is tellable" ("le malheur est le dicible") (1973: 206). Grivel was in effect anticipating studies on eventfulness and tellability that have flourished in literary studies since then (see Hühn 2010, 2014 [2009]; Baroni 2014 [2009]), and this at a time when such considerations were generally confined to the study of conversational narratives. Grivel also focuses on narrative strategies aimed at arousing suspense and curiosity, highlighting, like Barthes, the importance of textual reluctance in the dynamics of reading:

> *Narrative is mystery. It is constituted as a disturbance of communication.* . . . The reader witnesses the blurring of the drama, he is faced with an event, a behavior, etc. whose meaning is unclear and whose consequences remain hidden to him. (Grivel 1973: 261–62)

Even Genette proposed a functionalist interpretation of "paralipsis": a figure described as an open omission of some important aspects of the story. This figure, associated with "completive analepsis," constituted for Genette a dynamic sequence similar to the "hermeneutic code" described by Barthes:

> This principle of deferred or postponed significance [meaning] obviously fits perfectly into the mechanism of *enigma*, analyzed by Barthes in *S/Z*; and that so sophisticated a work as the *Recherche* should use this mechanism perhaps surprises those who place this work at the antipodes of popular novels—which it no doubt is in its significance and aesthetic value, but not always in its techniques. (Genette 1980 [1972]: 57)

With this short review, I hope I have succeeded in demonstrating that "type B" statements were far from being ruled out by French critics, even at the height of structuralism. And if we consider the publication dates of Todorov, Barthes, Bremond, Grivel, and even Genette, these authors can be considered as precursors of some of the most fundamental developments of narrative theory we have witnessed in the past decades with the rise of rhetorical, functionalist, psychoanalytical, and cognitive theories. As explained by Gerald Prince:

> Classical narratology, as it is often called nowadays, makes room for pragmatics. Where it differs from its postclassical expansive successor is in the kind of room it makes and . . . in the location it assigns that room in its house. Classical narratology, though it acknowledges the significance of context, frequently neglects it by (temporarily) bracketing it, (artificially) restricting it, or making it part of the text and (unintentionally) drowning it. (2016: 17)

3. WHY NOT LOOK AFTER NARRATIVE INTEREST?

I think that the reason why type B perspectives have been minimized in French narratology is not only epistemological, but also—and maybe more profoundly or more unconsciously—ideological and aesthetic. A hint of the true nature of the problem can be found in the above quotation from Genette, where the author feels impelled to justify the fact that the mechanism of enigma can be found in a masterwork like *À la recherche du temps perdu*. Also, when Todorov was dealing with suspense and curiosity, he was using these concepts to make a distinction between two popular genres: "whodunit" and "hardboiled" novels. As for Grivel, he was dealing only with popular novels selected from one decade of the nineteenth century. The case of Barthes is even more obvious because he repeatedly insisted on the fact that both hermeneutic and proairetic codes were aspects of the novel that contemporary literature was trying to challenge. Besides, we find in Barthes's writings many criticisms of the aesthetics of suspense, described as a commercial lever aimed at pushing the reader to "'throw away' the story once it has been consumed ('devoured'), so that we can then move to another story, buy another book" (2002 [1970]: 15–16).

There is also a striking convergence between the ideological values underlying most literary theories of the '60s and '70s in France and the rise of the aesthetics of the Nouveau Roman. At that time, Alain Robbe-Grillet and Jean Ricardou talked about "plot" either as an "outdated concept" (Robbe-Grillet 1963: 31–32), inadequate for contemporary literature, or as a symptom of some kind of "totalitarianism" (Ricardou 1967: 171–72). In other words, in France, the seductive power of plot, suspense, curiosity, and all the questions revolving around tellability or narrative interests were associated with commercial issues and with outdated, popular, conservative, or right-wing aesthetics, while for all serious intellectuals true art belonged necessarily to the "writerly" (*scriptable*), in other words, the potentially unreadable or unsellable but definitely left-leaning avant-garde. Here again, I don't think that many English-speaking critics would follow French critics in considering that a successful novel must necessarily belong to popular literature, as theorized by Pierre Bourdieu in *Les Règles de l'art* (1998) through the naturalized opposition between *art* and *money*.

Even though French structuralists occasionally summoned up the workings of narrative interest and the dynamics of plot, most considered those aspects to be of little interest, and consequently they were never studied in the masterpieces of modernity. Functionalist concepts were thus marginalized in narrative theory and separated from reflections on the "logic" of the "*fabula*," of "narrative sequence" or "plot," all of these concepts being considered in formalist terms.

4. FRENCH NARRATOLOGY AFTER THE CLASSICS

When considering recent developments in narrative theory, it is important to realize that French narratology didn't freeze up entirely in the '70s. First of all, at the beginning of the '90s, there occurred a spectacular twist in the semiotic theory of Greimas. For example, Greimas developed with Jacques Fontanille a new theory called "semiotics of passions" (Greimas and Fontanille 1991). Building on this new paradigm, authors like Jacques Fontanille and Claude Zilberberg proposed a reconceptualization of plot that can be considered as a transition from model A to model B or, more accurately, as an attempt to integrate type A models into type B models.

> [At the level of] discursive transformation, the sensible form is that of the *event*, characterized by its brightness and salience, and its intelligible and extensive conversion generates a *process*, often defined as a "whole," quantifiable and divisible into aspects; conversely, the process can be grasped by the *feeling* subject only if it is modulated by the intensity that makes it an event for the observer. The correlation at the foundation of the narrative schematization of speech would thus be as follows:

event ↔ process
intensity ↔ extensity[13]
(Fontanille and Zilberberg 1998: 77)

Cognitive science has also influenced narrative theory in French-speaking countries. In the mid-1980s, Michel Fayol (1985; Fayol and Monteil 1988) helped to develop cognitive models of narrative production that incorporated reflections on the structure of intentional actions and scripts. On the side of reception theory, Bertrand Gervais wrote an essential book building bridges between Ricoeur's conception of prefiguration (or *Mimesis* I), AI studies, cognitive models, and narrative theory. Here again, we can find a typical definition of a type B model of plot:

> Suspense[14] is . . . the anticipation of what is to come together with uncertainty about what is currently happening. . . . This tension can be produced by sudden changes in the intentional portrait of the hero or by the representation of unrelated actions; and it can be the result of a play on the cognitive dimension of the action or on the practical consequences of this action, its results, its effects on the world. (Gervais 1990: 345–47)

Yet, these essays seem to have remained virtually unnoticed by English-speaking cognitive narratologists. This ignorance reveals that if, during the 1960s and '70s, a serious narratologist was supposed to be able to read French, today, it is quite the opposite: French narratologists are obliged to read and publish in English if they want to be heard by the international community of narrative theorists.

I will complete this survey by mentioning what happened to the type B model of plot in French textual linguistics and in discourse analysis. This is very important in the French context because, as stated by John Pier:

> Theoretically oriented research on narrative continued [in France], but not always under the label of narratology, some of it in non-literary fields. French discourse analysis appears to offer a conceptual and methodological framework for addressing the concerns of postclassical narratology. (2011: 336)

---

13. This definition is close to the theory of eventfulness recently developed by German narratologists such as Wolf Schmid (2003) and Peter Hühn (2010, 2014 [2009]).

14. Note that for Gervais, "suspense" must be understood as a generic term for both curiosity and suspense as described by Todorov or Sternberg. To avoid ambiguity, I have proposed to call it "narrative tension" (see Baroni 2007: 100–10).

While this is true, it still remains that there are crucial differences between some francophone linguists, notably between the text-oriented model developed by Jean-Michel Adam (1985, 1997 [1992]) and the socio-discursive interactionist perspective adopted by Jean-Paul Bronckart (1985, 1996). Following the tradition inaugurated by Propp, Adam refuses to link narrative tension to the unfolding of the narrative sequence. This reluctance is justified in his eyes by a modular conception of texts that isolates the sequential level from other pragmatic or rhetorical aspects that belong, according to him, to different layers of textuality:

> The components which Baroni reproaches text linguistics with excluding from its conception of the sequence, put briefly, *pathos* in general, as already postulated by Aristotle, do not in my opinion have anything to do with the sequential module (L2), but rather with the semantic (L3), enunciative (L4), and illocutive-argumentative (L5) modules, governed by the generic module and by intertextuality. This is the way the sequential plot is densified and dramatized. Last, it is the modular nature of this theory of text and discourse that explains why, unlike Baroni, I do not situate the thymic elements [i.e., narrative devices aiming at arousing tension] within sequential structure. (Adam 2011: 12)

In contrast to this position, I think that a "cardinal function," in arousing a "dramatic interest" (such as suspense or curiosity) that fuels the reader's "desire for resolution" (as described by Tomashevsky, Todorov, Bremond, Barthes, and others), is a sequence of some kind, maybe not in the sense of an immanent textual structure based on an internal logic of the *fabula*, but undoubtedly in an experiential sense. In any case, Adam's position contrasts with the way Bronckart describes the "dialogic status" of the narrative sequence and the way this status is connected to a strategy of "emplotment":

> While it is rarely defined as such, the dialogical status of the narrative sequence is nonetheless clear. As we have shown, whether ternary, quinary or more complex, this sequence is always characterized by the emplotment of the events narrated. [Those events] are organized in order to create and resolve a tension, and the suspense thus aroused contributes to maintaining the addressee's attention. (Bronckart 1996: 237)

In the initial version of his model (dating from 1985), Bronckart insisted even more on the centrality of textual devices whose primary function is to arouse and (later) to resolve tensions, thus grounding his analysis of the construction of textual sequences (or "planning" in his terminology) on the analysis of the interaction between the crafting of the discourse and its impact on the audience. Bronckart claims that in types of discourse related to what he characterized as "the autonomous mode" (including theoretical discourse and narration), the distance between what is discussed and the discursive act facilitates "the formulation of an overall project (or 'model of the future') geared to the purpose of the language action engaged" (1985: 51). And he continues:

> This project is characterized by "macropropositions" organized in successive phases designed to create and then resolve a tension. As noted by Labov, the goal of the narrator is to prevent his discourse from being interrupted with a "So what?" by the time he reaches the end of his discourse.... The expected effect of mono-managed planning ["planification monogérée"] can be viewed as a sheet of paper bulging up in the middle; the degree of declivity produced represents the intensity of the resulting tension, and thus the spectacular appearance of the resolution or the fall; if the declivity is insufficient, the text will be considered "flat," without "relief" and tension, and this may well risk drawing the disparaging remarks or onomatopoeia mentioned above. (51)

Here again, the function filled by narrative tension in discursive interaction governs the interpretation of the sequential organization of the discourse, thus placing pragmatic considerations before any formal description of the phases of the discourse or of the narrated actions. Even though he had the feeling he was dealing with issues closely related to the "textual sequence" theory developed by Adam (1985, 1997 [1992]), Bronckart insisted that his conception of "narrative planning" was situated wholly at the discourse level and was thus relatively independent from the logic and chronology of the *fabula*:

> Tomashevsky distinguished FABULA from SYUZHET, Genette STORY [*histoire*] from NARRATIVE DISCOURSE [*récit*], Fayol the NARRATED from NARRATION, and the distinction which exists between INVENTIO and DISPOSITIO in classical rhetoric is frequently equated with these oppositions (actually, it would be more relevant, at this level, to oppose COMPOSITIO to DISPOSITIO). Such planning operations, as we have just defined them, are clearly related to the "surface arrangement" [*disposition superficielle*] side of these conceptual pairs; the superstructural molds thus relate exclusively to SYUZHET, NARRATIVE DISCOURSE, NARRATION, or DISPOSITIO. (1985: 51)

So, in this pragmatic conception, the definition of narrative sequence is based on what Barthes calls the "hermeneutic code," and not on the "proairetic code" alone. Planning the narrative sequence is aimed at producing an effect on the audience (arousing tension and desire for a resolution), and it is only indirectly that we can link this function to some internal features of the *fabula*. For Jean-Michel Adam (1997: 48–51), in contrast, the complication phase of the narrative sequence (Pn2) has always been described as the disturbance of an initial state at the story level, this conception being directly inspired by the formalization of *fabula* as found in Larivaille (1974), a model which is itself based on Propp's morphology. Thus, there are important differences between the models developed by Adam and Bronckart: For the former, textuality and story logic come first, and pragmatic aspects (narrative tension, narrative interest of the discourse, its meaning or "point," etc.) are additional layers of the text (e.g., an explicit moral at the end of the story or a stylistic variation highlighting the expressivity of the language or the pathos of the story); for the latter, social interaction is at the foundation of the discursive planning, and thus the structure of the discourse derives from its function in a specific context. In conclusion, we see that in textual linguistics and discourse analysis developed by French and Swiss linguists since the mid-'80s, there have always been alternatives to the type A model.

5. NARRATIVE TENSION BEYOND POPULAR STORYTELLING?

I shall finish with a personal anecdote. When I first published my book on narrative tension, I thought that I was working on a general theory of plot, a theory that could be applied to all kinds of narratives, or at least to most fictions. But in France, many critics thought that I had developed a tool whose main function would be to highlight one of the essential attributes of popular storytelling.[15] Of course, narrative tension plays a major role in popular culture, but it was not my aim to use this concept in order to make a distinction between commercial productions and high-brow literature because I was (and still am) convinced that most fictions (good or bad, popular or elitist, commercial or artistic) offer infinite variations of this essential aspect of narrativity: The dynamics of plots always involves a dialectical tension between repetition and innovation, readability and writability, or (in Eco's words) over-

---

15. See, for example, the review of my book by Viviane Asselin (2007).

coded, undercoded, and creative abductions.[16] Also, after Aristotle, I believe that the aesthetic tensions we experience in fictions are probably linked to the most fundamental anthropological functions we can associate with mimetic representations. That is why I have had to deal continuously with issues concerning the literary value of plot and suspense (Baroni 2012). I have also tried (with some success, I hope) to apply my model to novels of the twentieth century (e.g., works by Michel Butor, Alain Robbe-Grillet, Charles-Ferdinand Ramuz, and Julien Gracq).[17] But in literature departments, in France and even in French-speaking Switzerland, I still feel that there is a reluctance to apply the study of the dynamics of plot to canonized literature.[18] In the best case, critics consider that this aspect has no particular interest, and in the worst case, some remain completely blind to the fact that narrative tension truly belongs to the novels they cherish.[19] Here again, my experience shows that the difference between French-speaking and English-speaking critics might lie more in aesthetics and in ideology than in epistemology.[20]

WORKS CITED

Adam, Jean-Michel. 1985. *Le Texte narratif*. Paris: Nathan.

———. 1997. [1992]. *Les Textes: Types et prototypes. Récit, description, argumentation, explication et dialogue*. 3rd ed. Paris: Nathan.

———. 2011. "The Narrative Sequence: History of a Concept and a Research Area." Paper presented at the 1st Congress of the Réseau romand de narratologie, Fribourg, May 20, 2011. http://www.unil.ch/webdav/site/fra/shared/The_narrative_sequence.pdf.

Asselin, Viviane. 2007. "L'intérêt du récit." *Acta Fabula* 8, no. 6. https://www.fabula.org/revue/document3619.php.

Baroni, Raphaël. 2007. *La Tension narrative. Suspense, curiosité et surprise*. Paris: Seuil.

———. 2012. "La valeur de l'intrigue." In *La valeur de l'œuvre littéraire, entre pôle artistique et pôle esthétique*, edited by Philippe Voisin, 23–38. Paris: Classiques Garnier.

———. 2014. [2009]. "Tellability." In *Handbook of Narratology*, 2nd ed., edited by Peter Hühn, Jan Christoph Meister, John Pier, and Wolf Schmid, vol. 2: 836–45. Berlin: De Gruyter.

———. 2017. *Les Rouages de l'intrigue*. Genève: Slatkine.

Barthes, Roland. 1975. [1966]. "An Introduction to the Structural Analysis of Narrative." *New Literary History* 6, no. 1: 237–72.

---

16. On abduction and narrative configurations, see Pier (2004, 2016: esp. 32–33).

17. See Baroni (2017).

18. It is interesting to notice that things seem to change more quickly in literary didactics. At a time when literary studies are threatened, it is has become essential to work again on narrative interest and the dynamics of empirical reading so as to spur the interest of students.

19. For a case study applied to Ramuz, Gracq, and Robbe-Grillet, see Baroni (2017).

20. I am grateful to John Pier, Federico Pianzola, Clara Mallier, Marie-Laure Ryan, and Emma Kafalenos for their helpful comments on this chapter.

———. 2002. [1970]. *S/Z*. Translated by Richard Miller. Oxford: Blackwell Publishing Ltd.
Bartlett, Frederic. 1995. [1932]. *Remembering*. Cambridge: Cambridge University Press.
Bourdieu, Pierre. 1998. *Les Règles de l'art*. Paris: Seuil.
Bremond, Claude. 1973. *Logique du récit*. Paris: Seuil.
Bronckart, Jean-Paul. 1985. "Les operations langagières." In *Le Fonctionnement des discours*, edited by Jean-Paul Bronckart et al., 37–58. Neuchâtel: Delachaux et Niestlé.
———. 1996. *Activité langagière, textes et discours. Pour un interactionnisme socio-discursif*. Neuchâtel: Delachaux et Niestlé.
Brooks, Peter. 1992. [1984]. *Reading for the Plot: Design and Intention in Narrative*. Cambridge, MA: Harvard University Press.
Chambers, Ross. 1984. *Story and Situation: Narrative Seduction and the Power of Fiction*. Minneapolis: University of Minnesota Press.
Dannenberg, Hilary P. 2008. *Coincidence and Counterfactuality: Plotting Time and Space in Narrative Fiction*. Lincoln: University of Nebraska Press.
Eco, Umberto. 1979. *The Role of the Reader: Explorations in the Semiotics of Texts*. Bloomington: Indiana University Press.
Fayol, Michel. 1985. *Le Récit et sa construction*. Neuchâtel: Delachaux et Niestlé.
Fayol, Michel, and Jean-Marc Monteil. 1988. "The Notion of Script: From General to Developmental and Social Psychology." *European Bulletin of Cognitive Psychology* 8: 335–61.
Fludernik, Monika. 1996. *Towards a 'Natural' Narratology*. London: Routledge.
Fontanille, Jacques, and Claude Zilberberg. 1998. *Tension et signification*. Paris: Mardaga.
Genette, Gérard. 1980. [1972]. *Narrative Discourse: An Essay in Method*. Translated by Jane E. Lewin. Ithaca, NY: Cornell University Press.
Gervais, Bertrand. 1990. *Récits et actions. Pour une théorie de la lecture*. Longueuil: Le Préambule.
Greimas, Algirdas Julien, and Jacques Fontanille. 1991. *Sémiotique des passions*. Paris: Seuil.
Grivel, Charles. 1973. *Production de l'intérêt romanesque*. Paris: Mouton.
Herman, David. 2002. *Story Logic: Problems and Possibilities of Narrative*. Lincoln: University of Nebraska Press.
Hühn, Peter. 2010. *Eventfulness in British Fiction*. Berlin: De Gruyter.
———. 2014. [2009]. "Event and Eventfulness." In *Handbook of Narratology*, 2nd ed., edited by Peter Hühn, Jan Christoph Meister, John Pier, and Wolf Schmid, vol. 1: 159–78. Berlin: De Gruyter.
Kafalenos, Emma. 2006. *Narrative Causalities*. Columbus: The Ohio State University Press.
Keen, Suzanne. 2007. *Empathy and the Novel*. Oxford: Oxford University Press.
Kukkonen, Karin. 2014. "Plot." In *Handbook of Narratology*, 2nd ed., edited by Peter Hühn, Jan Christoph Meister, John Pier, and Wolf Schmid, vol. 2: 706–19. Berlin: De Gruyter.
Larivaille, Paul. 1974. "L'analyse (morpho)logique du récit." *Poétique* 19: 368–88.
Passalacqua, Franco, and Federico Pianzola. 2016. "Epistemological Problems in Narrative Theory: Objectivist vs. Constructivist Paradigms." In *Narrative Sequence in Contemporary Narratology*, edited by Raphaël Baroni and Françoise Revaz, 195–217. Columbus: The Ohio State University Press.
Phelan, James. 1989. *Reading People, Reading Plots: Character, Progression, and the Interpretation of Narrative*. Chicago: The University of Chicago Press.
Pier, John. 2004. "Narrative Configurations." In *The Dynamics of Narrative Form: Studies in Anglo-American Narratology*, edited by John Pier, 239–68. Berlin: Walter de Gruyter.
———. 2011. "Is There a French Postclassical Narratology?" In *Current Trends in Narratology*, edited by Greta Olson, 336–67. Berlin: De Gruyter.

———. 2016. "The Configuration of Narrative Sequences." In *Narrative Sequence in Contemporary Narratology*, edited by Raphaël Baroni and Françoise Revaz, 20–36. Columbus: The Ohio State University Press.

Prince, Gerald. 2016. "On Narrative Sequence, Classical and Postclassical." In *Narrative Sequence in Contemporary Narratology*, edited by Raphaël Baroni and Françoise Revaz, 11–19. Columbus: The Ohio State University Press.

Ricardou, Jean. 1967. *Problèmes du nouveau roman*. Paris: Seuil.

Robbe-Grillet, Alain. 1963. *Pour un nouveau roman*. Paris: Minuit.

Ryan, Marie-Laure. 1991. *Possible Worlds, Artificial Intelligence, and Narrative Theory*. Bloomington: Indiana University Press.

Schmid, Wolf. 2003. "Narrativity and Eventfulness." In *What is Narratology? Questions and Answers Regarding the Status of a Theory*, edited by Tom Kindt and Hans-Harald Müller, 17–33. Berlin: Walter de Gruyter.

Segal, Eyal. 2011. "The 'Tel-Aviv School': A Rhetorical-Functional Approach to Narrative." In *Current Trends in Narratology*, edited by Greta Olson, 297–311. Berlin and New York: De Gruyter.

Shen, Dan. 2013. "Implied Author, Authorial Audiences, and Context: Form and History in Neo-Aristotelian Rhetorical Theory." *Narrative* 21, no. 2: 140–58.

Sternberg, Meir. 1978. *Expositional Modes and Temporal Ordering in Fiction*. Bloomington: Indiana University Press.

———. 1992. "Telling in Time (II): Chronology, Teleology, Narrativity." *Poetics Today* 13, no. 3: 463–541.

———. 2011. "Reconceptualizing Narratology: Arguments for a Functionalist and Constructivist Approach to Narrative." *Enthymema* 4: 35–50.

Terlaak Poot, Luke. 2016. "On Cliffhangers." *Narrative* 24, no. 1: 50–67.

Todorov, Tzvetan. 2013. [1966]. "The Typology of Detective Fiction." In *Modern Criticism and Theory*, edited by David Lodge and Nigel Wood, translated by Richard Howard, 225–32. London: Routledge.

Tomashevsky, Boris. 1965. [1928]. "Thématique." In *Théorie de la littérature*, edited and translated by Tzvetan Todorov, 263–307. Paris: Seuil.

van Dijk, Teun Adrianus. 1972. *Some Aspects of Text Grammars*. The Hague: Mouton.

Villeneuve, Johanne. 2004. *Le Sens de l'intrigue, ou la narrativité, le jeu et l'invention du diable*. Laval: Presses de l'Université Laval.

CHAPTER 2

No-Narrator Theories/ Optional-Narrator Theories

Recent Proposals and Continuing Problems

SYLVIE PATRON

The narrator is the fundamental concept of classical narratology and has carried on into most postclassical forms of narratology (*pan-narrator theories*). For these theories, the presence of a fictional narrator, whether overt or covert, is constitutive of the definition of fictional narrative. I propose to survey the recent scholarship challenging pan-narrator theories and favoring optionalism: the argument for the optional nature of the narrator in the theory and analysis of fictional narrative. By "recent" I mean articles or book chapters belonging to the period of new or postclassical narratology (Walsh 1997, 2007a; Gaut 2003; Kania 2005; Thomson-Jones 2007, 2009; Currie 2010; Köppe and Stühring 2011; Margolin 2011a), as distinct from those written in opposition to classical narratology (Kuroda 2014a [1973]; 2014b [1974]; 2014c [1976]; Banfield 1973, 1978a, 1978b, 1982) or even prior to the date generally thought to mark its coming into being (Hamburger 2003 [1957, 1968]).

After a few preliminary remarks concerning terminology, I will briefly present the various proposals mentioned above and the relations that exist (or not) between them as well as the proposals of the first generation (those of Kuroda and Banfield in particular). I will offer a synthesis of the main arguments put forward in favor of the optional-narrator theory. The first argument concerns the inadequacy of the arguments of the opposing theory,

---

Two prior versions of this article, in French and English, have been published in Patron (2015: 165–86, 2019: 153–68).

although optional-narrator theorists also base their views on other theoretical or critical-interpretive data. In the second section of my essay, I will emphasize the absence of historical perspective in most of the proposals in question and identify a few errors or approximations in certain presentations of the history of the concept of the narrator. In the third and final section, I will outline a contribution that could be made to the debate between pan-narrator theories and optional-narrator theories by a history of literary theories based on the model of the history of linguistic theories, as understood by the so-called French school, which is closely linked to epistemology rather than to historiography alone.

1. A SURVEY OF RECENT PROPOSALS

1.1. Terminology

A few terminological clarifications need to be established before starting in order to make the proposal clear and avoid certain epistemological ambiguities. The expression "non-narrator theory" was first used, to my knowledge, in an article by Marie-Laure Ryan (1981) to describe the positions of Émile Benveniste (1971 [1959, 1966]), Käte Hamburger (2003 [1957, 1968]), Ann Banfield (1973, 1978a, 1978b), and S.-Y. Kuroda (2014c [1976]): "This position . . . is known to specialists as the non-narrator theory of narrative fiction" (Ryan 1981: 519). The expression is used again in Ryan (1991: 67) in the form of "The No-Narrator Theory of Fiction" as well as in Ryan (1993: 601, 2001: 146, 150) and in other subsequent works and articles. This is an inadequate expression and leads to confusion; it was never used, moreover, by the theorists in question. It is inadequate because none of the theorists in question deny the fact that there is a fictional narrator in some fictional narratives. What they dispute is the assumption that there is always a fictional narrator in all fictional narratives. The prefix "no" in "no-narrator theory" can only be understood as a "passage to the limit," leading the negative part of the theory to completely absorb the positive part. The expression was never used by either Kuroda or Banfield (the other theorists being outside of the confrontation proper, both for reasons of date and reasons connected to their epistemological project). We do find an article called "No-Narrator Theory" signed by Banfield in the *Routledge Encyclopedia of Narrative Theory* (2005), but this is a commissioned article whose title was given by the editors of the volume. Among the theoretical opponents of Kuroda and Banfield, the use of the expression "no-narrator theory" is often accompanied by the idea that this theory, or different versions of it, lacks a unified model to account for fictional narratives as a whole, or even the category of fictional and nonfictional narrative together. We find one formulation of this idea in Ryan (1981: 519–20, 1991: 69). A closer examination reveals that this idea is simply a consequence of the way Ryan presents this theory, or certain versions of it, which could very easily be presented differently. Henrik Skov Nielsen (2004: 135) takes up this idea, but without offering any justifications or critical examination. Nielsen also provides us with the most clear-cut formulation of the idea, already put forward by Ryan (1991: 69), according to which this theory and its different versions cannot account for cases of fictional narrative that do have a narrator: "It has seemed impossible to make room for fictional first-person narrative in a theory that does not have room for the narrator" (Nielsen 2004: 135). This opinion is a revealing discursive fact ("no" in "no-narrator theory" is not understood as a passage to the limit over a two-sided theory, but confused with an absolute negation). However, it cannot be considered as a serious proposition concerning the structure of Hamburger's, Kuroda's, and Banfield's theories. The second-generation theorists, who will receive more attention in the rest of this essay, do not use the expression "no-narrator theory." The expression that Tilmann Köppe and Jan Stühring adopt to refer to their version or other versions of the theory is "optional-narrator theory," which is more adequate on a descriptive level (regarding this adequacy, see Kania 2005: 47; Köppe and Stühring 2011: 59 passim; Margolin 2011a: 43–44). Optional-narrator theory is opposed to pan-narrator theory, which is also itself an adequate description of the theory referred to above, according to which there is a fictional narrator in all fictional narratives.

1.2. Second Generation Optional-Narrator Theorists

Among second-generation theorists, the challenge to the theory that all fictional narratives have a fictional narrator (henceforth pan-narrator theory) takes various forms:

1. an interrogation into the identity of the narrator—in other words, and in particular, an interrogation into the endo-consistency of the concept of the narrator in narratology (see Walsh 1997, 2007a);
2. a demonstration of the argumentative weaknesses of pan-narrator theory (see Gaut 2003; Kania 2005; Thomson-Jones 2007, 2009; Köppe and Stühring 2011); and

3. a rethinking of the relationships between the author and narrator, leading to a challenge of the idea of the omnipresence of a certain type of narrator in fictional narratives (see Currie 2010).

Uri Margolin's article (2011a) needs to be presented in a little more detail. Its title, "Necessarily a Narrator or Narrator if Necessary," represents a paraphrase of the opposition between pan-narrator theory and optional-narrator theory. The article, however, does not challenge pan-narrator theory (for Margolin is the only one of the theorists in question to consider the arguments put forward by pan-narrator theory and optional-narrator theory as having equal weight). Instead, he sets himself the goal of describing the considerations (linguistic, philosophical, literary-theoretical, etc.) "which can motivate a narratologist to judge the narrator category/instance as an indispensable or as a merely optional element of his general model of literary narrative." He concludes by invoking "two recent theoretical moves which tend to circumvent the need for such a choice" (Margolin 2011a: 43): the redefinition of narratology's field of objects and reconsideration of the criteria for evaluating concepts and models. It is reasonable to suppose, however, that the refusal to choose between pan-narrator theory and optional-narrator theory and the appeal to a new transgeneric and "cognitive-instrumentalist" narratology, which would make this choice easy to circumvent, conceals an inclination toward the dominant theory, namely pan-narrator theory (see also Margolin 2009, 2011b[1]).

Among all the theorists in question, with the exception of Margolin, the challenge to pan-narrator theory is based on a certain conception of fictionality (see Walsh 1997 and especially 2007a, 2007b; Köppe and Stühring 2011; Currie 2010) or on a certain conception of art or artisticity, though in a more implicit way (this appears in particular in the comparison between literary narrative and film: see Gaut 2003; Kania 2005; Thomson-Jones 2007, 2009; see also Currie 2010). Richard Walsh is the only one of the theorists in question to explicitly take up the relationship he has with the first-generation theorists, characterized by their linguistic orientation: "Notable dissenters, on linguistic grounds, have been Käte Hamburger (2003), Ann Banfield (1982), and S.-Y. Kuroda (2014). My own objections to the narrator are based upon representational rather than linguistic criteria; hence, I shall be arguing that certain 'narrators' are outside representation, not that certain narratives function outside communication" (Walsh 2007a: 174, n. 1). In the conclusion to

---

1. The revision of Margolin 2009 (see 2014), which differs from the previous version only in section 3.6, does not offer any significant change from this point of view.

their article, Köppe and Stühring invoke the argument of the lack of theoretical unity advanced by the pan-narrator theorists against the first-generation optional-narrator theorists (see Köppe and Stühring 2011: 74 and 78, n. 43). However, it is difficult to know whether this invocation should be interpreted as an expression of solidarity with the first-generation theorists or, on the contrary, as in the case of Walsh, a desire to differentiate or highlight what is singular about their own contribution to the debate.

1.3. Arguments in Favor of Optional-Narrator Theory

In synthesizing the main arguments advanced in favor of optional-narrator theory, it is useful to make a distinction between a first part, which focuses on the scientific weakness of the arguments for pan-narrator theory, and a second part, which comprises positive arguments in favor of optional-narrator theory. We can note that most of the time, the arguments for pan-narrator theory have been advanced in response to the so-called no-narrator theory, Kuroda's and Banfield's versions of the optional-narrator theory in particular (this is a point that does not appear frequently enough in the work of the second-generation optionalists; see Köppe and Stühring 2011: 78, n. 41). The names of the arguments, on the other hand, are due to the second-generation optionalists. The fact that these arguments are reproduced from one theorist to another can be considered as a form of legitimation via consensus.

The Analytic Argument. This is presented in Gaut (2003: 235–37) and in Thomson-Jones (2007: 83) as the "a priori argument," and in Kania (2005: 47–48), Thomson-Jones (2009: 301), and Köppe and Stühring (2011: 63) as the "analytic argument." It aims to prove the existence of a fictional narrator in all fictional narratives. It is called "analytic" because its proof is based on expressing what is implicitly contained in the concept of narrative (or narration). Even though it is formulated in different ways by different theorists, the structure of the analytic argument remains globally the same:

1. Narration is an activity (an "activity of telling or showing a story," according to Thomson-Jones [2007], or "speech acts," according to Köppe and Stühring).
2. Every activity implies an agent ("someone who utters them," according to Köppe and Stühring).
3. Therefore, narration implies an agent ("the utterer," according to Köppe and Stühring). It is this agent that is called the narrator in pan-narrator theory.

For Gaut, Kania, Thomson-Jones, and Köppe and Stühring, the analytic argument does not prove what it is supposed to prove, namely the existence of a fictional narrator in all fictional narratives. What it establishes is the existence of a narrative agent, which may be called a narrator, for all narratives (see also Currie 2010: 65–67). It says nothing, however, as to the ontological status of the narrator or, shall we say, of the second narrator in the case of fictional narratives. The conclusion that all narration implies a narrator does not necessarily mean that all fictional narration implies a fictional narrator. On the other hand, if pan-narrator theorists tend to use the term "narrator" when talking about a fictional narrator, this does not mean that every instance of this term must be understood as referring to a fictional narrator. Use of the term "narrator" to refer to the author, the person in the real world who utters the story (orally or in writing), can be found among such eminent scholars as Robert Scholes and Robert Kellogg or Roland Barthes (see Spearing 2005: 17–18; Patron 2016 [2009]: 24–25).

The Ontological Gap Argument. This argument is presented under this name, but with slightly different content, in Kania (2005: 48–50) and in Köppe and Stühring (2011: 64–65). Thomson-Jones (2007: 83–84, 2009: 300–301), for her part, uses the expression "argument from means of access," which must be considered as synonymous with Kania's ontological gap argument. The ontological gap argument also aims to prove the existence of a fictional narrator in all fictional narratives. It rests on two premises:

1. We can reasonably expect an answer to how films or literary narratives are able to give us access, perceptually in the case of film, linguistically in the case of literary narrative, to information concerning fictional worlds—for brevity's sake, to fictional worlds. The obvious answer is that somebody gives us access to these fictional worlds (see Kania 2005: 48).
2. Only fictional individuals can have access to fictional worlds and thus give this access to other individuals (see Kania 2005: 48; Köppe and Stühring 2011: 64, 65).

The conclusion is that only a fictional person, who may be called a narrator and who, this time, is clearly characterized as fictional, can give us access to the fictional world of the film or of the literary narrative.

The ontological gap argument is subject to several criticisms. In Kania, in Thomson-Jones, and in Köppe and Stühring, we can identify two main ones. The first concerns the arguable nature of the first premise. Is it really reasonable to ask ourselves how films or literary narratives are able to give us access to fictional worlds? Kania draws first on George Wilson (1997: 309), a pan-narrator theorist, to remind us of the fact that there may be paradoxes or incoherencies at the very base of fictional works (we can think of narratives where the narrator is a dead character). He adds that, more commonly, whether the narrator is thinking the words we are reading, speaking them aloud, or has written them down remains indeterminate, as does the question of how we might have obtained a transcription or a copy of these words (see Kania 2005: 49; see also Thomson-Jones 2007: 84, 2009: 300–301). Similarly, Currie (2010: 77) invokes Bram Stoker's *Dracula*, where it is indeterminate how we have obtained a collection of narratives from various sources presented as forming a unity.

The other main criticism that can be made of the ontological gap argument is that postulating a fictional narrator does not resolve the problem of our access to the fictional world. The second premise suggests that a real person (the filmmaker, the actual author of the text) cannot have access to a fictional world, because he or she is situated on a different ontological level from that of the characters and events of this world. At the same time, the fictional narrator is located on an ontologically different level from the one we occupy as readers, who are real people. We are thus still faced with the same problem: that of understanding how the narrator is supposed to bridge the gap between the real world and the fictional world of the film or the literary narrative in order to provide us access to the fictional world (see Kania 2005: 51; Thomson-Jones 2007: 84; see also, formulated somewhat differently, Köppe and Stühring 2011: 65).

The Blocked Inference Argument. This argument is found under this name only in Köppe and Stühring (2011: 65–67). Actually, it represents a reformulation and further specification of the second stage of Kania's ontological gap argument (2005: 50–51) used in Thomson-Jones (2009: 299–300). It is also found in Walsh (2007a: 74) and in Margolin (2011a: 49) in an incidental manner. Its aim is to prove the necessity of attributing the illocutions (assertions, condemnations, etc.) of a fictional narrative to a fictional narrator on the basis of the fact that it would be false or absurd to attribute them to the author.

The structure of the blocked inference argument can be presented in the following way:

1. All fictional illocutions have to be attributed to someone.
2. Fictional illocutions cannot be attributed to the author.
3. Therefore, fictional illocutions have to be attributed to someone else who can be called a narrator and who must be fictional.

In the case of Köppe and Stühring, the blocked inference argument is logically fallacious due to an ambiguity in its terms. The confusion in question occurs between two interpretations of the expression "fictional illocutions," in particular in the proposition "Fictional illocutions cannot be attributed to the author." In the first interpretation, "fictional illocutions" refers to illocutions that a fictional character makes fictionally (which we can represent as "Fictionally, S utters p"). An example is "I came to Comala because I had been told that my father, a man named Pedro Páramo, lived here" in the first sentence of Juan Rulfo's *Pedro Páramo* (1994 [1955]: 3). In the second interpretation, the expression refers to illocutions concerning fictional states of affairs (represented as "S utters that, fictionally, p"). An example is "The first time Aurélien saw Bérénice, he found her frankly ugly" in the first sentence of Louis Aragon's *Aurélien* (2003 [1944]: 17; my translation). For Köppe and Stühring, while the proposition "Fictional illocutions cannot be attributed to the author" can be considered to be true according to the first interpretation, the same cannot be said in relation to the second. The theory of fiction they rely on specifically establishes that fictional illocutions in the sense of the second interpretation are precisely what the author of fictional narrative does: "A utters that, fictionally, p." For example, Aragon, in the opening sentence of *Aurélien,* generates the fictional truth that the first time Aurélien saw Bérénice, and so on. The case where fictional illocutions generate the fictional truth that a fictional narrator fictionally makes illocutions is considered as a special case. Comparable theoretical propositions can be found in Walsh (2007a: 78, 80) and in Currie (2010: 66, 70–71). On the other hand, if the proposition "Fictional illocutions cannot be attributed to the author" can be considered to be true according to the first interpretation, which concerns a special type of fictional illocutions, the two premises are not enough to establish the truth of the conclusion, which is supposed to concern all illocutions of a fictional narrative.

The Distinction of Fiction Argument. This argument bases the necessity of the author/narrator distinction on the necessity of accounting for the "distinction of fiction" (according to the expression of Cohn 1999), that is to say, what differentiates fictional discourse from nonfictional discourse. For Köppe and Stühring (2011: 67), this argument is invalid to the extent that the concept of the fictional narrator must itself be explained, and this can only be achieved on the basis of a theory of fiction. The distinction of fiction argument effects a simple reversal of the order of explanations. This idea is also at the heart of Walsh's challenge to pan-narrator theory (2007a: 72, 80). Another criticism concerns the function of the narrator in the distinction of fiction argument. Walsh puts it very clearly:

The function of the narrator is to allow the narrative to be read as something known rather than something imagined, something reported as fact rather than something told as fiction. . . . But such a view of the matter suffers the embarrassment that some of the things such an extradiegetic heterodiegetic narrator is required to "know" are clear indices of the narrative's fictional status, and so they contradict this rationale for positing such an agent. The most obvious of these occurs with internal and free focalization—that is, the narrative's access to the mind of another. (2007a: 73)

The passage goes on to reject the explanatory pertinence of the concept of the omniscient narrator, a criticism also found in Currie (2010: 68–69).

The Argument from Mediation. This argument is presented in Köppe and Stühring (2011: 68–72). It is also found in Currie (2010: 83–84) and in Thomson-Jones (2007: 78, 2009: 301) in an incidental manner. It can be presented as follows:

1. All fictional narratives display some sort of mediation.
2. There is no mediation without a mediator.
3. All fictional narratives have a mediator who can be called a narrator.

The first criticism that can be made of this argument is that "mediation" is an umbrella term that covers a variety of quite different phenomena that call for different explanations. Köppe and Stühring select three types of phenomena: the particular description of fictional events in the narrative (they speak of the "coloring" of fictional events), explicit commentaries, and evaluations. For them, to attribute mediation, in the sense of the particular description of fictional events, to a mediator or narrator should not be considered as an argument in favor of pan-narrator theory, but rather as a consequence of the prior adoption of this theory. They go on to show that the framework of optional-narrator theory can very well account for mediation: "The difference between the narratorless account of coloring and the narrator-based account can be said to be this: while the narrator-based account involves imagining of a narrator that he describes certain events under a particular description, the narratorless account involves imagining certain events under a particular description" (Köppe and Stühring 2011: 70). This position can be illustrated by the first sentence of Flaubert's *A Sentimental Education*: "On the morning of 15 September 1840 the Ville-de-Montereau was lying alongside the Quai Saint-Bernard, belching clouds of smoke, all ready to sail" (Flaubert 2008

[1869]: 3). I will return to Köppe and Stühring's analyses of explicit commentaries and evaluations in relation to the relationships between theory, analysis, and interpretation.

1.4. Other (Positive) Arguments

The positive arguments in favor of optional narrator-theory can in turn be divided into two categories: those that establish the superiority of optional-narrator theory over pan-narrator theory from the point of view of the rational criteria concerning the theory as such, and those that establish the superiority of optional-narrator theory from the point of view of its practical utility, that is, for the practice of literary interpretation.

Kania insists on the simplicity of his theory, which he calls "a minimal theory":

> As Wilson points out, if there is a fictional narrator it is usually pretty obvious from the work. If the story is told in the first person, ostensibly by someone with a different name from the author's, and it is sold as a novel, we have many good reasons to suppose that within this fiction being told there is also a fictional telling by a fictional agent. Sometimes the signs are much more subtle, as in the popular example of Henry James's "The Liar." But sometimes we have simply no reason to suppose there is a fictional telling of the story we read or see. In *The Heart of the Matter*, Graham Greene spins a good yarn, but there is no reason to posit an overarching fictional telling within it or coextensive with it. (Kania 2005: 51–52)

We find this simplicity again in Köppe and Stühring's formulation of the basic tenet of optional-narrator theory: "The basic tenet of ON [Optional-Narrator Theory] is that there is a narrator if we have good reasons to postulate a narrator. According to ON we have good reason to do this if a text explicitly or implicitly authorizes us to imagine that the story is told by a narrator" (Köppe and Stühring 2011: 73). I will not return to the criterion of theoretical unity, which is as present in Walsh (2007a: 78) as it is in Köppe and Stühring (2001: 74). To these criteria, Köppe and Stühring add that of falsifiability when they present the idea that in order to disprove optional-narrator theory on the basis of a counterexample, it would be necessary, first, to demonstrate that the example can be analyzed adequately only with recourse to a fictional narrator, and second, that the example is characterized as narratorless by optional-narrator theory—in other words, that the example chosen is indeed an authentic counterexample. On the other hand, Köppe and Stühring are much weaker on an epistemological level when they stress that the fact that a fictional narrative can be analyzed adequately only with recourse to a fictional narrator is precisely a good reason to postulate a fictional narrator. What they establish in this way is that the demonstration of falsity is impossible and thus that the theory is unfalsifiable. The revisions in the theory also need to be assessed in the light of what the new model represents better than the former one: This is the meaning of Kania's claim that "one advantage of [his] theory is that it can deal with all literary fictions," including those that have "storytelling narrators," that is to say fictional narrators who clearly signal the fictionality of the stories they tell (see Kania 2005: 52; for the notion of "storytelling" vs. "reporting narrators," Walton 1990: 368–72). Köppe and Stühring also raise the case of "storytelling narrators," presented as a possible instance of heterodiegetic narrators, that is to say narrators who are not present as characters in the story they tell (see Köppe and Stühring 2011: 62).

From the point of view of its practical, critical-interpretative applications, the first advantage of optional-narrator theory is that it allows us to eliminate "silly questions" (in the words of Walton 1990: 174–83, also used by Gaut 2003: 244, 246–47; Currie 2010: 58–60, 77) or "non-questions" (expression used by Chatman 1990: 130, quoted in Kania 2005: 49). Whether they are considered to be "silly" questions" or "non-questions," it is clear that they are illegitimate to pose and to attempt to answer (pan-narrator theorists admit this as much as the optionalists). For example, how can the narrator have direct access to the mental states of other characters? How can the narrator recount fictional events that are supposed to have occurred in the absence of any witnesses? Why, in some cases, does the narrator withhold information about the mental states of characters or other facts of the story? And so on (see Walsh 2007a: 74; Gaut 2003: 244, 247). These are logical and fully justified questions once we affirm the existence of a fictional narrator in all fictional narratives. But they no longer arise once one considers that fictional events, including events that take place inside the mind of the characters, can be given to us to imagine directly. In Kania, the antithesis of "non-questions" is "interesting critical questions":

> Whether we posit a fictional narrator in *The Heart of the Matter* or "The Liar" is a question of what it would buy us in terms of understanding these works. If I understand these works correctly, the supposition of a fictional narrator in *The Heart of the Matter* would get us no further than the intuitive understanding that Greene himself is telling the tale. On the other hand, the supposition of a fictional narrator in "The Liar" makes sense of its boss-eyed

view of the action, and gives rise to further interesting critical questions. (2005: 52)

We find the same kind of comment in Kania (2005: 52) and in Walsh (2007a: 78–79) regarding the advantage that may be gained by positing an unreliable narrator in order to account for certain inconsistencies in a narrative. As for Köppe and Stühring, they return to their analysis of explicit commentaries and evaluations in fictional narratives in order to establish the superiority of optional-narrator theory over pan-narrator theory:

> We argued that it is a matter of interpretation whether the evaluation is done by a narrator, or by some other fictional agent, or whether the passage in question is to be understood as an invitation to the reader to imaginatively evaluate a fictional state of affairs in a particular way. Now, by assuming right away that there is a narrator, could not interpreters run the risk of forgetting about some of these possibilities, and especially the possibility of there not being any fictional agent who does the evaluating? In this sense, might ON [Theory] not be pragmatically superior to PN [Theory]? (Köppe and Stühring 2011: 73)

We can mention finally that Margolin, in the first part of his article devoted to the narrator "as cognitive instrument," poses more or less the same questions but from the opposite perspective from that of the other theorists (Margolin aims rather to show the advantage that may be gained from positing a narrator, even in problematic cases; see 2011a: 55). He admits, however, that very little is to be gained by employing this concept in the case of third-person past-tense heterodiegetic narratives, in which respect he is closer to optional-narrator theorists, although without actually adopting this position (see Margolin 2011a: 56, 2011b).

The proposals of Walsh, Kania, and Köppe and Stühring, like Margolin's, remain very general. These theorists content themselves with talking about interpretation in general, at most the interpretation of such-or-such a fictional narrative, but without ever going into details. What we need now are detailed analyses of the greatest possible number and variety of fictional narratives. Only then can we understand what the relationships between theory, analysis, and interpretation in pan-narrator theory and optional-narrator theory really are and appreciate the heuristic superiority of optional-narrator theory over pan-narrator theory (see Patron 2010a, 2010b, 2013). I started doing this work in Patron (2010a), where I sought to identify the problems encountered by analysis and interpretation raised by pan-narrator theory in the case of Juan

Rulfo's *Pedro Páramo*. This montage novel is composed of two distinct parts (even though they interpenetrate in places), the first involving a fictional narrator and the second not having this narrator and being best understood as having no fictional narrator at all. In Patron (2013), which forms a pair with the first article, I tried to show the interest of optional-narrator theory not only in negative terms but also in positive terms. The example in the 2013 article is Mario Benedetti's "Cinco años de vida" ("Five Years of Life"), a "fantastic short story" in the words of the author, or an "unnatural" narrative in the terminology of contemporary unnatural narratology.

2. A GENERAL LACK OF HISTORICAL PERSPECTIVE

A common feature of the work of the second-generation optional-narrator theorists, which they also share with most of the work of the pan-narrator theorists of the same generation, is their lack of historical and meta-historical perspective (a perspective that would include reflections on the models that represent the evolution of narrative theories). I will address this question in three points, devoted, respectively, to the structure of the optional-narrator theorists' horizon of retrospection, to certain errors or approximations in reference to the history of the concept of the narrator and, finally, to the absence of what could be called the *historical argument* among optional-narrator theorists.

2.1. The Horizon of Retrospection

I borrow the notion of horizon of retrospection (*horizon de rétrospection*) from the history of linguistic theories. It refers to previous knowledge that a scientific work draws on, whether the knowledge in question is commonly shared but not referenced or comes from identifiable sources (see Auroux 1987; Puech 2006). In the case of optional-narrator theorists, the horizon of retrospection is not empty (there are more or less numerous names or references: not very many in Kania 2005, lots in Köppe and Stühring 2011). But it is fragmentary, arbitrary (why one reference rather than another?) and lacks historical depth (the oldest references are Hamburger 2003 [1957, 1968] and Kayser [2000] 1957). Above all, it seems to reflect the interests and chance readings of the individual theorist. In some cases the referencing process is absent, which does not mean a total absence in the horizon of retrospection, but rather that elements of knowledge are present in a vague way as shared knowledge. As we have seen, Walsh (2007a: 73) raises the question of the indices of fictionality, but he does not refer there or elsewhere to the work of Hamburger, who was nevertheless the first to address this question. Other elements of knowledge are referred to the most recent contributor to the debate, which signifies both a presence and an absence in the horizon of retrospection. Thus Currie (2010: 76) attributes the use or even the invention of the term "effaced narrators" to Wilson (2007). In the case of Köppe and Stühring (2011) and in that of Margolin (2011a), it is clear that the multiplication of references, including references that are not strictly contemporary, still do not take us outside a profoundly ahistorical presentism. Everything is placed on the same level: the arguments of the pan-narrator theorists in Köppe and Stühring (2011), the (linguistic, philosophical, literary-theoretical, etc.) considerations these arguments are attached to, and those of the optional-narrator theorists in Margolin (2011a).

We can also observe that references to the theories of Hamburger, Kuroda, and Banfield do not have the same status as references that are co-present with the activity of the optional-narrator theorists (e.g., Genette 1980 [1972] for Walsh; Searle 1975 or Cohn 1990 for Walsh and Köppe and Stühring; Walton 1990 for Kania, Currie, Köppe and Stühring; the works of the film theorists for Gaut, Kania, and Thomson-Jones). We have seen this in Walsh (2007a: 174, n. 1), who refers to the theories of Hamburger, Kuroda, and Banfield and simultaneously excludes them from the field of co-presence, that is to say from being used or refuted in the discussion—in short, from the dialogue with previous theories. Köppe and Stühring dilute them in a mass of uncategorized and unranked references, none of which belong to the field of co-presence: "We are by no means the first to criticize PN. Previous discussions include Banfield 1982, Morreall 1994, Weismar 1994, Walsh 1997, Ryan 2001, Gaut 2003, Kania 2005, Banfield 2005, Patron 2006, Walsh 2007, chapter 4" (Köppe and Stühring 2011: 75, n. 3). As for Margolin, he also excludes them almost immediately from his field of attention: "The arguments against the universal narrator position cited so far are familiar to us from the work of Banfield, Kuroda, and Hamburger, and have been reiterated by Patron. But this is only one part of the story, since several additional kinds of consideration are as relevant in this context. And this is where our attention turns next" (Margolin 2011a: 47). Under these conditions, there is nothing surprising in the fact that certain proposals of the optional-narrator theorists

> unknowingly repeat some of Banfield's proposals in particular: for example, the criticism of the inverted hierarchy between the fictional narrator and the language of fiction: "to treat a represented instance of narration as ontologically prior to the language doing the representing is to press the logic

of representation beyond representation itself and to make the subordinate term superordinate—that is, to assert a paradox in the name of logic" (Walsh 2007a: 80);

appear as a regression in relation to some of Hamburger's, Kuroda's, and Banfield's strong proposals: such is the case of the proposals that quite simply assimilate the role of the author of the fictional narrative with that of the narrator, either factual or fictional: "The answer I am proposing to my original question, 'Who is the narrator?' is this: the narrator is always either a character who narrates, or the author" (Walsh 2007a: 78); "unless there is some particular reason for thinking otherwise, I see no problem with the intuitive view that the person telling the story is the one who made it up— the author" (Kania 2005: 53); "we can say that Watson is the *internal* author/narrator and Doyle the *external* author/narrator"; "In the simplest cases, we have just an author/narrator, who tells a story, and in the story itself there is no narrator" (Currie 2010: 67, 74).

2.2. History of the Concept of the Narrator

Some works of the optional-narrator theorists contain errors, overt or covert, due to insufficient knowledge of the history of the concept of the narrator.

Overt: Walsh writes that "the narrator's promotion, as a concept, from a representational effect to a structural principle has occurred specifically in response to the qualities of fiction, not narrative per se" (Walsh 2007a: 69). Walsh is alluding here to the promotion of the narrator, as a concept, in classical narratology, inspired by structuralism. In this sense, his claim is false: In Barthes (1966), a major reference for Genette (1980 [1972]), the promotion of narrator is a response to the need to guarantee an "immanent" approach to fictional narrative (understood as an approach to the fictional narrative itself, removed from all external considerations; see Patron 2016 [2009]: 25–26, 32). If we go much further back in time, however, we can say that the birth of the concept of the narrator did in fact occur specifically in response to the qualities of fiction, notably with the memoir novel or first-person novel in the original sense of the term. The need for the concept of narrator, as distinct from both the author and the other fictional characters, appeared with the genre of the memoir novel, a form of autonomous first-person fictional narrative that is not embedded within a third-person fictional narrative. The issues it encapsulates are as follow:

- an "I" that is not that of the author but that of a fictional character (see above for the distinction of fiction argument and the argument from mediation);
- a "truth pact" within the fiction, it being supposed that the narrator is telling a factual story—in this case his or her life story (see above for the ontological gap argument);
- a restriction of the narrative information to what the narrator can know (see the function of the narrator in the distinction of fiction argument), but also to what the narrator can plausibly remember; and
- a more or less marked opposition between the experiencing "I" and the narrating "I."

These points can be illustrated by Marivaux's *La Vie de Marianne,* Smollett's *Adventures of Roderick Random,* and Goldsmith's *Vicar of Wakefield*—all examples taken from Anna Laetitia Barbauld in what is probably the first theoretical account of the narrator according to the traditional conception (see Barbauld 1977 [1804, 1959]; Patron 2016 [2009]: 15–17 passim, 2011 passim, 2012b: 164, 166).

Covert: Walsh takes Genette (1980 [1972]) as his point of departure and devotes a number of pages to demonstrating the incoherence of his typology of narrators, based on the double opposition "homo-/heterodiegetic" (i.e., present or absent as characters in the story they are narrating) and "extra-/intradiegetic" (i.e., present as narrators in first- or second-level narratives). Walsh is right to point out that in three out of four cases, the narrator is a character in the fiction: "There is nothing about the internal logic of fictional representation that demands a qualitative distinction between narrators and characters. Such narrators [i.e., homodiegetic extradiegetic narrators], because they are represented, *are* characters, exactly as intradiegetic narrators are" (Walsh 2007a: 72). But he should have known and made clear on this occasion that the concept of narrator was introduced into the theory precisely in order to account for the case of narratives that are homodiegetic and extradiegetic in one of the senses Genette gives to this term (it actually concerns single-level narratives, for which the distinction between intra- and extradiegetic is irrelevant). A case in point is Marivaux's *La Vie de Marianne*. The work of Kania, Currie, and Köppe and Stühring shows the same kind of errors or omissions. I will just quote Kania on the fictional character of the narrator: "The claim is *not* that the narrator is a character in the traditional sense (though this may be the case—for example, in most novels narrated in the first person), merely that it is not to be posited at the level of actuality, but rather at the fictional level" (Kania 2005: 47; see also Currie 2010: 74 and Köppe and Stühring 2011: 63–64, 67).

As for Margolin's definition of the narrator (2009: 351), taken up again in later works (2011a: 43, 44 and 2014), I refer the reader to the discussion published in the *Living Handbook of Narratology* (see Patron 2011; Margolin 2011b).

2.3. The Historical Argument

Nowhere do optional-narrator theorists appeal to what could be called the historical argument when taking on their opponents. I understand by this not the argument according to which the first concept of the narrator would be the best one (it is the best-founded empirically, but limited from the point of view of its extension) but the more general argument according to which things have not always been as they are now. The lines of history could have resulted in a different state of affairs: Nothing says that pan-narrator theory is not destined to disappear for a period of time and then possibly reappear at a later time in the same or in another form. In short, it is a relativistic argument coming within a scientific perspective that integrates history as the primordial given in narrative theory.

3. TOWARD A HISTORY OF CONCEPTS IN NARRATIVE THEORY

In the field of narrative theory, it is important to encourage historical research that combines questions concerning the structure of theories with an examination of the genesis of concepts. We can clearly see the interest of such an approach in the discipline's current state of development: It creates the conditions for this development to be effectively cumulative and not cyclical, and it means that, for example, a question such as that of the narrator, whether universal or optional, is not periodically posed and resolved in the same terms.

3.1. Principles

This type of research is based on a number of principles that have been established for some time by historians of linguistics for their discipline (see the work of Auroux and of the *Histoire des théories linguistiques* Laboratory; see also Colombat, Fournier, and Puech 2010 for a general survey).

The first principle is that of the *commensurability* of theories: However diverse the approaches and periods may be, it must always be possible to compare theoretical texts and evaluate them in terms of their aims, methods, and priorities with regard to the production of knowledge. In the case we are concerned with, we need in particular to examine the weight and validity of traditions in poetics, render these traditions commensurable with the modern theorization of the narrator, and show the continuity of sets of problems that often have the interest of being seen as radically distinct.

The second principle is *anti-teleology*. Generally speaking, the historian should refrain from appealing to teleology, in other words, explaining the past by the future. An opposition such as that between pan-narrator theories and optional-narrator theories can be a way of organizing the debate so that it harmonizes what appears as disjointed in a chronology that is neither linear nor directed by a program or end. But there are also other oppositions that partly, but only partly, overlap with the previous one (on the opposition between communicational theories of narrative and noncommunicational or poetic theories of fictional narrative, see Patron 2016 [2009], 2010a, 2012a, 2012b).

Another principle consists in accepting that every discipline has a *sanctioned* history and a *forgotten* one. A discipline does not destroy its past but integrates, assesses, and rewrites it (Auroux 1980: 8). Auroux uses the term "rate of reinscription" (*taux de réinscription*) to measure the capacity of a discipline to integrate its acquired knowledge. He opposes disciplines with a high rate of reinscription (such as mathematics) to those with a low rate of reinscription (such as linguistics, to which we could add literary theory or poetics). Where there are many theoretical ruptures in a discipline and a low rate of reinscription, the previous states of the discipline maintain a direct theoretical interest.

3.2. The Narrative Model in Historiography

Historians of linguistic theories challenge the idea that the narrative model (linear, unified, teleological) is adequate for representing the evolution of theories in the domain of the humanities. They suggest replacing this traditional model with that of series or "lines of history," which are numerous and able to intersect, become entangled, remain more or less independent, and may be longer or shorter in duration and even disappear (see Auroux 1989: 33ff., 1994: 20, 2012). It seems to me that this model can be profitably applied to the history of narrative theories. I give a few examples below, borrowing most of my characterizations of historical lines from Auroux (2012) while remaining aware that my examples are less varied and empirically grounded than those of Auroux.

A short line, with an outcome that is not universally recognized (at least among literary theorists) and that has few current extensions, is the challenge on linguistic grounds to pan-narrator theory by Kuroda and Banfield.

A long line, whose origins go back to Plato, with oscillations (and no limit moving along the timeline to the right), is the classification of modes of narration according to which either the author (more precisely the "poet") narrates or else tries to give the illusion that it is not he who is narrating but a fictional character. Walsh (1997, 2007a), Kania (2005), and Currie (2010) are clearly situated on this line. Genette (1988 [1983]: 101–2), cited in this regard by Köppe and Stühring (2011: 75, n. 2), occupies it on certain points.

There is, however, an element here that might appear problematic. Kania writes in a note that "the actual author *constitutes* the fictional world by his narration; the fictional world of *Vanity Fair* had no existence prior to Thackeray's telling, against which his reliability could be judged" (2005: 54, n. 36). In the same way, Köppe and Stühring stress the difference between David Hume telling *The History of Great Britain* and Charles Dickens telling the story of *David Copperfield*: "The latter *invites us to imagine* the story of David Copperfield without being in any way accountable for the truth of the tale. David Hume, in contrast, is committed to the truth of what he says about the history of Great Britain" (2011: 64; see also 68). Comparable claims can be found in Currie (2010: 69). They can be interpreted as the intuition of a problem concerning the use of the verb "narrate" (or "tell"), which does not mean the same thing when it refers to the author of the fictional narrative who constitutes the fictional world as it does when it refers to the narrator, real or fictional (at least in the case of reporting narrators), for whom the real or fictional world exists prior to the act of narration. In this sense, the line on which Kania, Köppe and Stühring, and Currie are situated intersects with another line of history, also long, characterized by sporadic reappearances, with one theoretical reappearance in particular provoking a rupture to the left (called an "epistemological rupture"): theorization of the role of the author of fictional narrative in opposition to that of the author of historical narrative; theorization of the role of the epic author in Hamburger.

Another line of history intersects with the preceding ones: the apprehension of the first-person fictional narrative as a particular or *marked* case of fictional narrative. This conception dates from the first theorizations of the first-person novel. It is found both in Hamburger (2003 [1957, 1968]) and in Searle (1975), although Hamburger and Searle are usually opposed to each other in other respects. Köppe and Stühring take it up, but apply the marked feature to the whole category of fictional narratives with a narrator, based on, but according to them not reducible to, the category of first-person fictional narratives: "In general, . . . it is not true that every work of fiction necessarily has a fictional narrator. The prescription to imagine being told something by a narrator is part of particular works of narrative fiction only" (2011: 62). Kania, on the other hand, shows that he is not situated on the same line of history when he writes: "Let us make clear that I do not deny the existence of fictional narrators. They most obviously exist in first-person narrated novels. Indeed, it may be that *most* novels have fictional narrators" (2005: 47).

We can furthermore note that Genette (1980 [1972]: 243–45, 1988 [1983]: 97) introduces something that was not in any of the series concerning the narrator or narration up to that point: the idea that all narratives, fictional or nonfictional, are in the first person, in other words are enunciated by an "I," whether explicit or implicit, apparent or effaced, but which, if effaced, can always be reinstated. This is the basis of the refutation undertaken by Kuroda and Banfield regarding a certain type of sentence found in fictional narratives, Japanese in the case of Kuroda, English and French in Banfield.

We can see that lines of history allow us to make the opposition between optional-narrator theorists and pan-narrator theorists more complex, since opposed theorists do not always occupy opposite lines and since some theorists are not always found on the lines where they would be expected to be. We may also find in the plurality of historical lines an explanation of the fact that "the general class of literary narrations for which any of these theorists deny a narrator is significantly unclear," according to the estimation of Wilson (2007: 77, n. 7). This effectively represents a problem for optional-narrator theory as a whole, considered in particular from the perspective of its falsifiability.

•

Unsurprisingly, the existence of a narrator in first-person fictional narratives (in a slightly broader sense than the original meaning of first-person fictional narratives, in which a character tells his or her story *or* that of another character that he or she has witnessed) is uncontroversial for optional-narrator theorists as well as for pan-narrator theorists. This narrator, in effect, is not a theoretical fiction or entity, but rather an immediate empirical object. The whole question is to know how far we can extend the application of this concept of the narrator to other sorts of fictional narratives without stripping it of its empirical determinations. This question underlies the challenge made by certain second-generation optional-narrator theorists. But these theorists themselves are not clear as to the status and place of the traditional concept of the narrator in their model.

Since reconstituting the history of a discipline is a good indicator for assessing the particular epistemological situation in which this discipline finds itself, it seems to me that the introduction of a historical perspective into the reflections of optional-narrator theorists would mark an important step in the evolution of narrative theory.

Translated from the French by Melissa McMahon

WORKS CITED

Aragon, Louis. 2003. [1944]. *Aurélien*. Paris: Gallimard.

Auroux, Sylvain. 1980. "L'histoire de la linguistique." *Langue française* 48, no. 1: 7–15.

———. 1987. "Histoire des sciences et entropie des systèmes scientifiques: les horizons de rétrospection." In *Geschichte der Sprachtheorie*, edited by Peter Schmitter, vol. 1: 20–42. Tübingen: Gunter Narr.

———. 1989. *La Révolution technologique de la grammatisation: Introduction à l'histoire des sciences du langage*. Liège: Pierre Mardaga.

———. 1994. "Introduction." In *Histoire des idées linguistiques*, edited by Sylvain Auroux, vol. 1: 13–37. Liège: Pierre Mardaga.

———. 2012. "Échelles de temps et échelles d'objets dans l'histoire de la grammaire française." *Congrès mondial de linguistique française—CMLF 2012*. http://www.shs-conferences.org or http://dx.doi.org/10.1051/shsconf/20120100337.

Banfield, Ann. 1973. "Narrative Style and the Grammar of Direct and Indirect Speech." *Foundations of Language* 10: 1–39.

———. 1978a. "The Formal Coherence of Represented Speech and Thought." *PTL* 3, no. 2: 289–314.

———. 1978b. "Where Epistemology, Style and Grammar Meet: The Development of Represented Speech and Thought." *New Literary History* 9: 415–45.

———. 1982. *Unspeakable Sentences: Narration and Representation in the Language of Fiction*. London: Routledge.

———. 2005. "No-Narrator Theory." In *Routledge Encyclopedia of Narrative Theory*, edited by David Herman, Manfred Jahn, and Marie-Laure Ryan, 396–97. London: Routledge.

Barbauld, Anna Laetitia. 1977. [1804, 1959]. "Three Ways of Telling a Story?" In *Novelists on the Novel*, edited by Miriam Allott, 258–60. London: Routledge and Kegan Paul.

Barthes, Roland. 1966. "Introduction à l'analyse structurale des récits." *Communications* 8: 1–27.

Benveniste, Émile. 1971. [1959, 1966]. "Relationships of Person in the Verb." In *Problems in General Linguistics*, translated by Mary E. Meek, 195–215. Coral Gables, FL: Miami University Press.

Chatman, Seymour. 1990. *Coming To Terms: The Rhetoric of Narrative in Fiction and Film*. Ithaca, NY: Cornell University Press.

Cohn, Dorrit. 1990. "Signposts of Fictionality: A Narratological Perspective." *Poetics Today* 11, no. 4: 775–804.

———. 1999. *The Distinction of Fiction*. Baltimore: The Johns Hopkins University Press.

Colombat, Bernard, Jean-Marie Fournier, and Christian Puech. 2010. *Histoire des idées sur le langage et les langues.* Paris: Klincksieck.

Currie, Gregory. 2010. "Authors and Narrators." In *Narratives and Narrators,* 65–85. Oxford: Oxford University Press.

Flaubert, Gustave. 2008. [1869]. *A Sentimental Education: The Story of a Young Man.* Translated by Douglas Parmée. Oxford: Oxford University Press.

Gaut, Berys. 2003. "The Philosophy of the Movies: Cinematic Narration." In *The Blackwell Guide to Aesthetics,* edited by Peter Kivy, 230–53. Oxford: Wiley-Blackwell.

Genette, Gérard. 1980. [1972]. *Narrative Discourse: An Essay in Method.* Translated by Jane E. Lewin. Ithaca, NY: Cornell University Press.

———. 1988. [1983]. *Narrative Discourse Revisited.* Translated by Jane E. Lewin. Ithaca, NY: Cornell University Press.

Hamburger, Käte. 2003. [1957, 1968]. *The Logic of Literature.* Translated by Marilynn J. Rose. Bloomington: Indiana University Press.

Kania, Andrew. 2005. "Against the Ubiquity of Fictional Narrators." *The Journal of Aesthetics and Art Criticism* 63, no. 1: 47–54.

Kayser, Wolfgang. 2000. [1957]. "Wer erzählt den Roman?" In *Texte zur Theorie der Autorschaft,* edited by Fotis Jannidis et al., 127–37. Stuttgart: Reclam.

Köppe, Tilmann, and Jan Stühring. 2011. "Against Pan-Narrator Theories." *Journal of Literary Semantics* 40: 59–80.

Kuroda, S.-Y. 2014a. [1973]. "Where Epistemology, Style and Grammar Meet—A Case Study from Japanese." In Patron 2014, 38–59.

———. 2014b. [1974]. "On Grammar and Narration." In Patron 2014, 60–70.

———. 2014c. [1976]. "Reflections on the Foundations of Narrative Theory—from a Linguistic Point of View." In Patron 2014, 71–101.

Margolin, Uri. 2009. "Narrator." In *Handbook of Narratology,* edited by Peter Hühn, John Pier, Wolf Schmid, and Jörg Schönert, 351–69. Berlin: Walter de Gruyter.

———. 2011a. "Necessarily a Narrator or Narrator If Necessary: A Short Note on a Long Subject." *Journal of Literary Semantics* 40: 43–57.

———. 2011b. "Response to Patron (Margolin Narrator Entry)." In *The Living Handbook of Narratology,* edited by Peter Hühn, Jan Christoph Meister, John Pier, and Wolf Schmid. http://hup.sub.uni-hamburg.de/lhn/index.php/Talk:Narrator.

———. 2014. "Narrator." In *The Living Handbook of Narratology,* edited by Peter Hühn, Jan Christoph Meister, John Pier, and Wolf Schmid. http://www.lhn.uni-hamburg.de/article/narrator.

Nielsen, Henrik Skov. 2004. "The Impersonal Voice in First-Person Narrative Fiction." *Narrative* 12, no. 2: 133–50.

Patron, Sylvie. 2010a. "The Death of the Narrator and the Interpretation of the Novel: The Example of *Pedro Páramo* by Juan Rulfo." Translated by Susan Nicholls. *Journal of Literary Theory* 4, no. 2: 253–72.

———. 2010b. "Introduction." In *Théorie, analyse, interprétation des récits/Theory, analysis, interpretation of narratives,* edited by Sylvie Patron, 1–18. Berne: Peter Lang.

———. 2011. "Discussion: 'Narrator.'" Translated by Susan Nicholls. In *The Living Handbook of Narratology,* edited by Peter Hühn, Jan Christoph Meister, John Pier, and Wolf Schmid. http://hup.sub.uni-hamburg.de/lhn/index.php/Talk:Narrator.

———. 2012a. "Narrative Fiction Prior to 1850: Instances of Refutation for Poetic Theories of Narration?" Translated by Susan Nicholls. *Amsterdam International Electronic Journal for Cultural Narratology* 6. http://cf.hum.uva.nl/narratology/a11_sylvie_patron.htm.

———. 2012b. "[Interview with] Sylvie Patron." Translated by Susan Nicholls. In *Narrative Theories and Poetics: 5 Questions,* edited by Peer F. Bundgård, Henrik Skov Nielsen, and Frederik Stjernfelt, 159–69. Copenhagen: Automatic Press/VIP.

———. 2013. "Unspeakable Sentences: Narration and Representation in Benedetti's 'Five Years of Life.'" Translated by Susan Nicholls. *Narrative* 31, no. 2: 243–62.

———, ed. 2014. *Toward a Poetic Theory of Narration: Essays of S.-Y. Kuroda.* Berlin: De Gruyter.

———. 2015. *La Mort du narrateur et autres essais.* Limoges: Lambert-Lucas.

———. 2016. [2009]. *Le Narrateur. Un problème de théorie narrative.* Limoges: Lambert-Lucas.

———. 2019. *The Death of the Narrator and Other Essays.* Trier: Wissenschaftlicher Verlag Trier.

Puech, Christian, ed. 2006. *Histoire des théories linguistiques et horizons de rétrospection.* Special issue, *Histoire, Épistémologie, Langage* 28, no. 1.

Rulfo, Juan. 1994. [1955]. *Pedro Páramo.* Translated by Margaret Sayers Peden. New York: Grove Press.

Ryan, Marie-Laure. 1981. "The Pragmatics of Personal and Impersonal Fiction." *Poetics* 10, no. 5: 517–39.

———. 1991. *Possible Worlds, Artificial Intelligence, and Narrative Theory.* Bloomington: Indiana University Press.

———. 1993. "Narrator." In *Encyclopedia of Contemporary Literary Theory: Approaches, Scholars, Terms,* edited by Irena R. Makaryk, 600–601. Toronto: Toronto University Press.

———. 2001. "The Narratorial Functions: Breaking Down a Theoretical Primitive." *Narrative* 9, no. 2: 146–52.

Searle, John. 1975. "The Logical Status of Fictional Discourse." *New Literary History* 6, no. 2: 319–32.

Spearing, A. C. 2005. *Textual Subjectivity: The Encoding of Subjectivity in Medieval Narratives and Lyrics.* Oxford: Oxford University Press.

Thomson-Jones, Katherine. 2007. "The Literary Origins of the Cinematic Narrator." *British Journal of Aesthetics* 47, no. 1: 76–94.

———. 2009. "Cinematic Narrators." *Philosophy Compass* 4, no. 2: 296–311.

Walsh, Richard. 1997. "Who Is the Narrator?" *Poetics Today* 18, no. 4: 495–513.

———. 2007a. "The Narrator and the Frame of Fiction." In *The Rhetoric of Fictionality: Narrative Theory and the Idea of Fiction,* 69–85, 174–75. Columbus: The Ohio State University Press.

———. 2007b. *The Rhetoric of Fictionality: Narrative Theory and the Idea of Fiction.* Columbus: The Ohio State University Press.

Walton, Kendall L. 1990. *Mimesis as Make-Believe: On the Foundations of the Representational Arts.* Cambridge, MA: Harvard University Press.

Wilson, George M. 1997. "*Le Grand Imagier* Steps Out: The Primitive Basis of Film Narration." *Philosophical Topics* 25: 295–318.

———. 2007. "Elusive Narrators in Literature and Film." *Philosophical Studies* 135, no. 1: 73–88.

CHAPTER 3

Narration outside Narrative

RICHARD SAINT-GELAIS

A novel is a narrative; it is also a book. It is, on the one hand, a discourse relating a story, involving a narration, temporal ordering, characters, actions, and settings. It is also, on the other hand, a physical object we may hold in our hands, composed of innumerable signs that include, but are not limited to, those making up the narrative. As a discipline, poetics has always been uncomfortable with this twofold dimension, which it tends to treat separately as two different sets of phenomena and questions, each calling for its own notions and methodology. In this, poetics follows the example set by Gérard Genette, who has devoted two studies to these questions, *Discours du récit: essai de méthode* in 1972 (English translation: *Narrative Discourse: An Essay in Method*, 1980) and *Seuils* in 1987 (English translation: *Paratexts: Thresholds of Interpretation*, 1997). The former is devoted to the "internal" study of narrative from an immanent perspective that puts aside extratextual factors such as the author in particular. The latter concerns the "external" approach to studying elements that belong to the book, but not to the narrative properly speaking, of which they serve as a threshold, the "undecided zone" lying between the "inside" and the "outside" of the text: the cover, illustrations, introduction, footnotes or endnotes, and so on. I say "external approach" not only because the paratext is, according to a spatial metaphor, "outside" the narrative, but mainly because the paratext is seen as the site of various negotiations between extranarratorial and extratextual agents: writer, publisher, commentators, and readers—both in the sense that a given paratext may result from such negotiations (e.g., the discussions between publisher Gaston Gallimard and writer Jean-Paul Sartre concerning the novel that was finally published under the title *La Nausée*[1]) and that paratexts play a crucial part in the emergence of reader's "horizon of expectations." The implication here is that paratextual elements are supposed to be read unproblematically, that they influence, and to some extent guide, readers when interpreting texts, but without introducing factors (uncertainties, ambiguities, contradictions) calling for elucidation.

The rationale for this methodological and conceptual split is that narrative and paratext are produced by two distinct agents, a fictional one (the narrator), and extrafictional ones (the writer, publisher, graphic artist, etc.). So we see that behind this dividing up of the bookscape there lies an ontological distinction between fiction on one side and reality on the other. This seems reasonable enough, and it may explain why narratology and paratextual studies have evolved as two independent sectors of literary theory.

Difficulties arise, though, as soon as we realize that the border between what pertains to the author and to the narrator is a blurry one. This ambivalence has traditionally been recognized through the notion of authorial intrusion, by which some critics consider segments of narratives (such as maxims, for instance) they read as more or less direct expressions of the writer's stance. This move is by no means neutral: As we all know, the claim that authors may interfere with the content of the narrative has been contested by the reaffirmation—frequent among narratologists—of the autonomy of narrative. This is not to say that writers don't have a say in the narrative of their novels, of course, but that we should, according to this view, assign such considerations to an altogether different interpretive strategy than the one called for by fiction. I deliberately use this notion of interpretive strategy, associated with Stanley Fish,[2] to stress the (often underestimated) importance of reading options when it comes to such questions. After all, there are no textual factors that compel us to ascribe a given sentence to a narrator, an implied author, or a real author; such decisions tell more about a critic's or a theoretician's set of assumptions (which is not to say that the latter are indifferent; far from it). This makes rather shaky not so much the distinction between the "inside" and the "outside" of narrative as it does the idea that this distinction exists by itself, independently of the reading process.

Consider, for instance, the famous opening of Franz Kafka's *Amerika*, in which Karl Rossmann, on entering New York City, sees the Statue of Liberty's

---

1. On this episode, see Michel Contat and Michel Rybalka's notice in the "Bibliothèque de la Pléiade" edition of *La Nausée* (1981: 1667–68).

2. *Is There a Text in This Class? The Authority of Interpretive Communities* (1980).

"arm with the sword [rising] up as if newly stretched aloft" (Kafka 1946 [1927]: 1). The sword, replacing the real statue's torch, is conspicuous enough for readers to look for a way of dealing with this anomaly. We cannot rule out that this is an authorial mistake; Kafka, after all, never went to New York City (even though he could easily have checked up on this detail). As it happens, critics are far more inclined to assume an intentional discrepancy, the purpose of which may be symbolic—but symbolic of what? Is the sword "an omen of the many chastisements in store for Kafka's victim-hero," as Adam Kirsch (2009) surmises? Or is it there "to warn the reader not to confuse Kafka's bizarre, hallucinatory landscapes with the real U. S. A.," as another commentator wrote (Heinegg 2002)?[3] Undergraduate students I have shown Kafka's description to were prone to see in this sword the effect of Karl Rossmann's mistake, not Kafka's: Seeing the Statue of Liberty in a "sudden burst of sunlight," the character, they argued, may well be experiencing here the first of many misperceptions he will have over the course of the novel. However, there is yet another possibility, namely, that this sentence is neither a mistake nor a symbol but a plain and faithful description of the Statue of Liberty—of *this* Statue of Liberty, in what would then be some kind of parallel America.

What I want to put forward, though, is not any of these interpretations but their very multiplicity and this multiplicity's consequences. Here is a text in which the theoreticians' occasional confidence about the borders of fiction is quite difficult to maintain, a point at which the reader is uncertain about the intra- or extrafictional status of a textual feature. Are we to accept this swordbearing Statue of Liberty as a reliable component of *Amerika*'s narrative and fictional world? Or is it perhaps something—blunder or symbol—superimposed on this narrative from the outside? We cannot say for sure, and this uncertainty dispels any hope not only of knowing what to make of this sword but also of tracing a clear line separating the inside and the outside of the narrative domain. Moreover, we should not restrict this "blurriness" to cases of inward-bound interferences, that is, narratives we might suspect of bearing the author's imprint. What I would like to examine in this chapter bears more on the opposite situation: cases in which we may ask ourselves whether the narrative is "spilling over into" the paratext or into elements thereof.

Let's start with relatively simple examples. Are all elements of the paratext to be attributed in every case to an extratextual agent, be it the author ("real" or "implied") or some other agent, such as the publisher? Who, for instance,

---

3. See also Klaus Mann's preface to *Amerika* in which he observes that Rossmann is "welcomed by . . . *a* Statue of Liberty furnished with an upraised sword," observing later on that "every detail of Kafka's description of American life is quite inaccurate, and yet the picture as a whole has poetical truth" (Mann 1946: viii, ix; emphasis added).

is to be held responsible for the title, the epigraph, or the segmentation of a narrative into chapters? The critical consensus about such matters seems to be that these textual zones lie outside the narrator's reach and jurisdiction, even though they may affect the interpretation of the narrative (as the title and epigraph do) or its rhythm and configuration (as the chapters do). Indeed, these factors can have significant repercussions. What is to be made, for example, of a segmentation that affects the body of the narrative but that is unbeknownst to the narrator? In a stimulating essay published thirty years ago, Randa Sabry observed that texts generally maintain "a rather massive and almost disdainful silence about the paratext. A text," she continued, "is not supposed to tell us about its title, its publication date, not even its author's name; and if the purpose of the preface and of the table of contents is, each in its own way, to give an account of the text, the text seems not even to suspect their presence which, however, remains close by" (Sabry 1987: 83; my translation). Sabry's observation suggests that this silence tends to be interpreted as a sign not so much of the text's discretion as of its effort to operate at a different level from that of the book, its producer, and its readers.

Most studies on paratextuality take this segregation for granted. Ugo Dionne's otherwise thorough study of chapter segmentation, *La voie aux chapitres. Poétique de la disposition romanesque*, has not much to say about the narrator's acknowledgment—or rather, lack of acknowledgment—of this paratextual form of segmentation (2008: 207–11). Yet, this plays directly into the reader's oscillation, on passing from one chapter to another, between two modes of apprehension, one material, the other fictional: on the one hand, turning the page and searching for the first line of the next chapter; on the other, the almost imperceptible suspension of and resumed attention to the characters and their imaginary actions and temporal and spatial settings. Segmentations of this type also contribute to the relative fragility of the narrative's always-to-be-reestablished abstraction from the materiality of the book, especially when this narrative is assumed by a narrator who may be unaware of or indifferent toward this fragmenting of the narrative flow.

Epigraphs confront us with a similar situation. Normally, they are treated as fragments that pertain to the text as a literary work, and not as belonging to the narrative or as being chosen and displayed by its narrator.[4] Reading them, we look for some meaning that the author—not the narrator—wants to impart to us. As with all conventions, this one, too, can be subverted, as it quietly is in Arkady and Boris Strugatsky's *Beetle in the Anthill* (translated from

---

4. Genette considers the possibility of attributing epigraphs to narrators in *Paratexts* (1997 [1987]: 121–22, 143).

the Russian). This novel has as its epigraph a "poem by a little boy": "Animals stood / By the door. / They didn't hide. / They were / Shot at, and / They died" (Strugatsky and Strugatsky 1980 [1979]: x). Most readers will see this as a quotation from some unidentified (but real) little boy that one, or both, of the Strugatsky brothers knew or met until, well into the novel, they come onto a scene in which a little boy shouts an almost identical poem he has composed (53). Suddenly, the epigraph is no longer an external addition clapped onto the book; it now turns out to be a fragment of the fictional world, even though the discrepancies somewhat muddle matters: The two versions of the poem differ slightly.[5] But whichever way we interpret it, this affects our assumptions about the relationship between narrative and paratext: The latter, to borrow a term from Jean Ricardou, is "captured" by the former, either because the reader considers that the epigraph belongs to the narrative or because he or she concludes that, while it lies outside the world portrayed by the narrative, the authors somehow quote a fictional character. This opens up another series of questions, of course, since authors are supposed to imagine, not quote, their characters. This is made even more striking by the fact that *Beetle in the Anthill* is a *science fiction* novel, making the idea of any contact between authors and characters especially problematic.

It is uncertain, though, whether readers will be eager to consider the alternative: that the epigraph is chosen and put there by the narrator. A similar case seems to confirm this view. Jean Ricardou's third novel, *Les lieux-dits. Petit guide d'un voyage dans le livre* (1969; English translation: *Place Names. A Brief Guide to Travels in the Book*, 2007), is dedicated to "Ed. Word." Now, this Ed. Word is not one of Ricardou's acquaintances but a character from his second novel, *La Prise de Constantinople* (1965). Here, too, we witness an apparent overflowing of fictional discourse onto the paratext. But as with the epigraph to *Beetle in the Anthill*, it is doubtful whether many readers will conclude that the narrator of *Place Names* knows Ed. Word personally (who would, then, break out of *La Prise de Constantinople*'s fictional frame) and that this narrator takes responsibility for the dedication. Still, this shows the fragility of the narrative/paratext distinction—not only in obvious cases, such as introductions written by a character in the novel, but also in more unexpected cases such as the ones considered so far. This suggests that virtually no dimension of the paratext is safe from fictionalization.

Such fictionalization may also apply to strata of the paratext that are usually deemed indifferent to their materiality, such as typography. Take, for

---

5. Such is the case in the French version of the novel. In the English translation, only punctuation distinguishes the little boy's rendition from the epigraph. I have not been able to ascertain how things stand in the Russian original.

instance, *Fools* (1992), a science fiction novel by Pat Cadigan that confronts the reader with a dazzling and disconcerting narrative in which the characters' identities seem perpetually to be on the verge of dissolution and recomposition. *Fools* is set in a futuristic world in which various technologies enable people to buy, franchise, or even snatch other people's memories and personalities. Its main three characters (Marva the actress, Marceline the "memory junkie," and Mersine the "Brain Police" agent) are caught up in such a whirl of ambiguities that the reader consistently wonders who is "possessed" by whom. Marceline is a character "played by" (in the peculiar sense that *Fools* gives to playacting) Marva until she achieves "escape velocity" and becomes convinced that she is a real person, not a theatrical character. But it appears later that Marva herself may be only an "imprint," a fake persona adopted by Mersine during a Brain Police mission. . . . One thing, though, helps readers to find their bearings: The sections narrated, respectively, by Marva, Marceline, and Mersine are printed in three different typefaces. Once this convention is understood, the reader can proceed with relative ease through the novel. However, this realization comes only gradually: The first sections make one wonder not only who the narrator is (and whether there is only one or several), but also what exactly these typographical variations mean.

So *Fools* is a text whose typography, far from being indifferent, clearly contributes to the narrative's meaning.[6] One could even reverse the relationship postulated by most comments on Cadigan's novel, in which typography serves as a clue to the characters' identities, and say that these identities emerge (to the extent that they do emerge) from the variations of typeface; that, strictly speaking, these identities are *textual* identities (to the extent the text allows them to be identities—that is, not very much).

But even the reader who is willing to grant the material text this degree of influence over its fiction will recognize that typography, in *Fools*, works in an abstract way: The three fonts do not mean anything by themselves, but only,

---

6. Cadigan's novel thus belongs to a category of novels that are "to be looked at as much as they are to be read" (Maziarczyk 2011: 169). Maziarczyk sees this as an instance of "technological metareference": "The manipulation of the physical properties of the printed codex as an object . . . makes the reader aware of the novel's dependence on the technological medium of print" (175). In the same volume, John Pier analyzes, in addition to various intricate uses of typography, the opening pages of William Gass's *Willie Masters' Lonesome Wife* (1968/69), in which a photograph of a woman "is leaning into the text at a 45-degree angle from the left, the top of her head, like her trunk, extending beyond the edge of the page as her open mouth, slightly above and to the left of the first line, seems either to exhale onto, or about to take in, a block held in her hand containing an oversized letter 'S,' the initial letter of the first word of the book" (2011: 111–12). Given that the similarity between the woman's upper lip and the "S" makes this an example of "intermedial imitation," the fact that the woman character interacts with the printed word tends to diegetize the latter.

in a Saussurean manner, through their mutual differences. Moreover, nothing suggests that the characters (none of whom gives any indication that she is *writing* her narrative) are in any way aware of this typographical device, which clearly operates on a paratextual (but narratively meaningful) level as mere indices of each segment's narrator.

In this respect, *Fools* can be contrasted with another novel using typographical features: *Murder by Fax* (1992 [1991]), by the Dutch writer Henk Elsinck. Here, too, the reader has no choice but to take notice of the material dimension of the text, since *Murder by Fax*, which is both a thriller and an epistolary novel, is made up of facsimiles of faxes that the various characters (police, members of a terrorist organization, and other people involved) send to each other. In spite of this unusual formal device, this is a bona fide detective novel in which the reader collects clues, considers suspects, and formulates hypotheses about the outcome. What is remarkable, though, is that among these clues are typographical ones: If the readers look closely enough, they may arrive at the solution to the mystery by taking into account not only the content and wording of the faxes but their printed features, as well. The main difference from Pat Cadigan's *Fools* is that the characters of *Murder by Fax* are aware of these details, for the faxes belong to the fictitious universe in which they are written, sent, and received. Consequently, a formal dimension of the text is included in the diegesis, the typography of the text being turned into a physical feature of fictitious objects.[7]

It is thus that the typographical features of the printed book potentially have crucial implications, for they may compel readers to revise the usual relationship between text and fiction. As shown by the examples above, the text may not represent the fiction but become part of it. *Murder by Fax* is thus a "fictional artifact": a text that pretends to originate, *as text*, from the fictional realm itself.[8] This, of course, is a fiction—a second-level fiction, if you will—but a fiction that the reader has no choice but to accept and build inferences from.

It would be misleading to confine this phenomenon to marginal cases such as *Murder by Fax*. The kind of narrative/book relationship I have in mind includes all kinds of cases where this book is implicated, in full or in part, in the narrative—cases in which there occurs a fictionalization of the book as such. Take, for instance, the situation that arises when a given narrator

---

7. My use of the adjective "fictitious" (and elsewhere in this chapter, "fictional") follows the distinction established by Jerzy Pelc: "'*Fictitious*' may apply to things, persons, properties, relations, events and phenomena. By '*fictional*,' on the other hand, we propose to call *expressions, sentences, writings, texts* or *works* referring to fictitious entities" (1986: 1).

8. See chapter 8 of my book *L'empire du pseudo* (1999).

is presented as responsible not only for the narrative in the strict sense but for its publication as well—in other words, situations in which the narrator assumes the role not only of an author but of *the* author of what we are reading. Such narrators, in contrast to narrators who speak or of whom one cannot say what they concretely do as narrators, not only write; they write books that exist and are read in two universes: ours and the characters'. Classical detective novels, and especially detective novel series, seem to be fond of this formula.⁹ The vast majority of Arthur Conan Doyle's novels and short stories about Sherlock Holmes are told by Holmes's friend and fellow lodger at 221B Baker Street, John H. Watson, whose well-meaning but ineffective assistance gives the stories much of their quaint charm. But Watson's diegetic role is also to provide the public with reports on Holmes's investigations. These publications even have a retroactive effect on the diegesis. This becomes clear when, at the beginning of *The Sign of Four* (1986a [1890]), Holmes comments on the way his chronicler accounted for his investigation in *A Study in Scarlet* (1986a [1887]):

> "I glanced over it," said he. "Honestly, I cannot congratulate you upon it. Detection is, or ought to be, an exact science and should be treated in the same cold and unemotional manner. You have attempted to tinge it with romanticism, which produces much the same effect as if you worked a love-story or an elopement into the fifth proposition of Euclid." (Doyle 1986a [1890]: 108–9)

This outwardness of Holmes and Watson from a book in which they were characters is slightly dizzying but is, upon reflection, the logical consequence of common assumptions about narratives. A narrator enunciates. Sometimes, this enunciation takes the form of writing. And what is more natural than to publish what one has written? But this has the disturbing effect of telescoping the inside and the outside of the narrative in a textual equivalent of a Möbius strip. We read, in the series, an account of what becomes of this series in the world of the characters. But since we, too, as readers, hold these very texts in our hands, it is tempting to assimilate our situation into that of the fictitious audience of Watson's works, as though these works were able to straddle the fictional frame and reach us not only as narratives but also *as books*.

A similar situation—the creation of a fictituous publication context by the text itself—can be found in the second volume of Cervantes's *Don Quixote*,

---

9. Tzvetan Todorov's claim that detective novels are made of narratives that "never recognize their status as books" (1971: 58; my translation), an admission that in his mind would be tantamount to stressing the imaginary character of the story, must thus be dismissed.

in which Quixote and Sancho Panza meet people who have read the first volume of their adventures. As with the public existence of Watson's texts, this results in an ontological metalepsis[10] that is highlighted, in Cervantes's novel, by the visible presence of readers in the fiction—a fiction dilated enough to include them in its scope. Doyle's device is less daring, but it rests on the same assumptions—assumptions that were later adopted by many classical detective novelists in order to justify the presence, alongside the detective, of an assistant whose main function is to see (without understanding) and to recount (without revealing too much too soon). The writerly posture of the "Watson" figures also helps to explain curious textual features that may otherwise betray the (real) author's hand. For instance, why do these narrators conceal solutions they already know perfectly well when they begin their (retrospective) narratives? The obvious answer is that they do this in order to preserve the pleasure (real) readers will experience from trying to solve the mystery by themselves. At the same time, this implies an embarrassing intrusion by the real author and may compromise verisimilitude. We thus see the advantage of having the Watson figure writing and publishing: This makes his secretiveness understandable, since he, too, has readers to baffle.

This is not to say that the narrator-as-author device plays a strictly instrumental role, for it opens the possibility of developing a second fictional strata that, however elusive, contributes to some remarkable trompe-l'œil effects. For instance, Watson scatters enticing allusions in his narratives to mysteries that Holmes has untangled (e.g., the giant rat of Sumatra, or the case of the politician, the lighthouse, and the trained cormorant[11])—mysteries that he, Watson, has not told. Thus, in the opening lines of "The Problem of Thor Bridge," (1986b [1922]: 564) Watson points out that the notes for these "unchronicled cases" are kept in a dispatch box he has deposited at Cox & Co., a bank located at Charing Cross. This incidental remark has enticed generations of Holmesians to dream (tongue in cheek) of finding this treasure box or to imagine that it was (conveniently) destroyed during the London blitz, and so on. These fans playfully extend the Watson-as-author fiction, following the tradition of Holmesian studies found in publications such as the *Baker Street Journal*. The main tenet of Holmesology consists in pretending that Watson is indeed the author of the texts, to which Holmesian scholars attribute a referential status: The presence of the name of Arthur Conan Doyle on the book covers is

---

10. See McHale (1987: 119–21, 222–27), Ryan (2006: 207–11), and Pier (2016 [2014]: § 3.2). On the use of metaleptical devices in the second volume of *Don Quixote*, see Dällenbach (1989 [1977]: 87–89, 92–93).

11. See Doyle's "The Adventure of the Sussex Vampire" (1986b [1924]: 534) and "The Adventure of the Veiled Lodger" (1986b [1927]: 624).

explained away by making him the "literary agent" of the "real" author, John H. Watson. This assumption has many implications, the main one being that Watson, as a *factual* writer, is liable to mistakes, thus enabling Holmesians to correct certain details of his narratives (dates, for instance) whenever they lead to inconsistencies (as they quite often do). What would be quite problematic in the case of fiction—namely, the identification and correction of "wrong" narratorial assertions—thus becomes licit in this curious literary game.

Once again, I would like to caution against the temptation to marginalize such cases, however zany they may seem. Holmesians are not deluded readers, unable to distinguish fiction and reality, but sophisticated readers who feign to confuse the two and, in so doing, map out a complex, collective fiction: the fiction of Holmes's and Watson's historical existence, of the latter's authorship—and the fiction of Watson's texts' nonfictionality.

This is not the only example of a fiction overlapping with the world in which the book is read. In the 1930s, Leo Bruce, in *Case with No Conclusion* (1939), took the narrator-as-writer device to parodic heights. His detective, Sergeant Beef, admonishes his companion-cum-chronicler, Townsend, for having cast him in a bad light in his previous novels; he even blames Townsend, metaleptically, for having failed to provide him with the kind of criminal cases that would have made him as famous as his "competitors," Nicholas Blake's Nigel Strangeways and Philip Macdonald's Anthony Gethryn, both of whom he explicitly mentions in his diatribe (Bruce 1984 [1939]: 7).

One of the later Maigret novels by Georges Simenon, *Les Mémoires de Maigret* (1950; English translation: *Maigret's Memoirs*, 1963), presents us with yet another variation on the narrator-as-author formula: Whereas the other novels of the series recount the commissaire's investigations through a heterodiegetic narration, *Maigret's Memoirs* has as its narrator Maigret himself, who endeavors to rectify the version of his career, life, and habits given in the previous volumes of the series. For Maigret—*this* Maigret—has read the novels that feature him. He has met Georges Simenon, whom he has befriended and to whom he has confided that he would like to write a book that would set things right: a narrative that, for once, would not be a novelization of his life and career but a truthful account thereof. This fascinating situation—in which a character corrects "his" author—is made conspicuous, in the first French edition, by an ingenious cover layout in which Simenon's name is crossed out and replaced in handscript by Maigret's, thus embodying the authorial substitution carried out in the text itself.[12]

---

12. Penguin's online edition of *Maigret's Memoirs* adopts a similar design (https://www.penguin.co.uk/books/288967/maigret-s-memoirs/).

As with Watson's authorship of Doyle's stories about Sherlock Holmes, the idea that *Maigret's Memoirs* were written by Maigret, not Simenon, is of course a fiction. But isn't fiction what readers expect when they read novels? Why should we be surprised here? The point is that normally, fictions are framed by peritextual indications (such as "novel") stipulating that they are to be read as fictions. But this works only if these indications are read confidently as lying—and operating—*outside* fiction. The texts I am considering here extend this fiction, effectively making them swallow up their own frame. The original cover of *Les Mémoires de Maigret* materializes this situation: It displays a peritext that is somewhat "invaded" by fiction and that, as a consequence, becomes a part of the fiction it is supposed to frame. Readers are thus prompted to enclose this "peritextual fiction" in a new frame that *they* have to supply in order to consider it as the fiction it is.

Granted, fictitious characters usually don't sign books—that is, real books—even if this practice was once far more frequent (consider the examples of *Gulliver's Travels* or *Robinson Crusoe*) than it is nowadays.[13] The fact remains that readers are always faced with having to make decisions about the exact limits of the fictional frame. Readers of novels such as *Murder by Fax* are asked to turn typography into an integral part of each narration. Conversely, readers who consider spelling errors as typos exclude them from the narrative realm. One may adopt a similar line of thought about factual mistakes, as does John Searle when he states the following:

> The test for what the author is committed to is what counts as a mistake. . . . [I]f Sherlock Holmes and Watson go from Baker Street to Paddington Station by a route which is geographically impossible, we will know that Conan Doyle blundered even though he has not blundered if there never was a veteran of the Afghan campaign answering to the description of John Watson, M. D. (Searle 1979 [1975]: 72)

Searle's argument seems reasonable enough even though, in fact, it rests on an imaginary example: Holmes and Watson never went from Baker Street to Paddington by a "geographically impossible" path, whatever this might mean. Holmesology, though, shows us that existing inconsistencies (of which,

---

13. An intriguing recent example is Richard Castle, a character (played by actor Nathan Fillion) in the ABC series *Castle*, in which he is a best-selling mystery writer solving "real-life" (in the fictituous world, that is) mysteries. Since then, several of "his" novels have been published by Hyperion Press, with Fillion—who admits to his not being their author, whose real identity is still uncertain, as far as I know—appearing as Richard Castle on the back covers and at book signings.

as already mentioned, there are quite a few in the Sherlock Holmes stories) may be interpreted as the narrator's blunders, not the author's. As we have seen, *Amerika*'s sword-bearing Statue of Liberty is not necessarily ascribed to Kafka's (hypothetical) ignorance about the monument's features—a hypothesis that is probably less likely to arise than other interpretations (either symbolic or diegetic) between which readers may hesitate.

•

I insist on this uncertainty of interpretation, for it seems to me that narrative theory, and especially narratology, has not always paid sufficient attention to the ambivalent status of its object. Narratives are, in a sense, fragile constructions caught between text and fiction; they are made of words but cannot disentangle themselves from the diegesis they belong to, if only because they treat characters and fictitious events as being real. (This is, after all, the classical rationale for the distinction between author and narrator: The former imagines a story, whereas the latter reports it as fact.) Narratologists like to describe their discipline as a formal one, which it is, but in the specific sense that it offers analytic instruments for describing the text's mooring in an imaginary context. To put it in another way: Narratology's way of dealing with narrative consists in exploring this narrative's—and the narrator's—status within, and relationship with, diegesis. Enlightening as it is, Pelc's distinction between the fictitious and the fictional (see note 7 in this chapter) thus appears to be porous. Narrators and their narratives are fictional, since they belong to the level of discourse, but they are also fictitious: They cannot be disentangled from the realm of fiction.

What we must understand, here, is that narration and all the phenomena coming under its scope (narrator, narrative stance, focalization, and so on) is, to a larger extent than narratologists are usually willing to admit, the combined result of writing and interpretive processes and strategies. To read a text as narrative involves a series of decisions that mold one's relation to both text and fiction. A useful tool for describing this is, I submit, the notion of *parafictionalization*.[14] Parafictionalization is what a reader does when he or she treats a textual feature as embodying a diegetic element. Such a process does not so much erase this textual feature as "translate" it into a component of the diegesis. Consider a simple example. In a famous scene from *Madame Bovary* in which Charles asks Rouault for his daughter's hand, the former addresses the latter, first as "Maître Rouault," then as "Père Rouault" (Flau-

---

14. See Saint-Gelais (1994: 165–71).

bert 1986 [1857]: 84). This slight difference, lost in the English translation (in which Charles sticks to "Monsieur Rouault"), is likely to be noticed by readers of the French text, who will not deem it meaningless but will probably see in it instead the sign of Charles's understanding of the significance of Rouault's favorable, if tacit, response. To parafictionalize is to infer diegetic results from a given textual feature while at the same time seeing these results as forming part of the content of the work, and not as products of the reading process. My students' supposition that *Amerika*'s Karl Rossmann does not see the Statue of Liberty correctly is also a parafictionalization, as is, on another level, my own hypothesis that Kafka's novel depicts an alternate-world New York (and America). In contrast, Adam Kirsch's symbolic interpretation, or the supposition of a mistake committed by Kafka, are not parafictionalizations, for they do not result in a *diegetic* account of a textual phenomenon.

Now, narration and narrators are, to a larger extent than we usually admit, results of such a parafictionalization process. A text "has" a narrator when, and if, readers feel justified in performing the relevant parafictionalization, that is, when and if they assign textual features (such as evaluative utterances) to a fictitious enunciator, however impersonal and abstract they may be.[15] I would go as far as to suggest that a narrative may be seen as having a narrator or not as the reader goes through it and is alternately encouraged to and prevented from attributing a narrator to what is read. *Madame Bovary*'s famous opening pages, with their soon-to-vanish narratorial "nous," immediately come to mind in this respect. But one could also mention Jean Ricardou's *La Prise de Constantinople*, in which various I-narrators appear and disappear through the pages, or even S. S. Van Dine's Philo Vance mysteries, in which the homodiegetic narrator (named Van) becomes so inconspicuous after a few introductory pages that most readers probably end up forgetting there was a narrator (and a corresponding character!) in the first place.

The limits one sets to this parafictional process determine what one is ready to put under the narrative scope, and what to set aside from it. We've seen that paratexts, as a general rule, are excluded from narratives: Readers don't normally include them in parafictional operations. But such an exclusion is suspended as soon as readers have reasons to conclude otherwise, as with *Beetle in the Anthill, Murder by Fax*, or *Maigret's Memoirs*.

This approach does not resolve controversies, but it does help, I think, to see what is at stake when they arise. Take, for instance, the curious debate about the authorship of *Pale Fire*. The novel was, of course, written by Vladimir Nabokov; that is not an issue. What is contentious, however, is the fic-

---

15. Sylvie Patron's contribution to this volume states a similar position, albeit from a different perspective than mine.

tional authorship of the text, or rather texts, since *Pale Fire* is made up of several segments: a long poem ("Pale Fire," by the fictitious poet John Shade) preceded by a verbose introduction and followed by an even longer commentary by one Charles Kinbote, who snatched Shade's manuscript from his widow and set himself up as its editor. The reader who accepts these attributions performs simple forms of parafictionalization, reading, for instance, the poem's themes and style as expressing John Shade's (rather than Vladimir Nabokov's) poetic stance, or by seeing the commentary's striking peculiarities as a sign of Kinbote's madness. More sophisticated but less expected forms of parafictionalization can be found, though. Kinbote's many unreliable claims (among other things, he fancies himself as Charles the Beloved, exiled king of Zembla) suggest an insane imagination whose exact scope is uncertain. This brought the critic Page Stegner to wonder whether it is Kinbote who authors not only the commentary but also the poem.[16] This surprising thesis has been opposed by Andrew Field's counter-thesis, according to which Kinbote and his delirious gloss on Shade's poem may well be inventions of Shade himself (Field 1967: 291–332). For several years now, *Pale Fire* studies have been divided up between "Shadeans" and "Kinboteans" of this byzantine controversy. What is striking, though, is the postulate shared by both camps, namely that parafictionalization of narrative agents, once set into motion, may be difficult to stop. Turning *Pale Fire* into an intricate battlefield between its two enunciators, these commentators agree to wage their dispute in the fuzzy but fascinating zone where narration seems to extend beyond narrative.[17]

But in so doing, critics inevitably show that narrative features are not a given, that narrators and their narrative acts are fictions whose salience and scope rest on interpretive strategies. This suggests less the centrality of narrators than the strength of many readers' desire to provide narrative discourse with a (fictitious) origin, to see narrators as the source, not the result, of what they read. Texts "have" narrators inasmuch as we read these narrators into these texts. But to be established as such, narrations and their agents need to be framed, as all fictions have to be, so that a clear, if invisible, border enables readers to know where the game begins and where it ends. Seen under this light, paratextual studies and narratology are not distinct from one another, but rather are mutually dependent disciplinary fields, as readers may dizzily realize when narrators, overstepping the limits of "their" narratives, purport to be nothing less than the authors of the books they hold in their hands.

---

16. "It is even possible, perhaps probable, that Gradus and Shade are as much figments of Kinbote's imagination as Charles the Beloved and the far-distant land of Zembla. Although it is difficult, if this is true, to explain where the poem came from, it is conceivable that Kinbote wrote it himself" (Stegner 1967: 129).

17. For a detailed examination of this debate, see Boyd (1999: 114–26). See also Pier (1992).

WORKS CITED
Primary Sources

Bruce, Leo. 1984. [1939]. *Case with No Conclusion*. Chicago: Academy.

Cadigan, Pat. 1992. *Fools*. New York: Bantam.

Doyle, Arthur Conan. 1986a. *Sherlock Holmes: The Complete Novels and Stories*, vol. 1. New York: Bantam.

———. 1986b. *Sherlock Holmes: The Complete Novels and Stories*, vol. 2. New York: Bantam.

Elsinck, Henk. 1992. [1991]. *Murder by Fax*. Translated by H. G. Smittenhaar. Fairfax, VA: New Amsterdam.

Flaubert, Gustave. 1986. [1857]. *Madame Bovary*. Paris: Garnier-Flammarion.

Kafka, Franz. 1946. [1927]. *Amerika*. Translated by Edwin Muir. New York: New Directions.

Ricardou, Jean. 1965. *La Prise de Constantinople*. Paris: Minuit.

———. 2007. [1969]. *Place Names: A Brief Guide to Travels in the Book*. Translated by Jordan Stump. Champaign, IL: Dalkey Archive.

Simenon, Georges. 1966. [1950]. *Maigret's Memoirs*. Translated by Helen Thomson. Harmondsworth, UK: Penguin.

Strugatsky, Arkady, and Boris Strugatsky. 1980. [1979]. *Beetle in the Anthill*. Translated by Antonina W. Bouis. New York: Macmillan.

Secondary Sources

Boyd, Brian. 1999. *Nabokov's* Pale Fire. *The Magic of Artistic Discovery*. Princeton, NJ: Princeton University Press.

Contat, Michel, and Michel Rybalka. 1981. "*La Nausée*, Notice." In *Œuvres romanesques*, by Jean-Paul Sartre, edited by Michel Contat and Michael Rybalka, 1657–87. Paris: Gallimard.

Dällenbach, Lucien. 1989. [1977]. *The Mirror in the Text*. Translated by Jeremy Whitely and Emma Hughes. Chicago: The University of Chicago Press.

Dionne, Ugo. 2008. *La voie aux chapitres. Poétique de disposition romanesque*. Paris: Seuil.

Field, Andrew. 1967. *Nabokov: His Life in Art*. Boston: Little, Brown.

Fish, Stanley. 1980. *Is There a Text in This Class? The Authority of Interpretive Communities*. Cambridge, MA: Harvard University Press.

Genette, Gérard. 1980. [1972]. *Narrative Discourse: An Essay in Method*. Translated by Jane E. Lewin. Ithaca, NY: Cornell University Press.

———. 1997. [1987]. *Paratexts: Thresholds of Interpretation*. Translated by Jane E. Lewin. Cambridge: Cambridge University Press.

Heinegg, Peter. 2002. "One Weird Country." *America: The Jesuit Review*, November 11, 2002. http://americamagazine.org/issue/culture/one-weird-country.

Kirsch, Adam. 2009. "America, 'Amerika.'" *New York Times, Sunday Book Review*, January 2, 2009, 23. http://www.nytimes.com/2009/01/04/books/review/Kirsch-t.html.

Mann, Klaus. 1946. Preface to *Amerika* by Franz Kafka. New York: New Directions.

Maziarczyk, Grzegorz. 2011. "Print Strikes Back: Typographic Experimentation in Contemporary Fiction as a Contribution to the Metareferential Turn." In *The Metareferential Turn in*

Contemporary Arts and Media: Forms, Functions, Attempts at Explanation, edited by Werner Wolf, 169–93. Amsterdam: Rodopi.

McHale, Brian. 1987. *Postmodernist Fiction.* London: Routledge.

Pelc, Jerzy. 1986. "On Fictitious Entities and Fictional Texts." *RS/SI* 6, no. 1: 1–35.

Pier, John. 1992. "Between Text and Paratext: Vladimir Nabokov's *Pale Fire.*" *Style* 26, no. 1: 12–32.

———. 2011. "Intermedial Metareference: Index and Icon in William Gass's *Willie Masters' Lonesome Wife.*" In *The Metareferential Turn in Contemporary Arts and Media: Forms, Functions, Attempts at Explanation,* edited by Werner Wolf, 97–124. Amsterdam: Rodopi.

———. 2016. [2014]. "Metalepsis." In *The Living Handbook of Narratology,* edited by Peter Hühn, Jan-Christoph Meister, John Pier, and Wolf Schmid. http://www.lhn.uni-hamburg.de/article/metalepsis-revised-version-uploaded-13-july-2016.

Ryan, Marie-Laure. 2006. "Metaleptic Machines." In *Avatars of Story,* 204–30, 246–48. Minneapolis: University of Minnesota Press.

Sabry, Randa. 1987. "Quand le texte parle de son paratexte." *Poétique* 69: 83–99.

Saint-Gelais, Richard. 1994. *Châteaux de pages: la fiction au risque de sa lecture.* LaSalle: Hurtubise HMH.

———. 1999. *L'empire du pseudo. Modernités de la science-fiction.* Québec: Nota bene.

Searle, John R. 1979. |1975]. "The Logical Status of Fictional Discourse." In *Expression and Meaning, Studies in the Theory of Speech Acts,* 58–75. Cambridge: Cambridge University Press.

Stegner, Page. 1967. *Escape into Aesthetics: The Art of Vladimir Nabokov.* London: Eyre and Spottiswoode.

Todorov, Tzvetan. 1971. "Typologie du roman policier." In *Poétique de la prose,* 55–65. Paris: Seuil.

CHAPTER 4

Narrator on Stage

Not a Condition but a Component for a Postdramatic Narrative Discourse

BENOÎT HENNAUT

This contribution aims to show how the mise en scène of narration becomes an original creative tool within a kind of theater whose main objective was not to narrate. Examples will be drawn from a body of work produced in the 1980s and '90s known under the collective term "post-dramatic" (Lehmann 2002 [1999]). This term has been widely commented on in the field of theater studies since its initial use. It designates a type of production whose main point is not governed by the staging of a text (Western dramatic tradition), but instead arises from the encounter between the combination of different staging techniques (visual, auditory, choreographic, and even textual). Artistic and dramaturgic choices are prioritized according to the production's performative dimension at the expense of a plot driven by characters' psychology. The examples considered are drawn from two highly recognized artists from this theater movement: Elizabeth LeCompte and the Wooster Group in the US, and Jan Lauwers and the Needcompany in Belgium.

Before demonstrating how narration and narrative performance are creative staging elements in a theater that is deliberately distanced from a narrative tradition, I would like to clarify two points. It is necessary, first,

---

This chapter is adapted from Benoît Hennaut, *Théâtre et récit, l'impossible rupture. Narrativité et spectacle postdramatique (1975–2004)* (2016) and is published here with authorization from the publisher, Classiques Garnier (Paris, France).

to demonstrate the position that theater and dramatic art have currently assumed in narrative analysis despite the *repoussoir* role that theater long played for many traditional narratologists. It will then be necessary to explain how the narratorial instance is not a condition for the existence of a theatrical narrative in order for it to be able to become one dramaturgic instrument among others.

1. THEATER AS A VALID OBJECT FOR NARRATOLOGICAL STUDY

Analysis of the dramatic genre in classical and even in postclassical narratology has never been an easy topic. The nature, position, and existence of a narrator were (and still are) usually debated as the crucial points upon which theater is either rejected or accepted as a valid medium of narrative discourse (in short, Genette versus Chatman). I have elsewhere addressed the key aspects of the relationships that have been developed between narratology and theater writing (Hennaut 2013, 2016). Here I will only consider the main points.

Generally speaking, it is nowadays accepted that theater can be studied from a narratological angle. We must first recall the work of Thomas Pavel (1976, 1985), who, in seeking to distance himself from the orthodoxy of structuralist theory, developed a generative grammar of narrative and plot on the basis of Corneille's tragedies and English Renaissance drama. In terms of theater studies, Manfred Pfister (1988 [1977]) was the first to consider the narrative dimension in an extended study of dramatic theory as early as 1977 (as discussed in Richardson 2001: 682 and in Fludernik 2008: 355), soon followed up by one of the founders of semiological studies applied to theater, Keir Elam (1980). As for the history and theory of theater, several analyses develop narratological tools such as plot structure and temporal structure or make use of the term "focalization," thus introducing the concept of point of view. A number of studies devoted to defining a "narratology of drama" incorporate thematic criteria that are specific to narratological approaches. In addition to the possibility of identifying, in theater, forms of temporal construction that are specific to narrative (story/discourse; see Richardson 1987), these studies explore categories such as character, plot, time, space, and so on that were developed in narrative analysis. In more contemporary performance studies, the conjunction of the terms "theater" and "narrative" is often encountered in bibliographies (Lavandier 2008 [1994]; Le Roux 2012; Meyer MacLeod and Pralong 2012; Breger 2012). In this particular field, however, it is notable that the question of whether theater can be dissociated from narrative has never actually been asked.¹

Narratological analysis applied to drama has therefore been established. Nevertheless, a problem, or rather a limitation, surfaces almost immediately: The question often debated remains the possibility of a narrator's existence (see Hühn and Sommer 2014 [2009]: 427). It is useful to quickly address the main points of this debate.

To take two classic examples, the seminal positions of Gérard Genette (1980 [1972], 1988 [1983]) and Franz Karl Stanzel (1984 [1979]) are well known in this regard: The conditions of narrativity (and therefore the existence of a "narrative") are based on the textual existence of a mediating, narratorial voice function. Theater is an exclusively mimetic art, founded on the direct representation of actions, not their narrative retelling. In a word, theater, which is deprived of a narrator, is excluded from narratology in this approach.

In contrast, Seymour Chatman's contributions to this debate were essential to the inclusion of the dramatic genre in the narratological melee. Chatman's seminal thoughts and initial argument (1978) about the narrator as an organizing principle governing choices as to the manner in which film sequences are presented have had numerous echoes among theorists of drama.

In "The Literary Narrator," Chatman takes a clear position on the inclusion of theater and drama in the field of narrative. He claims that neither more nor less than in third-person narrative, drama incarnates a type of narrative: "Once we decide to define Narrative as the composite of story and discourse (on the basis of its unique double chronology), then *logically*, at least, narratives can be said to be actualizable on the stage or in other iconic media" (Chatman 1990: 114). All text types may be the specific media actualization of a same function, which consists in presenting a story and endowing it with a chronological construction that is complex on multiple levels (the argument dear to formalist narratologists). Chatman therefore explicitly opposes Genette by bringing the diegesis/mimesis distinction together under the single banner of "Narrative," the distinction that, for the French structuralist, constituted the narrative frontier. Nevertheless, by identifying a narrator in film, Chatman remains faithful to the idea that all forms of narrative are subject to narratorial organization. He thus creates the "Presenter" figure, a neutral term that is potentially disembodied and dehumanized and that takes charge of organizing the discourse in the form of "telling" or "showing" (Chatman 1990: 116).

---

1. A question I have specifically analyzed in my own work; see Hennaut (2016).

This is also the case with André Gaudreault, who uses the terms "monstrator" or "mega-narrator." This other influential film analyst, however, makes a precise distinction as early as 1988 between the specificity of a "scenic narrative" (in theater) and "filmic narrative" (in film) as opposed to "scriptural narrative" (texts and literature). Gaudreault therefore proposes to distinguish narration from monstration in order to account for the particularity of drama's scenic narrative discourse. But although Gaudreault creates the foundations for a specifically visual narrative, he was himself pleading for the existence of a "mega-narrator, narratologically responsible for any actualized theater discourse" (Gaudreault 1988: 89).

More recently, critical studies of the possible existence of a narrator or narratorial instance specific to theater (and correlated point of view concepts) tend either to establish themselves in response to classical narratologies that excluded theater from their arguments (on this question, see Jahn 2001 and Nünning and Sommer 2008) or to document the different narratorial functions identified in a specific body of work and analyze their function (Richardson 1988, 2001).[2] In a wider perspective inspired by the works of Chatman, the desire to base narratological analysis of theater on the existence of an "actantial" narrator (whatever form this narrator might take) amounts nevertheless to admitting *in fine* the necessity of this instance as a defining criterion of narrative discourse (even if disembodied and nonhuman, as Chatman suggested). All in all, it still seems difficult to take a step back from the narratorial instance criterion as an all-powerful and key parameter of dramatic narrativity in the majority of studies that founded and enriched the relationships between theater and narratology.[3]

2. BEYOND THE NARRATORIAL CONDITION

And yet, certain analyses forge a path for the possibility of including the performing arts in a narrativity defined otherwise than by the existence of a verbal mediator or a theoretical figuration of a narrator. These analyses share a common intuition, although it is not always pursued to its conclusion: the specificity of a staged narrative discourse that is not anchored in a theoretical

---

2. Alber and Fludernik (2014 [2009]: 319–22) discuss theater under "mediacy/narrative mediation" and also recapitulate the studies mentioned here.

3. Even in contemporary studies, among those researchers most inclined to identify a narrative function in spectacular performance, analysis remains determined essentially by the search for a narratorial presence. See Martens and Elshout (2014).

analogy of textual function. I will refer briefly to the works of Manfred Jahn (2001) and Monika Fludernik (2008).

Although Jahn begins by developing the arguments in favor of a narratorial instance specific to theater writing, he takes care to situate himself among the dominant analytic trends as to the purpose of theater analysis. Jahn opts for a median position between analyzing theater as written text and theater exclusively as performance. He indeed integrates performance aspects into a definition of a theater-specific narrative discourse. In his 2001 article, Jahn alters Chatman's typology of text types. He calls for a dialogue between the "written/printed" mode and the "performed" mode (rather than the "diegetic" and "mimetic" labels adopted by Chatman). As in Chatman, both of these modes fall under the narrative type. A theater "script" (the written piece), a textual mode that Jahn ranks along the lines of the novel and short story as written or printed narrative genres, must be approached as a complete medium in and of itself. It poses specific questions when we approach it as an "act of language" (instructions, description) and in terms of narratorial identity. It must be distinguished from the performance,[4] which belongs to the category of performed narrative types (along with opera). According to Jahn, in theater, these modalities complete each other in accomplishing narrative discourse. He distinguishes the textual concretization (in the strict sense) of a lyric or of a dramatic text from its performed identity, thus identifying two possible incarnations of a narrative type. This is progress compared with Chatman, who did not perceive performance as a constitutive element of narrative structure, but as a "simple medium" for actualizing story (Chatman 1990: 109). Nevertheless, as soon as he formulates this intuition, according to which the performative dimension could, in itself, assume the narrative function and incarnate "discourse," Jahn finds it necessary to reinforce the existence of a dematerialized and "super-generative" narratorial instance.

---

4. This distinction between text and performance has actually been at the heart of theater studies since they were initiated. In France, Anne Ubersfeld (1977, 1981) and Patrice Pavis (2007 [1982]) worked on this difference in their early works, but always considering the priority of text over performance. For French theater semiology, the dramatic text has always been considered as the backbone of the upcoming performance and its meaning. In the US, by contrast, Richard Schechner (1982, 1988, 2006) founded "performance studies" on the fact that performance as such can be an independent artistic vector and discourse. From this perspective, performance is the first level of analysis, progressively including textual material as a tool to work with (in addition to various drama elements, if necessary). For performance studies, text is a potential, not a prerequisite. Nowadays, European theater studies have extensively integrated Schechner's proposals in their theoretical approach. This contribution defends the priority of performance over text in the theatrical construction of the works analyzed here. In this sense of "theatrical actualization," performance should not be confounded with works related to the live-art and body-art tradition.

In my opinion, the location of narrative discourse is in fact the primary issue for the narratological study of theater forms. Is it necessary to limit narrative discourse to the content of the dramatic text (*fabula* elements to which stage directions are eventually added)? Or should it, on the contrary, be considered in terms of performance, including all aspects of its realization, thereby attributing a discursive[5] specificity to the performance narrative outside of a narratorial analogy specific to textual media?

Monika Fludernik develops this consideration in a clear and well-supported analysis.

As early as 1996, Fludernik declared in her *Towards a 'Natural' Narratology* that theater is undoubtedly "the most important narrative genre whose narrativity needs to be documented" (348). She based her argument on the criteria for *experientiality*[6] in order to qualify the dramatic event and performance as a form of narrative in its own right. Theater shares with a text (in the strict sense of the term) "the same cognitive parameters which are operative in the re-cognization of narrative structures" (Fludernik 1996: 336).

In her article dating from 2008, Fludernik addressed the narrative issue specific to theater more precisely, abandoning the criteria of plot[7] and narratorial mediation. According to her, it is necessary to consider the narrative analysis of theater writing in terms of discourse[8] and its absolutely specific performative particularity, thereby distancing itself from the necessity of identifying a narrator, regardless of form (whether anthropomorphic or not): "Dramatic 'discourse' would be equivalent to the medium of enactment and performance" (2008: 359).

It is important to stress Fludernik's essential contribution: demonstrating theater's capacity to inscribe narrative discourse within the performance itself, beyond any required verbal mediation. However, like Jahn, Fludernik nuances this position by introducing the *playscript* "[that] incorporates features that take account of the performance, indicating visual and acoustic orchestration" (2008: 362). In the end, though, Fludernik cautiously maintains an ambiguous position.

On the one hand, she considers dramatic discourse strictly in terms of performance, the outcome of which is the conclusion that "drama . . . does not

---

5. In theater studies, Karel Vanhaesebrouck (2004) addressed this question by stressing the specificities of the performance envisaged as discourse in acts.

6. "There cannot be any narratives without a human anthropomorphic experience of some sort at some narrative level. . . . [Experientiality is] the quasi-mimetic evocation of a real-life experience" (Fludernik 1996: 13).

7. Which, of course, is in keeping with the position defended throughout *Towards a 'Natural' Narratology*.

8. And therefore not in terms of the *fabula* or of the narrative act.

have *one* discourse but . . . each performance has its discourse from which the audience extrapolates the plot and fictional world" (2008: 363). This radical and reception-oriented position in fact could rally to the idea of the *unique performance event* and transform the spectator into an active narratee who is extensively implicated in the final elaboration of the discourse and goes beyond the role of implied reader/audience (see section 3 below).

On the other hand, Fludernik considers narrative discourse as fixed in the playscript. The playscript is the final written text, given once and for all, which includes both the constitutive plot elements and the necessary performance indications (i.e., stage directions). It is on the basis of this playscript that a reader, using his or her imagination, would be able to extrapolate the performance (regardless of whether or not this reader is a director[9]). Here Fludernik joins Jahn (2001) in this description of a "privileged" relationship (which, however, is also highly unstable in the alternative narratological consideration she has of it) between the written, printed avatar (the script) and its corresponding "performance" of narrative discourse as applied to the stage. Like Jahn, Fludernik assumes a position situated between the literary "*drama reading*" tradition (for which the reference is the "dramatic text") and the "all for the performance" position, as vindicated by contemporary theater studies (for which the reference is the "performance text"[10]).

3. PERFORMANCE AS AUTONOMOUS DISCOURSE

Fludernik's contribution enriches the debate about narrativity within dramatic discourse and allows me to suggest the following: When it acts as a narrative, a theater performance (that is, the staged performance) can incarnate a narrative[11] function for which the spectator is the narratee. Indeed, in the postdramatic expressions considered here, the narrative function is neither limited nor motivated by exchanges between characters (narrators and narratees being on stage) in which the spectator would be part of an implied audience/reader. Narrative is rather considered as a functional aspect of the performance itself as a whole, given that the internal components of the performance are not

---

9. Again, the seminal works of Anne Ubersfeld (1977, 1981) extensively analyzed this question from a semiological point of view.

10. In Schechner's definition (2006), all of the constitutive elements of a performance process taken in its physical and concrete reality.

11. I differentiate between these two terms: a "narratorial instance" (i.e., a narrator that is physically or symbolically incarnated and who produces discourse), and the "narrative function" (i.e., the overall level of responsibility as to the elaboration of the organizing narrative discourse of a story, with or without narrator).

always decipherable in terms of established narrative structures and continuity. In this case, the *performance as such* is absolutely constitutive of the narrative discourse specific to a staged theatrical production, and spectators are considered as so many active narratees. Pursuing this approach, I would argue that in theater, the narrative function, as a form of creative mediation, can do without a narrator in the form of a disembodied super-agent (Chatman's rhetorical construction). In discursive terms, the narrative function exists in the staging of the performance itself, of which only the author (a combination of the playwright and the director or, in contemporary theater, the artist who signs off the performance) is *in fine* responsible. I thus consider performance to be a form of discourse insofar as it organizes and aligns a series of differentiated signs, thereby producing signification. At the same time, I consider narrative discourse to be defined, at a minimum, by the intentional[12] disposition of a series of temporally successive elements that structure and transmit a representation of the world or of experiencing the world. How then is the narrativity of a dramatic and performance discourse to be assessed if we forego the use of narratorial expression?

To begin with, defining the narrative capacity of a performance discourse is by no means an inconsequential endeavor. We can in fact distinguish three positions as to what constitutes narrative discourse and its expressive form:

1. The well-known traditional position found in structuralist narratology and its derivatives. The story (*fabula*) is first as the material given, whereas discourse (*sjuzhet*) organizes it. This involves creative distortions between the dual temporal level, the effects of focalization, and, of course, the possibility of transposing the story from one form of discourse to another (nonexclusively verbal) form.

2. The more rhetorical or phenomenological position: Discourse is first, and the act of narration engenders the *fabula*, which amounts to progressive reconstruction of the *fabula* by the receiver of the discourse. This is the position expressed by David Bordwell (1985), Monika Fludernik (1996), and Richard Walsh (2007), to name only a few. Advancing the primacy of discourse (consistent with advocating the auctorial gesture and creative mediation) supposes that it is the existence of narrative discourse that both exposes and unites a story's structure and components instead of there being a preexisting story.

---

12. I use this word in the aesthetic sense inspired by John Searle and expounded upon by Gérard Genette (1999 [1997]) and Jean-Marie Schaeffer (1996). Intentionality implies the intention used to produce an object and the attention given to it by its receptor. It is a bilateral cognitive relationship.

3. The position that separates narrativity and narrative, making the second a finished product of the first through narrative discourse. Narrative is only the final organized product of the latent or progressive narrativity of discourse. Narrativity in this sense can be based on a series of formal, mimetic, and pragmatic criteria (the stages of narrativity as formulated by Marie-Laure Ryan [1992, 2004, 2006]) as well as on the basics, narrative microdesigns, and macrodesigns elaborated by David Herman (2002, 2009) and on Werner Wolf's narratemes (2003, 2004). Seen as a finished product of narrativity, the well-formed narrative (whether considered to be dependent on verbal language or not) is distinct from a "narrative potential" or "sense of narrativity" elicited in a reader or spectator by a discourse that in some way evokes actions without necessarily connecting them temporally or teleologically.

In my opinion, it is useful to combine the last two positions in order to support the scope of the theoretical framework being proposed here. The object of theater, and even more so in contemporary and postdramatic theater, is first and foremost to produce an intentional artistic artifact. This artifact must be analyzed at the fundamental level of its discourse (as defined above, i.e., the organization, proclamation, and syntagmatic alignment of differentiated signs whose succession provokes signification; see previous page). Looked at in this way, discourse generates actions and events.[13] It delineates, produces, and contains a collection of elements constitutive of narrativity. It is on the basis of the eventfulness engendered by performance discourse that a given performance contains narrativity.[14] In the end, a theater performance might function like a narrative and be concretized as narrative by the receiver, even if it is not in itself complete at this level (or does not seek to be, which is generally the case with postdramatic productions; see Hennaut 2016).

More specifically, though, I will use tools specific to the transmedial orientation of narratology in order to refine this analysis. This approach is structured around the ideas defended by David Herman, Marie-Laure Ryan, and Werner Wolf. All three consider it possible to assess narrativity as a progres-

---

13. "Event" is understood here in the sense proposed by Peter Hühn of "type II event" or change of state, itself derived from Yuri Lotman's plot model and Wolf Schmid's "eventfulness," a notion that brings together the criteria of facticity and resultativity as well as the more context-dependent features of relevance, unpredictability, persistence, irreversibility, and noniterativity (Hühn [2014 (2009)]: 169–74; Schmid [2003]).

14. An approach similar to the one defended by René Audet (2006). For Audet, a discourse is inhabited by narrativity as soon as it delimits or organizes disruptive elements at its metalevel that are called "events."

sive property and, most important, to identify narrativity within the most diverse media. They do so by acknowledging the importance of communicated experience (Fludernik's heritage) while simultaneously maintaining the need for a signifying whole required of the narrative discourse as such. The combination of their positions convincingly reinforces the idea that theater performance as discourse can be analyzed in terms of narrativity without it being absolutely necessary to identify an organizing narratorial instance and, above all, without shackling performance as discourse exclusively to the function of being a narrative.[15]

In the body of work from which I draw the following examples, postdramatic performance does not claim narrative completeness. Performances such as these are not based on an organized tale or on a dramatic framework identified as such. Rather, postdramatic performance is a theater discourse that *can* be narrative. It develops a succession of events within a temporal structure and creates worlds by using actants, but it also flouts various codes. Most often, it fails to function as a fully constructed narrative. Or rather, it succeeds *in not doing so,* since that in itself was one of the primary aims of its dramatic project. In order to function as a unilateral and autonomous narrative discourse, it would require the framework provided by an unequivocal meaning as communicated by its author. However, it is precisely the absence of such meaning that the performance and its author seek to highlight, though not without problematizing and nuancing their use of the narrative tools, as well as the role of the spectator (see Hennaut 2016: 181–235, 285–327). In its contemporary or postdramatic form, performance discourse can throw the narrative function back to a secondary or even further removed distant level when compared with other aesthetic ambitions.

Nevertheless, the narratorial instance may persist at the performance level, even when the narrative function is denied or diminished in the production. In such cases, the narrator role is perceived more as a stylized mark of the narration or as a specific dramatic element. It is in this sense that I will use the adjective "stylistic" to designate a natural parameter that is amplified, isolated, or accentuated in order to produce a particular creative effect. The presence and use of onstage narrators, those narratorial instances that purvey narrative itself on stage, are largely problematized by the postdramatic performance. Running counter to the narratological tradition, their stylistic presence belongs to a non-narrative theatrical discourse.

---

15. For an in-depth analysis of this idea, focused on several of Romeo Castellucci's iconic productions, see Hennaut (2014).

4. THE NARRATOR AS A STYLISTIC DEVICE

The few examples that I am able to address in the limited space of this essay are drawn from the work of two artists, or actually groups of artists, since from the outset they have insisted on the collaborative aspect of their work.

The Wooster Group began in 1975 in New York as the result of collaboration between a group of actors from Richard Schechner's Performance Group. It has continued to operate until now under the leadership of director Elizabeth LeCompte (www.woostergroup.org). The Group's work, which has been well documented (see, among others, Savran 1986; Callens 2004; Quick 2007), questions the power of cultural representations and traditions, particularly those associated with theater. Often qualified somewhat hastily as postmodern due to its highly fragmented style, the Wooster Group's theater is highly rhythmic, visual, deliberately polemical, and almost expressionist. Some of the Group's more important productions are *Route 1&9* (1981), *L. S. D. (. . . just the high points . . .)* (1984), *Frank Dell's The Temptation of Saint Antony* (1987), *Brace Up!* (1991), and *House / Lights* (1998).

In 1986, Jan Lauwers and Grace Ellen Barkey founded the Needcompany in Brussels (www.needcompany.be). Like Elizabeth LeCompte, Jan Lauwers trained as a visual artist. He came to the theater in order to question representational codes, which he first addressed via the segmentation of major texts from the literary and theater traditions. To this he added a highly personal scenic language, combining music, dance, and sculpture. In doing so, Lauwers ensured that these creative media participated in creating the performance. His numerous productions (which have been analyzed in detail, primarily by Stalpaert et al. 2007) include the following: *Need to Know* (1987), *Julius Caesar* (1990), *Le Désir* (1996), *Needcompany's Macbeth* (1996), *Snakesong Trilogy— Integral Version* (1998), *Morning Song* (1999), *Images of Affection* (2002), and *Isabella's Room* (2004).

First, it must be said that there are several instances in postdramatic theater of onstage narrator figures, which has been very well documented elsewhere (often described as an "epic" dimension at the heart of the drama). Let us recall that in modern and contemporary dramatic literature, two recurrent examples of an onstage narrator are persistently cited by theater analysts and narratologists focusing on dramatic form: *The Caucasian Chalk Circle* (1945) by Bertold Brecht and *The Glass Menagerie* (1944) by Tennessee Williams. It is primarily on the basis of these examples that archetypical functions have been defined concerning the way in which an onstage narrator contributes to the development of the drama. To take but one example from the narratological field, Brian Richardson (1988) distinguished several types of narrators for the purposes of a literary and textual analysis of drama:[16] internal narrators (characters telling a story to others, soliloquies), the "monodramatic narrator" (an expression he borrows from Dorrit Cohn and that can perhaps be likened to Genette's autodiegetic narrator[17]), the generative narrator (who performs an ontological role in relation to the actions or figures that emerge from this narrator's discourse), and the frame narrator (the narrator of the prologue or epilogue, reminiscent of the chorus). Elsewhere, the memory play genre is often referred to as a somewhat particular case of the two narrator types: the frame narrator and the generative narrator. In a "memory" play, a narrator reveals autobiographical episodes onstage. In my opinion, the balanced triumvirate formed between the two narrator types (frame narrator and generative narrator) and the memory play genre provides the ideal tool to qualify postdramatic artists' structural use of the narratorial instances they stage.

Let us consider a few initial examples of a postdramatic onstage narrator who seemingly fulfils conventional archetypes, but whose discourse is quickly problematized or is not self-evident.

In *Le Désir* (1996), as in the complete version of the *Snakesong Trilogy* (1998), both by Jan Lauwers, the central figure of the Professor has the role of framing the performance. While this old man tells his life story, he engenders a series of performative episodes (dances, sketches, living sculptures). The "banal" narrative framework used in *Le Désir* (1996),[18] which later has the same function in *Snakesong Trilogy* in its *Integral Version* (1998), stresses the importance of the three texts read between the dances and performances.[19] These texts are themselves put into perspective by the actresses' distancing effect, and the end of the production (other actresses' ironic staging of the Professor's death) closes a circular process in on itself: The narrative framework offered by the Professor figure thematizes the very dramatization of the dramaturgic message. Hence, the first of three problems: *In the economy of the performance, the narrator's discourse serves another purpose than the traditional role of organizing the guiding tale.*

Also in Lauwers, we could potentially say that the figure of Mike (*Images of Affection*, 2002) is a "super generative" narrator. Mike represents the entire discourse and sequencing of the performance through his introductory speech

---

16. It must be pointed out, however, that Richardson does not take the staged or performative dimensions into account at all.

17. "The world of the play is largely coextensive with the narration of the character" (Richardson 1988: 209).

18. A life that is ending, a couple drifting apart, health problems, etc.

19. *Les Chants de Maldoror* (1869) by Isidore Ducasse comte de Lautréamont, *A Rebours* (1884) by Joris-Karl Huysmans, and *Salomé* (1891) by Oscar Wilde.

addressed to the audience: "I'm the narrator and I think it's really important you know exactly where I'm coming from. . . . It's my job to stay here and to make them stay [note: pointing at the other actors], because they rather want to be there with you." Then, after a short pause, Mike starts again in medias res with these words that, bit by bit, attempt to constitute a diegetic universe of the performance, whereas the other actors slowly come to life: "Then everything went silent . . . silent . . . and this silence . . . they knew . . . was their greatest enemy. They knew that this silence should not be. That this silence was not a silence but a threat."[20] Mike *is* in fact the performance in his role as generative narrator. He dramatizes and thematizes the performance in a self-referential manner. Throughout the entire performance, Mike, even when silent for long periods, remains present on stage, crouching in a corner in the shadows, the permanent incarnation of the sequence of events put into play. And yet, for all this, the performance remains a tough nut to crack for the spectator in terms of identifying a coherent plot. It will even explicitly contest the facts told by Mike. Second problem: *The narrator's discourse is highlighted as an enunciative structure but does not in any way guarantee the structure and reliability of a story/plot.*

In terms of the Wooster Group, the character of Frank may be described as a generative narrator in *Frank Dell's The Temptation of Saint Antony* (1988). He produces his own self-narrative, the reproduction of himself and of his televised show. The staged episodes may appear as hallucinated scenes from his own universe, borrowed from the world of sketches, stand-up comedy, cabaret, or the traveling fair show (knife throwers, hotel-based theater troupes, etc.).[21] Toward the end of this performance, in the exuberant scenes where the two female characters reproduce precisely these fair and cabaret moments, positioned above Frank, the actress Kate Valk herself becomes the generative narrator. She engenders the actions that are acted out, creates a double space between the "story" being shown (the vague kidnapping of a hotel director) and what is being said. Valk does not in fact stop telling abracadabra stories that are more or less illustrated in these vaudeville sequences. And finally, the third problem: *Here, onstage narrators multiply as the incoherencies mount or become linguistically unintelligible.*

We can easily guess that the purpose of this corpus, in terms of the narratorial instance, does not lie in illustrating phenomena already defined in dramatic literature (frame or autodiegetic narrator). In fact, postdramatic theater

---

20. Jan Lauwers (n.d., ca. 2001–2002), *Images of Affection* (performance in English; 10 front and back typed sheets, unnumbered). Needcompany archives.

21. All of these locations and traditions evoke the character of Frank Dell and his "father," the satirist Lenny Bruce, a very popular but highly controversial figure in 1960s America.

problematizes the supposedly linear character of narrative and its structuring of time and events. For these artists, the telling of a story is not self-evident. Theater's narrative function must be dismantled by the performance. Their dramatic project refuses narrative as the guiding structure of unambiguous meaning.[22]

These initial examples show that the onstage narrator often fulfils a utilitarian function. The frame narrator, or generative narrator, facilitates performative interstices. The narrator's role is only a pretext for staging developments at the heart of these productions. The narrator accentuates aspects of the performance whose raison d'être lies outside narrative discourse, in the strict sense. It is not a condition for or expression of an unambiguous discourse that constitutes the narrative thread of the performance. Should such a narrative thread exist, it can be pieced together only by the spectator making use of a few scattered elements, among them these narrated episodes.

In his analysis of Jan Lauwers's productions, Rudi Laermans specified that in addition to the fact that it triggers the performance, this narratorial framing function also implicitly reflects on the position of theater as staged in this discourse (is it theater within theater, or is it a continuity of representation?). Laermans points out that in the *Snakesong Trilogy*, the central figure of the Professor disintegrates over the course of the three show-episodes that constitute the trilogy. It deteriorates as a simulacrum of the traditional dramatic hero emerges, which is also a simulacrum of narrative and of "dramatic content" in these productions (Laermans 1998). The pseudo-narrative framework offered by the Professor's episodes in *Snakesong Trilogy* is in a sense the formal completion of Lauwers's calling narrative into question (whose source is in fact the voluntary dismantling of the Shakespearean story, a topic it is not possible to address here). While problematizing and refusing narrative as a hermeneutic structure of the performance, this pseudo-narrative framework assumes a role that positions it as a pretext for dramatizing something other than itself (this also stands out in *Images of Affection*, with the intrusion of the Mike character cited above).

On a slightly different note, the postdramatic narrator can change into the organizer and commentator of the performance, putting the narrator's own speech into play with the performance elements that take place. The most successful example of this figure is Kate Valk's role in the Wooster Group's *Brace Up!* (1991). This narrator is stylized: The narrator retains the contours and appearance of a narrator, but the narrator's traditional functions are rubbed out and attenuated. This character, explicitly designated as "narrator," acts as the

---

22. This argument is developed in Hennaut (2016: 85–143).

main narratorial instance and serves the purposes of the performance. However, yet again, the narrator does not really provide the key to the organizing discourse for the performance as a whole. The narrator serves the same metatheatrical function as that attributed to the Professor in the previous example, incarnating one of the dramaturgic ambitions of this production. In *Brace Up!* (a project that examines the text of Chekhov's *Three Sisters* using Japanese-style techniques; see below), the Wooster Group thematizes one of its favorite preoccupations. What possibilities remain for theater? Elizabeth LeCompte questions the survival of traditional theater in the contemporary world.

In *Brace Up!*, this narrator (played by Kate Valk) is also not only the narrator. The narrator is also a facilitator, governing the movements of people and objects on stage. The actress implements the framework and progression of the performance. This particular narrator function is based on a Japanese inspiration, combining the *kyogen* clowns (Noh drama comic interludes) with the *benshi* tradition (an actor/performer who narrated silent films in Japan at the beginning of the twentieth century, sometimes becoming more famous than the movie stars themselves). LeCompte attributes the additional function of stage manager to this commentator (see, among others, LeCompte 1993). This figure must move the performance along, in addition to filling gaps in the story that the performance "does not have the time" (read: the desire) to address. In this double role, this *benshi* narrator is extremely metaleptic,[23] even more so in that the narrator also accentuates the role of Paul Schmidt, the translator of Chekhov, who is the playwright associated with LeCompte in this performance. At the narrator's invitation, Schmidt intervenes on stage (and through video in the production's revival in 2003) in order to recall different episodes of the *Three Sisters* fable and to ask "Kate" (using her first name) to slow down the rhythm on this occasion! We could conclude that *Brace Up!* ascribes a dominant position to the story; however, the meta-theatrical threads simply cannot be swept away without being filtered through the *benshi* narrator. The tale that LeCompte highlights through Kate Valk (LeCompte's stage double, as several specialists of the Group like to say) is a dramaturgic discourse that considers the power and position of the theater performance. A clear response is provided in a comment later made by Kate Valk about *To You the Birdie! (Phèdre),* which is similarly based on a classic behemoth. "The size of the theatrical gesture had to be so huge to make the story interesting, to

---

23. The original definition of narrative metalepsis was put forth by Genette: "Any intrusion by the extradiegetic narrator or narratee into the diegetic universe (or by diegetic characters into a metadiegetic universe, etc.), or the inverse . . . , produces an effect of strangeness that is either comical . . . or fantastic" (1980 [1972]: 234–35).

stop it being boring melodrama," she unabashedly declared (quoted in Quick 2007: 160; see also Villeneuve 1991 on this point).

The postdramatic narrator, pushed to the limit in *Brace Up!*, is used to achieve a dramatic discourse that is rhetorical before it is narrative. This narrator incarnates the level of performance in this multipolar production that puts narrative material in relief without being enslaved to it. The story (even the "most boring melodrama") is performed just as much as it is commented on or recounted. It is a pretext for *doing theater,* as clearly demonstrated in the genetic analysis of this production with the addition, late in time, of the *Three Sisters* text to the already ongoing dramatic project that was to become, finally, *Brace Up!*[24]

With LeCompte, as with Lauwers, the narrator acts as a meta-theatrical tool, both in terms of the content of the story used and in terms of the form of the production. In her analysis of Lauwers, Janine Hauthal (2007) suggests that these are also post-epic or post-Brechtian techniques. They no longer simply serve to segment an action that is in essence already disrupted or to disrupt the illusion of a representational aesthetic that the Brechtian *Gestus* aimed to isolate for comment. Postdramatic production already achieves this with the plurality of its production methods and its inherent deconstructions. The aim of this critique is to expand the speaking space (the *Sprechraum*) so as to deliberately and structurally include therein the theater and spectators. According to Hauthal, and following Brecht, the dramaturgy of discourse (including addressing the audience) has definitively surpassed conversational dramaturgy (internal onstage).

Let us push this reasoning further in order to enrich my own analysis. In addition to the functions we have already attributed to the postdramatic narrator, this narrator, as used by LeCompte or Lauwers, would also be the materialization of their phenomenological claim in terms of the open and shared nature of the meaning of their creation. In this theater, artists constantly invoke the spectator as implicated in the development of signification. Thanks to the onstage narrator, the audience takes the stage.

---

24. The creation process used in *Brace Up!* was not dictated by a decision to "perform" *Three Sisters*. The choice to use *Three Sisters* came about toward the end in order to enrich a staging process, the collective research for which was inspired by Japanese culture. "We began to watch hours and hours of tapes on noh drama and kyogen theater. But they were hard to concentrate on in the beginning because the timing is so radically different from anything we're used to. So we switched over to Japanese films, and developed quite a palate for that—of directors we liked, of actors we liked. Finally, we bounced back and forth between Japanese films and noh and kyogen. So all these things were operating together: the dances and letting them transmutate into other things, the Japanese movies and plays. But we needed a text. Then Ron Vawter brought in Paul Schmidt's [translation of] *Three Sisters*. It fit like a glove" (Kate Valk, quoted in Mee 1992: 150).

But we must consider yet another aspect of the postdramatic production's emphasis on the narrator: the systematic weakening of the narrator. The narrator is punished or prevented in its role as organizer of the performance. The metalepsis that the postdramatic performance inflicts on its narrator is often violent. Usually, the narrator is highlighted in his or her role as a result of the narrator's weaknesses. The Needcompany's productions provide many examples of this.

In his first Shakespearean works, Lauwers's narrators correspond to an explanatory logic for the dismantling and reduction of Elizabethan drama (Sprang 2007; Van Kerkhoven 1997). They "simply" have an organizing principle approximating Kate Valk's initial role in *Brace Up!* They are there to frame the sequence of the performance and help the spectator overcome the difficulties of the reduction applied to the sequence of the expected narrative. What is more interesting is that this function also seems to address the actors onstage. I would venture to say that this is in fact the start of the postdramatic narrator's problems. The narrator of *Julius Caesar* (1990) is explicitly described thus: "The narrator provides the stage directions and helps the public to understand the narrative thread. She guides people in the right direction and delineates the possible boundaries of interpretation" (de Boeck 1995: 165; my translation). But in such directions, the narrator triggers the refusal and mutiny of certain actors who refuse to obey! Even if it presents itself as already "shaken up," this narratorial instance maintains a complete discursive integrity. In *King Lear* (2000), this discursive integrity is besieged by the eruption of a multitude of contradictions between the discourse spoken by the narrator and the discourse projected using subtitles that invade and distort the narrator's speech. There are also the various linguistic disturbances and screamed language used in the fifth act of this Needcompany production. In this case, the narrator's organizing function is itself besieged by the preeminence of the performance. This is exactly the violent fate that will be reserved for Mike in *Images of Affection,* where he is constantly contradicted and taken to task by the characters that he engenders on stage.

Postdramatic narrators do not go unnoticed. Their own weaknesses often stand out. They are even discredited when they are supposed to structure the piece as a whole. In other words, the natural function that they could occupy in the performance sequence is undermined by the incoherence of their discourse or their own condition as "weak" characters in the diegetic content that they do their best to create.

In the *Snakesong Trilogy* (Lauwers), the Professor is deaf, blind, and handicapped. With the character's progressive weakening, the pseudo-narrative framework that the Professor's discourse represents emerges (see above). The

Professor seems in fact to disappear in the meanderings of his narrative in order to give way to the performative episodes. Also, the character of the Professor is constantly interrupted in his narrator role, diminished by the comments and metaleptic play of the other actors.

Finally, Mike, in his introductory statements to *Images of Affection*, where he is supposed to be framed as a narrator, implies from the outset the degradation and self-cancellation of his role: "I am a bullshitter, a liar. Which is unfortunate for you because you need me to make sense of this thing. . . . I'm sad, I'm tired and I'm ugly. Look at my face."[25]

5. CONCLUSION

The meta-theatrical use of the narratorial instance in postdramatic theater undermines the role of the narratorial instance as a point of reference as well as its modulating, explanatory, and introductory functions. Narratorial mediation is used and distills elements that contribute to establishing certain levels of narrativity, but this is not always obvious. At times, it is as if postdramatic theater systematically uses all possible stylistic devices that problematize a narratorial instance in order to better undermine it: concurrently metaleptic, collective, unreliable, generative, and autodiegetic. Mike is all of this at once in *Images of Affection*.

In these examples, we understand that the narrator is not a condition for the existence of a dramatic or dramatized narrative discourse. The performance assumes the discursive level of theater, and the narrator becomes a creative component of this multimodal discourse, which in itself consists of theatrical and performative structures. In the end, possibly, but never necessarily, one of the keys to meaning or resolution may lie in narrative interpretation.

In its challenge to narrativity and to the world of narrative, the postdramatic production plays with certain narrative processes. It even plays with the first of these requisites: the narrator and the effects of perspective or focalization.[26] By incorporating or maintaining such methods in versions that are corrupted, weakened, or excessively dramatized, the artists included in this corpus illustrate the inadequacy, or at least the decay, of the narrative organization of discourse as an obvious vector for meaning in their theater. The nar-

---

25. Jan Lauwers (n.d., ca. 2001–2002), *Images of Affection* (performance in English; 10 front and back typed sheets, unnumbered). Needcompany archives.

26. It would be useful to consider in greater depth the effects on focalization that arise with the introduction of visual media or film in postdramatic productions.

rative act and the stories it conveys trigger the imaginary and accentuate the artistic project that inhabits the theater of the artists studied. Often, they reinforce meta-theatrical questioning as well as the reflexive, specular space that the postdramatic performance constitutes in relation to the power of drama. These artists have entrusted the continued development of a mimetic, realistic, narrative, and psychological theater to film and television. In their work, narrative is present in all its structural and discursive aspects in spite of the fact that it is never asserted by the artists themselves as an overall organizing discourse for the performance. These artists detest narrative as something explanatory and anticipatory, but they love it for the full range of its transgressive potential. By making stylistic use of the forms of narrative discourse, they condemn the obvious. As such, the spectator is unable to let go and experience the self-evident; there is an absence of the familiar lull of the narrative purr that carries a spectator in a clear, specific direction. In the end, it is the spectator who must extract vectors of signification necessary for understanding the spectacle from the overall discourse constitutive of the performance. These vectors are of course partially narrative, but they are also rhetorical, political, aesthetic, and poetic. That, however, is another story . . .

WORKS CITED

Primary Sources[27]

LeCompte, Elizabeth, and The Wooster Group. 1988. *Frank Dell's The Temptation of Saint Antony.* Premier performance September 16, 1988, The Performing Garage, New York.

———. 1991. *Brace Up!* Premier performance January 18, 1991, The Performing Garage, New York. Jan Lauwers and Needcompany.

———. 1996. *The Snakesong Trilogy—Le Désir.* Premier performance November 6, 1996, Kanonhallen, Kopenhagen.

———. 1998. *The Snakesong Trilogy, Integral version with live music.* Premier performance April 16, 1998, Lunatheater, Brussels.

———. 2002. *Images of Affection.* Premier performance February 28, 2002, Stadsschouwburg, Brugge. Script: [ca. 2001–2002] *Images of affection* (performance script in English; 10 front and back typed sheets, unnumbered), Needcompany archives.

Secondary Sources

Alber, Jan, and Monika Fludernik. 2014. [2009]. "Mediacy and Narrative Mediation." In *Handbook of Narratology*, edited by Peter Hühn, Jan Christoph Meister, John Pier, and Wolf Schmid, vol. 1: 310–25. Berlin: De Gruyter.

---

27. Only works discussed in detail are listed.

Audet, René. 2006. "La narrativité est l'affaire d'événement." In *Jeux et enjeux de la narrativité dans les pratiques contemporaines (arts visuels, cinéma, littérature)*, edited by René Audet et al., 7–35. Paris: Dis voir.

Bordwell, David. 1985. *Narration in the Fiction Film*. Madison: University of Wisconsin Press.

Breger, Claudia. 2012. *An Aesthetics of Narrative Performance: Transnational Theater, Literature and Film in Contemporary Germany*. Columbus: The Ohio State University Press.

Callens, Johan, ed. 2004. *The Wooster Group and Its Traditions*. Brussels: Peter Lang.

Chatman, Seymour. 1978. *Story and Discourse: Narrative Structure in Fiction and Film*. Ithaca, NY: Cornell University Press.

———. 1990. "The Literary Narrator." In *Coming to Terms: The Rhetoric of Narrative in Fiction and Film*, 109–23. Ithaca, NY: Cornell University Press.

de Boeck, Christof. 1995. "De achterkant van de beheersing. Het theater van Jan Lauwers." *Documenta* 13, no. 3: 158–72.

Elam, Keir. 1980. *The Semiotics of Theatre and Drama*. New York: Methuen.

Fludernik, Monika. 1996. *Towards a 'Natural' Narratology*. London: Routledge.

———. 2008. "Narrative and Drama." In *Theorizing Narrativity*, edited by John Pier and José Ángel García Landa, 355–84. Berlin: Walter de Gruyter.

Gaudreault, André. 1988. *Du littéraire au filmique. Système du récit*. Paris: Méridien Klincksieck.

Genette, Gérard. 1980. [1972]. *Narrative Discourse: An Essay in Method*. Translated by Jane E. Lewin. Ithaca, NY: Cornell University Press.

———. 1988. [1983]. *Narrative Discourse Revisited*. Translated by Jane E. Lewin. Ithaca, NY: Cornell University Press.

———. 1999. [1997]. *The Aesthetic Relation*. Translated by G. M. Goshgarian. Ithaca, NY: Cornell University Press.

Hauthal, Janine. 2007. "On Speaking and Being Spoken: Reading on Stage and Speaking with Accents in Needcompany's *Caligula*." In *No Beauty for Me There Where Human Life Is Rare: On Jan Lauwers' Theatre Work with Needcompany*, edited by Christel Stalpaert et al., 169–87. Ghent: Academia Press.

Hennaut, Benoît. 2013. "Narratologie et écritures théâtrales: quel dialogue possible?" *Cahiers de Narratologie* 24. http://narratologie.revues.org/6656.

———. 2014. "Building Stories around Contemporary Performing Arts: The Case of Romeo Castelluci's *Tragedia Endogonidia*." In *Beyond Classical Narration: Transmedial and Unnatural Challenges*, edited by Jan Alber and Per Krogh Hansen, 97–116. Berlin: De Gruyter.

———. 2016. *Théâtre et récit, l'impossible rupture. Narrativité et spectacle postdramatique (1975–2004)*. Paris: Classiques Garnier.

Herman, David. 2002. *Story Logic: Problems and Possibilities of Narrative*. Lincoln: University of Nebraska Press.

———. 2009. *Basic Elements of Narrative*. Chichester: Wiley-Blackwell.

Hühn, Peter. 2014. [2009]. "Event and Eventfulness." In *Handbook of Narratology*, edited by Peter Hühn, Jan Christoph Meister, John Pier, and Wolf Schmid, vol. 1: 158–78. Berlin: De Gruyter.

Hühn, Peter, and Roy Sommer. 2014. [2009]. "Narration in Poetry and Drama." In *Handbook of Narratology*, edited by Peter Hühn, Jan Christoph Meister, John Pier, and Wolf Schmid, vol. 1: 419–34. Berlin: De Gruyter.

Jahn, Manfred. 2001. "Narrative Voice and Agency in Drama: Aspects of a Narratology of Drama." *New Literary History* 32, no. 3: 659–79.

Laermans, Rudi. 1998. "De idiotie van het menselijke." *Etcetera* 16, no. 63: 28–32.

Lavandier, Yves. 2008. [1994]. *La dramaturgie: les mécanismes du récit, cinéma, théâtre, opéra, radio, télévision, B. D.* Cergy: Le clown et l'enfant.

Le Roux, Monique. 2012. "La nécessité d'un *théâtre-récit.*" *La quinzaine littéraire*, 1073.

LeCompte, Elizabeth. 1993. "Une bibliothèque de détritus culturels." *Theaterschrift*, 3.

Lehmann, Hans-Thies. 2002. [1999]. *Le théâtre postdramatique*. Paris: L'Arche.

Martens, Gunther, and Helena Elshout. 2014. "Narratorial Strategies in Drama and Theatre." In *Beyond Classical Narration: Transmedial and Unnatural Challenges*, edited by Jan Alber and Per Krogh Hansen, 81–96. Berlin: De Gruyter.

Mee, Susie. 1992. "Chekhov's *Three Sisters* and The Wooster Group's *Brace Up!*" *The Drama Review* 36, no. 4: 143–53.

Meyer MacLeod, Arielle, and Michèle Pralong, eds. 2012. *Raconter des histoires. Quelle narration au théâtre aujourd'hui?* Genève: Métis Presses.

Nünning, Ansgar, and Roy Sommer. 2008. "Diegetic and Mimetic Narrativity: Some Further Steps towards a Transgeneric Narratology of Drama." In *Theorizing Narrativity*, edited by John Pier and José Ángel García Landa, 331–44. Berlin: Walter de Gruyter.

Pavel, Thomas. 1976. *La syntaxe narrative des tragédies de Corneille*. Paris: Klincksieck.

———. 1985. *The Poetics of Plot: The Case of English Renaissance Drama*. Minneapolis: University of Minnesota Press.

Pavis, Patrice. 2007. [1982]. *Vers une théorie de la pratique théâtrale: voix et images de la scène*. Villeneuve-d'Ascq: Presses Universitaires du Septentrion.

Pfister, Manfred. 1988. [1977]. *The Theory and Analysis of Drama*. Translated by John Halliday. Cambridge: Cambridge University Press.

Quick, Andrew, ed. 2007. *The Wooster Group Workbook*. New York: Routledge.

Richardson, Brian. 1987. "'Time is out of joint': Narrative Models and the Temporality of the Drama." *Poetics Today* 8, no. 2: 299–309.

———. 1988. "Point of View in Drama: Diegetic Monologue, Unreliable Narrators, and the Author's Voice on Stage." *Comparative Drama* 22, no. 3: 193–214.

———. 2001. "Voice and Narration in Postmodern Drama." *New Literary History* 32, no. 3: 681–94.

Ryan, Marie-Laure. 1992. "The Modes of Narrativity and Their Visual Metaphors." *Style* 26: 368–87.

———. 2004. "Introduction." In *Narrative across Media: The Languages of Storytelling*, edited by Marie-Laure Ryan, 1–40. Lincoln: University of Nebraska Press.

———. 2006. "Narrative, Media, and Modes." In *Avatars of Story*, 3–30, 231–34. Minneapolis: Minnesota University Press.

Savran, David. 1986. *The Wooster Group (1975–1985): Breaking the Rules*. Ann Arbor, MI: UMI Research Press.

Schaeffer, Jean-Marie. 1996. *Les célibataires de l'art: pour une esthétique sans mythes*. Paris: Gallimard.

Schechner, Richard. 1982. *The End of Humanism: Writings on Performance*. New York: Performing Arts Journal Publications.

———. 1988. *Performance Theory*. New York: Routledge.

———. 2006. *Performance Studies: An Introduction*. New York: Routledge.

Schmid, Wolf. 2003. "Narrativity and Eventfulness." In *What Is Narratology? Questions and Answers Regarding the Status of a Theory*, edited by Tom Kindt and Hans-Harald Müller, 17–33. Berlin: Walter de Gruyter.

Sprang, Felix. 2007. "Turns on the Narrative Turn: Showing and Telling in Needcompany's Early Shakespeare Productions and *Isabella's Room*." In *No Beauty for Me There Where Human Life Is Rare: On Jan Lauwers' Theatre Work with Needcompany,* edited by Christel Stalpaert et al., 132–48. Ghent: Academia Press.

Stalpaert, Christel et al., eds. 2007. *No Beauty for Me There Where Human Life Is Rare: On Jan Lauwers' Theatre Work with Needcompany.* Ghent: Academia Press.

Stanzel, Franz Karl. 1984. [1979]. *A Theory of Narrative.* Translated by Charlotte Goedsche. Cambridge: Cambridge University Press.

Ubersfeld, Anne. 1977. *Lire le théâtre.* Paris: éditions sociales.

———. 1981. *L'école du spectateur, lire le théâtre 2.* Paris: éditions sociales.

Vanhaesebrouck, Karel. 2004. "Towards a Theatrical Narratology." *Image & Narrative* 9. http://www.imageandnarrative.be/inarchive/performance/vanhaesebrouck.htm.

Van Kerkhoven, Marianne. 1997. "L'adaptation d'œuvres de Shakespeare par Jan Lauwers." *Theaterschrift* 11: 112–30.

Villeneuve, Johanna. 1991. "Tchekhov revisité." *Jeu—Cahiers de théâtre* 61: 84–88.

Walsh, Richard. 2007. *The Rhetoric of Fictionality: Narrative Theory and the Idea of Fiction.* Columbus: The Ohio State University Press.

Wolf, Werner. 2003. "Narrative and Narrativity: A Narratological Reconceptualization and its Applicability to the Visual Arts." *Word and Image* 19, no. 3: 180–97.

———. 2004. "'Cross that border—Close that gap': Towards an Intermedial Narratology." *European Journal for English Studies* 8, no. 1: 81–103.

CHAPTER 5

The Poetics of Suspended Narrative

FRANÇOISE REVAZ

In his article "An Introduction to the Structural Analysis of Narrative" (1975 [1966]), Roland Barthes stressed the "prodigious variety of genres" that narrative encompasses. Nearly forty years later, Jean-Michel Adam concluded his book *Genres de récits. Narrativité et généricité des textes* with the observation "that there are still so many narrative genres left to identify and describe that [this] essay has turned out to be more of an outline than a sustained analysis" (2011: 297). Convinced that the field of narrative analysis remains virtually inexhaustible and stimulated by the current renewal of narrative theory, I would like to offer a personal contribution to this field by examining a fascinating yet still largely unexplored narrative genre: suspended narrative.[1]

---

1. Interest in narrative seriality has been on the rise in French-language as well as in English-language research, as can be seen in the latter case in the collection of essays edited by Frank Kelleter, *The Media of Serial Narrative* (2017), and in the cluster of essays on "Serial Narrative" that appeared in the January 2019 issue of *Narrative*. However, the particularities of suspended narrative as a serial genre distinct from "series" properly speaking have rarely been examined in their own right.

1. SUSPENDED NARRATIVE: FROM SERIAL NOVEL TO MEDIA SAGA

The genre of suspended narrative, which can be assimilated to the feuilleton or the media saga, is characterized by its fragmentary mode of distribution: the sequential release of a narrative in installments, with a frequency of publication dictated by the type of publication. From this perspective, it shares certain features of the rhetoric of seriality and imposes a particular mode of reception: that of discontinuous reading, and hence the impossibility for the reader to know what happens next until a subsequent episode is published.

The French term *feuilleton* appeared at the end of the eighteenth century to refer to the section in a newspaper containing nonfictional texts and short fictional narratives (tales or short stories) published in installments. The extension of the term "feuilleton" or "serial" to include long fictional narratives (novels) took off in the 1840s, and the term "serial novel" became the preferred designation of this new literary genre. During the same period, there arose, in parallel, a widespread practice of selling novels *en livraisons,* that is, in installments that appeared at various intervals and could even be discontinued before reaching the end. For instance, the novelist Eugène Sue's *Le Morne-au-Diable ou l'Aventurier* appeared in forty installments in the newspaper *La Patrie* between November 2, 1841, and February 4, 1842, and subsequently in two separate volumes, published by Gosselin, in 1842. In the early twentieth century, cinema and comics used the same serial approach, the former in episode films and the latter in daily or weekly strips telling a to-be-continued story. Thereafter, television adopted the technique and still offers today suspended narratives, that is, series that use the same dramatic devices as the lengthy nineteenth-century serial novels. Finally, over the last ten years or so, the term "feuilleton," meaning an ongoing media saga, has regularly been used in French newspaper and media jargon to refer to "affairs" (political conflicts, electoral processes, natural catastrophes, or financial scandals) whose twists and turns are reported on a daily basis until they reach their natural conclusion. As we can see, suspended narrative involves extremely diverse sociodiscursive practices (literature, the written press, comics, radio, television, and cinema), thus demonstrating its eminently transmedial nature.

In the context of this chapter, I will illustrate the genre of suspended narrative by drawing upon two contrasting corpora assembled in the course of research projects supported by the Swiss National Scientific Research Fund. One corpus brings together media feuilletons or sagas taken from the contemporary written press; the other consists of to-be-continued stories taken from Franco-Belgian comics of the 1940s and '50s.[2]

2. MULTILEVEL TEMPORAL SUSPENSION

Since Genette (1980 [1972], 1988 [1983]), the narrative text has been considered to be governed by a double temporality. On the one hand, there is the temporal plane of the "story," that is, the temporality of the events being narrated as they took place or are assumed to have taken place in the diegetic world. And on the other, there is the temporal plane of the "narrative," which corresponds to the order in which oral, written, or iconic-verbal discourse presents the events of the diegetic world. These two temporal levels can be in synchrony if the narrative relates events in the order in which they took place, but they can also be asynchronous in the well-known cases of prolepsis and analepsis. In the case of suspended narrative, we need to add a third level of temporality: that of periodic publication in the real world. Temporal suspension, then, can be observed at all three of these levels.

The fragmented mode of publication imposes a temporal suspension in the reader's world, since he or she can only read part of the ongoing media affair or comic adventure. This suspension of publication leads to a temporal interruption at the levels of both "story" and "narrative." While each new episode of a suspended narrative only provides a portion of the macro-narrative "ahead,"[3] observation of the media and fictional corpora shows that there is a significant difference between them at the level of the temporality of events. In the context of a media affair, the people involved do not suspend their activity between two narrated episodes. Events continue to unfold, life goes on, and the time of events does not stand still in between the narrative fragments provided day after day by journalists. This means that there is a referential continuity that journalists can draw upon to produce their daily articles. In comic-strip narratives, on the other hand, nothing seems to happen, in between two episodes, to the characters involved in the different adventures. No long temporal ellipsis is ever observed, allowing the reader to imagine that diegetic time has elapsed of which he or she is not aware. This is why

---

2. For further details, see Revaz (2017, 2018); Revaz and Boillat (2016); and Revaz, Boillat, Borel, and Oesterlé (2016).

3. In the particular context of the present article, an "episode" is defined as the narrative unit constituted by each new "installment": a daily article on a media affair, or the weekly strip of a to-be-continued story.

the rhythm of publication in weekly strips seems to result in a particular type of temporal suspension, different from that to be found in, for instance, the division of the novel into chapters. Indeed, division into chapters, whose "suspensive potentialities" are highlighted by Ugo Dionne (2008), may give rise to long interruptions in the diegetic world. It is not unusual to find a chapter beginning as follows: "Almost two years later Giovanni Drogo was sleeping one night . . . ," or again: "Another page turns, the months and the years go by" (Buzzati 2007 [1940]: 86, 236). In comic-strip adventures, when there is an ellipsis between the "shown" (what is visible in the image) and the "intervened" (what is assumed to have taken place between the previous and the following image),[4] the hiatus is of an extremely short duration and can easily be filled in. Often, the summary at the beginning of the strip mentions an element that makes it possible to understand the link between the last panel of the previous episode and the first panel of the following episode. For example, in the periodical magazine *Paris Jeunes,* the page of the "Atome 21–93" adventure dated May 30, 1946, ends with the image of two characters lying on the ground, having been knocked out by an invisible hand. A week later, the summary states that they "have come round," which enables the reader to understand why the first panel of the new episode shows them on their feet, though still dazed. In other cases, the temporal hiatus between two panels can be filled by referring to an actional script. The "Atome 21–93" page dated June 20, 1946, ends with an image of the same protagonists when they have just decided to go in search of their enemy. They are seen heading toward a sort of aircraft. One of them says: "We will fly over the area in my stratorocket. . . ." The following episode shows the two characters at the controls of the craft high in the sky. In this case, the temporal ellipsis can easily be filled by the reader, who will activate the "embarkation-on-an-aircraft and takeoff" script. As a general rule, however, the actions and movements of the characters carry on exactly from where the reader, involuntarily cut off from the text, left them the previous week. Thus it is not unusual to have a new episode that starts with chronological information such as: "A second later, the sharp blade penetrated deep into the body of the hyena" (*Vaillant,* no. 120, August 28, 1947), giving the impression that the character had remained immobile for a whole week poised, ready to strike, knife in hand, his movement literally "suspended." In some cases, it is a character's utterance that remains suspended at the end of a strip, and it is only a week later that the final word or

---

4. The concepts of the "shown" and the "intervened" are borrowed from Thierry Groensteen (2013).

sentence is uttered or the verbal exchange with a crony is concluded. Last, the suspended time of publication in the real world may be integrated, through the phenomenon of metalepsis, into the diegetic level when, for instance, the characters' frame of reference coincides with that of the strip's publication in weekly installments. In this case, the characters in the narrative comment on the unfolding of their own adventures while taking into account the rhythm of publication. Thus a character in the diegetic world will encourage another to wait "until next Thursday," which in fact corresponds to the publication date of the following episode in the world of the reader. As Alain Boillat points out with reference to the suspended narrative of *Little Nemo in Slumberland*, published weekly in the *New York Herald* from October 15, 1905, to July 23, 1911: "The segmentation of the narrative into episodes is not called into question by the diegetic pseudo-continuity, but rather is exhibited in the diegesis itself" (2013: 100).

3. A FRAGMENTED WHOLE

Conventionally, narrative is defined with reference to the criteria of unity and closure inherited from Aristotelian theory, itself based on the *Poetics*: "As in the other arts of representation a single representation means a representation of a single object, so too the plot being a representation of a piece of action must represent a single piece of action and the whole of it" (Aristotle 1932: 1451a30). In light of this definition, suspended narrative is problematic. Indeed, since it is most often written piecemeal as publication progresses, its narration is fragmented, and this may appear to compromise the narrative's unity: "Construction over time fragments and dilutes the coherence that a narrative composed as a whole would have possessed, and weakens its configuration" (Dubied 2004: 207). This position, inherited from certain structuralist and formalist approaches, gives the impression that the dimensions of unity and closure are dependent on the sole condition that the narrative be complete on publication (a finished novel or short story), and hence that it can be read from beginning to end. However, as Jean-Marie Schaeffer has pointed out, what matters "is not that there is a universal consensus as to what a complete and self-contained narrative actually is, but solely the fact that, for a narrative to be successful, the reader needs to consider it as complete and self-contained" (2010: 217). Under what condition(s), then, can a narrative be considered complete? Let us return for a moment to Aristotle and his notion of "the whole":

> A whole is what has a beginning and middle and end. A beginning is that which is not a necessary consequent of anything else but after which something else exists or happens as a natural result. An end on the contrary is that which is inevitably or, as a rule, the natural result of something else but from which nothing else follows; a middle follows something else and something follows from it. Well constructed plots must not therefore begin and end at random, but must embody the formulae we have stated. (Aristotle 1932: 1450b26)

A priori, this definition seems to describe the mere chronological succession of the three "moments" of any actional process: its "beginning," "middle," and "end." However, despite appearances, what in fact dictates the succession of the parts of a process is as much a logical constraint as a chronological order: The parts of the "whole" constituted by the "single" piece of action "must be so arranged that if one of them be transposed or removed, the unity of the whole is dislocated and destroyed. For if the presence or absence of a thing makes no visible difference, then it is not an integral part of the whole" (1451a32). Aristotle's affirmation, "A beginning is that which is not a necessary consequent of anything else but after which something else exists or happens as a natural result," underlines the logical link connecting the beginning and the middle. The beginning of an action can be defined as such not because nothing happened prior to it, but because there is no causal link between what happened previously and what follows. Likewise, the logical link connecting the end to the middle is one of necessity or probability. When Aristotle states that nothing else comes after the end, it is, again, with reference not to a chronological succession, but to a logical consequence: Events and actions may well take place after the end, but they are in no way the outcome of this conclusion. Beyond mere chronological succession, Aristotle seeks to demonstrate the indispensable causal link between events for, he says, "there is indeed a vast difference between what happens *propter hoc* and *post hoc*" (1452a20). In short, the continuity of a narrative depends on the fact that the relationship between its parts is not merely chronological (one part before another), but also logical (one part as a consequence of another). In the case of suspended narrative, the effect of completion (the temporal and logical links between distinct episodes) results from the presence of verbal or iconic elements whose function is to unify the distinct episodes through their integration into the structure of the forward-moving narrative—that is, to weave a unity that transcends the fragments, to highlight continuity, to suture the spatial and temporal gaps between episodes, and, in short, to confirm that we are still reading the same story.

4. A COHERENT WHOLE

Though a suspended narrative constitutes a whole once it reaches its conclusion, at its outset it is merely an emergent whole. Hence it is important that its frontiers (beginning and end) and semantic unity (thematic continuity between successive episodes) be clearly indicated. When Harald Weinrich states that "a text is a meaningful (i.e., coherent and consistent) sequence of language signs between two evident breaks in communication" and that the only breaks he envisages are the "the fairly long pauses in oral communication" and "the two boundaries of the covers of a book" (1973 [1964]: 13), he fails to recognize the existence of other types of breaks, namely segmentation into chapters and publication in episodes. We therefore need to observe carefully what it is that forms the boundary lines in suspended narratives and how the participation of each episode in a macro-narrative that progresses piecemeal is indicated.

4.1. Boundary Lines

There is a marked difference between the beginning and end markers of the narratives in media sagas and those in the to-be-continued stories found in comics magazines. Leaving aside the few cases of events that are programmed to occur in serial form (a sporting tournament or an election), in most cases the emergence of a media saga cannot be predicted: It is the happenstance of current events that suddenly turns a fleeting news item into an affair that rumbles on and becomes a saga. In this rather particular context, then, the beginning of the suspended narrative is rarely announced. At best, the possibility of an imminent news saga is raised: "It will be the political saga of the week, or even the coming months" (*Le Temps*, March 26, 2012). Similarly, it is never certain that a media saga will reach its denouement; some affairs remain unsolved forever. Moreover, as the journalist-narrator can hardly influence the course of events, he cannot decide artificially when the affair will end. At best he can take note of the fact that the narrative has reached its natural conclusion: "the end of the saga that has had everyone in England on tenterhooks throughout the weekend" (*La Liberté*, January 23, 2006). Sometimes, what was heralded as the end of an affair turns out to be not a definitive but a "dangling" end: "A positive outcome appeared to await this controversy-riven saga that has been going on for years. But the threat of a referendum has once more plunged the whole question into uncertainty" (*Le Temps*, June 6, 2012).

With the fictional stories in the comics corpus, the planning, announcement, and demarcation of the narrative's beginning and end are all under the control of the scriptwriter and publisher. Even if we are aware that certain authors have been known to submit their strips upon completion of each episode, without having a prior overall scenario and hence without knowing in advance where the week's plot twists were taking them,[5] their narratives all have a form of closure. On the other hand, their duration is variable (extending from a few weeks to several years), the only convention being that, in the "adventure story" genre that dominates the corpus, "the hero overcomes all the trials so that he can leave the world of Adventure and return to his own familiar world" (Letourneux 2010: 201). The beginning of an adventure may be more or less clearly marked. Sometimes it is only indicated by the recitative in the first panel (using the [French] imperfect tense to describe the canonical initial situation). But in most cases, the beginning is announced in the peritext, either on the cover page or on an insert between inside pages, one or two weeks before the effective start of the adventure. The announcement may take several forms and be made by various enunciative sources (the publisher, a character in the comic, even the scriptwriter himself). While the end of an adventure is often indicated by the words "The End," it may also be relayed by a character in the narrative, who observes: "There we are! Another adventure brought to a successful conclusion!" (*Spirou*, no. 907, September 1, 1955). Sometimes it is only a "dangling" ending, as the possibility of continuation is raised in the recitative in the final panel: "Jasmin sets off to rejoin the guard and, perhaps, experience further adventures . . ." (*Bayard*, no. 28, June 15, 1947). When a hero's adventure is part of a series, the ending is obviously the strategic place in which to announce a new forthcoming adventure: "Next Thursday . . . *Le Sphinx d'or* [The Golden Sphinx]" (*Tintin*, November 17, 1949).

4.2. Semantic Unity

With suspended narrative, semantic unity is marked by the presence of recurrent elements that ensure the cohesion and continuity of the various episodes. Thematic continuity between the episodes of a factual media saga may be ensured by the presence of a recurrent element (an "identifier") in the form

---

5. In one episode of the earliest adventures of Spirou and Fantasio, the commentary at the end of the strip, "Will Spirou save the day? He only has six days to do it in!" (*Le Journal de Spirou*, November 10, 1938), clearly refers to the activity of the scriptwriter, who needs to find a way out for the coming week's installment!

of key words present in display copy: "September 11," "DSK Affair," "Bird Flu," and so on. The repetitive use of an identical expression has an anaphoric function and, as Sophie Moirand points out, acts as "as a memory trigger and reminder of events that occurred before the present event" (2007: 56). On rare occasions, logos (drawings or photographs, sometimes accompanied by a caption) can be found that facilitate the association of an article with an ongoing news saga. In comics magazines, the semantic unity of the to-be-continued narrative is flagged by the systematic repetition of the title of the adventure at the start of each episode. This verbal identifier, whose typographic characters sometimes vary according to the type of adventure,[6] may appear on its own, but in most instances it is complemented with an illustration; these elements, taken together, then serve as a logo for the ongoing adventure. These illustrations represent mainly the *place* where the adventure happens, an *object* connected to the plot, the *face* of the hero, or again a combination of these elements. Sometimes, when the adventure is part of a series, a surtitle may be present, acting as an identifier for the series "A Further Adventure of Alix" or "Further Adventures of Tintin and Snowy."

5. A SUCCESSION OF EPISODES: BETWEEN OPENING AND CLOSURE

As soon as a suspended narrative begins, the reader anticipates a narrative "whole," which of course can only be an emergent totality, one momentarily fragmented into successive episodes, separated in both space and time. The linkage between episodes is ensured by recourse to suture markers that are to be found at strategic junctures constituted by the thresholds of the articles or strips. While these markers are different, depending on whether they concern a media saga or a to-be-continued story in a comics strip, their functions are nevertheless identical in both cases: Backward-facing sutures (summaries, repetitions, anaphoric resumptions), looking to the past, allow the reader to recall the previous episode, while forward-facing sutures (questions, hypotheses, and forecasts), looking to the future, question what is to come, suggest possible scenarios, and awaken the readers' expectations. Thus the impression of unity felt by all readers of a suspended narrative is due to the manifestation of a particular form of cotextuality that extends beyond the strict space of the daily or weekly episode. Usually the notion of cotextuality designates

---

6. The writing may seek to convey an atmosphere mimetically. We find, for instance, the title of an adventure that takes place in Baghdad written in characters that imitate Arabic calligraphy, or the letter *c*, in the title *On a marché sur la lune*, represented by a crescent moon.

the scope—to the left or the right—of a linguistic unit in a text and includes the relations of interdependence obtaining between copresent utterances. In suspended narrative, the notion must be broadened to allow for the different forms of linkage observable between successive episodes, that is, the horizontal interweaving of a left cotext (the previous episode) with a right cotext (the following episode). This form of cotextuality, which is external to the unit of the episode but internal to the macrotextual unit constituted by the suspended narrative, is in fact a phenomenon of "transtextual" cotextuality.

5.1. The Opening of an Episode

As the days go by, the journalist-narrator of a media saga reports fragments of the events in an emerging story while remaining ignorant of what is to come. Thus the whole built up by his discourse can be seen to be under permanent threat from the unpredictable course of ongoing events. As the scenario of events has not yet been written, the task of emplotment is largely one of anticipation, and it is the narrative's forward-facing sutures that will be dominant. As he has no hold on the course of events, the journalist who wishes to keep his readers on the edge of their seats can only imagine possible scenarios and make predictions. Which is why, besides presenting the latest developments, he is led to ask questions ("Will he sell or won't he?" [*Le Matin*, February 13, 2006]), advance hypotheses ("If the situation continues to deteriorate, the firm will become a prime candidate for asset-stripping" [*Le Temps*, January 27, 2006]), or suggest more or less probable future developments ("Alinghi can hope to win the Cup today" [*24 Heures*, July 3, 2007]). This prospective activity can be observed in both display copy and the body of the article itself. Backward-facing sutures, that is, reminders, are less frequent, as it is supposed that the reader will remember recently described events from one day to the next. It is only when, for want of fresh news, a saga is interrupted for too long that journalists consider it necessary to give a summary, or at least a brief reminder of the facts, in order to reconnect the reader with the emerging plot.

In comics-magazine serials, the linkage between episodes follows other conventions. First, in some adventures each episode is given a title at the start of the strip, with the title of the subsequent episode appearing at the end. In such cases, the suture consists in an exact repetition of this peritextual component in two successive installments. As for backward-facing sutures, the term of course refers to the summary that, by convention, can be found at the start of the strip and that serves as a reminder of the main events of the previous weeks. However, as in media sagas, it is the forward-facing sutures that are most important, the only difference being that the scriptwriter controls the turn of events that he himself imagines and can therefore end each episode as he wishes. Since the aim is to spur the reader to purchase the next issue, the end of the episode is a particular focus of attention. The strategy involves creating suspense in the last panel of the strip. In this connection, there are veritable end-of-strip topoi, which have sometimes been overused by certain scriptwriters. One frequently used technique is systematic recourse to suspensive effects: suspension of an action or a movement whose accomplishment will be represented "in the next episode." The strip then ends with a spectacular image corresponding to a climax of events, such as the fall of a character or an aggression. Another way of creating a forward-facing linkage is to ask a question at the end of the strip, for instance: "What's going to happen next?," "What will become of them?," "Will Superman be defeated . . . ?," and so on. A further possibility consists in putting the hero in an apparently inescapable situation in which he himself verbalizes the probable tragic outcome, as in the following example: "A big flat creature! I won't get away this time!" (*Le Journal de Spirou*, no. 41, October 9, 1941).

However, the degree of suspense present at the end of a strip is variable; some comic strips, depending on the type of periodical or adventure, will be observed to progress by proposing a series of events without much tension[7] and dividing the narrative up in a way that often seems quite arbitrary. Sometimes, even, a sort of zero degree of suspense is to be found when the indication "to be continued" and suspension points are insufficient to leave the reader impatiently waiting for the next installment. In this case, the linkage between episodes merely consists in the recurrent presence of the hero from one week to the next.

5.2. The Closure of an Episode

While each episode of a suspended narrative calls for a continuation in the near future, it also needs to provide a sense of completion. The genre therefore has to satisfy two requirements: It needs to ensure continuity by opening each episode onto what is to follow, and at the same time allow the episode a certain autonomy:

> We are familiar with the two antagonistic constraints of closure and opening, of folding and rebounding, between which every real serial is torn: it is essential that each episode close in on itself, and it is no less imperative that

---

7. See Baroni (2007) on the principle of "narrative tension."

it be imbued with considerable tension and frustration in order to create an impatient desire to know what happens next.... (Baetens 1998: 96–97)

Within the framework of the episodes of a media affair, as we have seen, the narrative is suspended because the journalist does not know what is going to happen next. In this particular epistemic context, each article has to appear to be as complete a "news item" as possible about the day's developments. From this perspective, the journalist is obliged to close each new article even if, within the narrative economy of the suspended macro-narrative, such closure can only be provisional.

In comics-magazine to-be-continued stories, narrative suspension largely has to do with a writing strategy that deliberately delays the presentation of diegetic events. The account of the opening of episodes given above may have given the impression that to-be-continued stories consist solely in a succession of exciting episodes told at a relentless, breakneck pace, which invariably ends with the suspension of a movement aimed at building up an atmosphere of suspense. However, it is to be observed that the sort of narrative dilation particular to the suspended genre gives considerable importance to closed episodes that end with an admittedly merely provisional denouement. From this perspective, the status of the episode's strip is paradoxical, as it is both a link in the narrative chain (and hence needs to indicate what connects it to previous strips and what "looks to" subsequent ones) and a relatively autonomous fragment (which is why it needs to produce an impression of completion). The author of a to-be-continued story can therefore make good use of its division into episodes and confer a certain degree of autonomy upon his weekly strip by, as it were, closing it in on itself. One way of indicating this fragmentation is to give each episode a title. In this connection, it may be useful to bear in mind Ugo Dionne's distinction between "numbered" and "titled" chapters:

> Numbered chapters reveal the continuity, the mobility of the narrative, making it a veritable sequence and the object of a logical, causal chain.... Conversely, titled but unnumbered segments act as barriers; they close each episode in on itself, confirming the impression of parataxis, of a garland of unconnected fables. (2008: 371)

As a general rule, in to-be-continued stories the titles do not appear at the start of an episode, but when they do it is clear that their function is to designate a semantic unit, as can be seen in the following short selection of consecutive titles from one of the "Tarzan" adventures published in the magazine *Vaillant* in 1946:

- "City of Vampires" (*Vaillant*, August 8, 1946)
- "The Vampire Goddess" (*Vaillant*, August 15, 1946)
- "Vengeance!" (*Vaillant*, August 22, 1946)
- "The Living Dead!" (*Vaillant*, August 29, 1946)
- "The Trap!" (*Vaillant*, September 5, 1946)
- "The Sacrifice!" (*Vaillant*, September 12, 1946)
- "A Strange Combat" (*Vaillant*, September 19, 1946)

Each title refers to either a thematic diegetic unit (place or character) or an event unit (action or event). These titles summarize the subject matter of the week's episode, but far from destroying all suspense by revealing forthcoming content ahead of time, they act as eye-catchers whose role is in fact to tempt people into reading. Moreover, this concern with keeping up the reader's interest undoubtedly explains the remarkable fact that in comics, unlike novels, the titles more often than not appear at the end of a strip rather than the beginning, together with a message containing "next week . . . ," the aim of which is of course to ensure their readers' loyalty: "Next week: The Cunning of Spendius" (*Vaillant*, May 14, 1950).[8] While the titling of episodes isolates each narrative fragment, and often appears to be a somewhat artificial device apparently aimed at fitting the narrative material into the model imposed by periodic publication, the presence of closed episodes may also be attributable to the unfolding of the plot itself. Indeed, some to-be-continued stories involve mini-plot twists that seem to evolve quite naturally in the limited space of a weekly strip. For instance, the "adventure" genre, so widely represented in the corpus, generally presents a hero entrusted with a mission or who, acting on his own initiative and out of personal interest, engages in a quest (for wealth, glory, a woman, etc.). These situations favor the accumulation of ordeals and obstacles that the hero needs to overcome before he can attain his goal. The weekly strip format provides the opportunity for a complete mini-plot that generally unfolds as follows: The hero is faced with danger; his strength and courage enable him to overcome his adversary; momentarily, the danger is averted. Or again: The hero finds himself at an impasse; he comes up with an ingenious solution (or a helper miraculously comes along and gets him out of trouble); he is then well positioned to pursue his quest. And the strip ends with a panel showing the positive denouement of the week's plot twist. This closure is of course only provisional and in no way prevents the reader from

---

8. Sometimes, each episode of an adventure is given a title at the beginning of the strip and ends with the announcement of the title of the following episode. In such cases there is a suturing effect due to the identical repetition of an element of the peritext in two successive installments.

eagerly looking forward to the next installment for, as the rules of the "adventure" genre imply, no sooner has the hero got out of one tight spot than he finds himself in another.

6. SERIAL OR SERIES?

In this chapter I have sometimes used the term "series." As such expressions as "serial" or television "series" are interchangeable in ordinary language, the terms might be thought to be synonymous. This is not the case, however. In *Memories and Adventures,* Sir Arthur Conan Doyle, the author of the famous Sherlock Holmes adventures, makes a very clear distinction between the two notions:

> A number of monthly magazines were coming out at that time, notable among which was *The Strand.* . . . Considering these various journals with their disconnected stories it had struck me that a single character running through a series, if it only engaged the attention of the reader, would bind that reader to that particular magazine. On the other hand, it had long seemed to me that the ordinary serial might be an impediment rather than a help to a magazine, since, sooner or later, one missed one number and afterwards it had lost all interest. Clearly the ideal compromise was a character which carried through, and yet installments which were each complete in themselves. (Doyle 2012 [1924]: 90)

As this extract shows, the term "serial" designates the specific mode of production of suspended narrative, whose dynamic is as follows: Each installment is a fragment of the forthcoming macro-narrative. The notion of "series," on the other hand, is characterized by a different dynamic: the return of the same well-known, familiar characters in successive episodes, which in each issue proposes a narrative that is both complete and completed. The series, then, is based not on the fragmentation of a narrative into successive episodes chronologically linked to each other, but on the principle of redundancy.[9] In a series, the hero never ages: In each new adventure, the reader finds him exactly as he was in previous adventures. Umberto Eco points out just how much the pleasure derived from reading a series depends on this very immutability: not

---

9. The same lack of distinction between "serial" and "series" can be found in O'Sullivan (2019), where "serial" is defined quite justly as "a continuing narrative distributed in installments over time" (50). However, the example given is the films of James Bond, which are actually "series."

just the same hero, with the same characteristics (clothes, character, habits, gestures, etc.), but also the same plot structure. Even if, in each new adventure, the hero is to be found in a different setting and faced with new obstacles, the convention that governs the series is "the repetition of a habitual scheme in which the reader can recognize something he has already seen and of which he has grown fond" (Eco 1984: 160). What must be underlined is the fact that, curiously enough, the predictability of events characteristic of the series seems in no way to diminish the element of suspense. Depending on the narrative genre to which the series belongs (adventure, Western, science fiction, etc.), the reader will have a rough idea of what is going to happen, but not of the way the hero will pull through: "The reader's pleasure consists in finding himself immersed in a game of which he knows the pieces and the rules—and perhaps the outcome—drawing pleasure simply from following the minimal variations by which the victor realizes his objective" (Eco 1984: 160). As Bruno Monfort points out: "In a series the movement is not from previous narrative to following narrative, but from the interior of each text toward the series as a virtual set" (1995: 65). Last, it should be noted that, while a clear distinction needs to be made between the notions of serial and series, various combinations of the two are possible. Some of the suspended narratives in the corpus of comics examined for this essay present a single adventure centered on a hero who never subsequently reappears, while others are continued as a series.[10]

7. SUSPENDED NARRATIVE: A TRANSMEDIAL GENRE

Suspended narrative clearly belongs to the narrative genre. It can be observed that, over and above their semiotic diversity, each of the texts in the corpus (from journalism or from comic strips) displays traits of narrativity that are common with the others. But suspended narrative is also distinguished from the classic narrative genres (fairy tale, fable, historical narrative, etc.) due to its particular mode of production, namely publication in fragments. This observation confirms the following postulate, formulated by Jean-Michel Adam:

> Genres are thus defined by contrast within a system of genres; they can be understood only within a set of resemblances and differences between genres and subgenres defined by a social group at a given moment of its history. (2011: 14)

---

10. The same phenomenon is also to be found in television series, among which some productions are actually serials (*Dallas, Top Models,* or *Lost*) while others are not (*Friends, Columbo,* or *Dr. House*).

While suspended narrative shares with other genres the fact of being narrative, its fragmented mode of production influences its mode of textualization. It is here that the decisive impact of genericity[11] on textuality can be noticed. The elements of textuality singled out in this essay are obviously constrained by their belonging to a "suspended" genre. For example, when a comics series develops over a long period of time (several months or even several years), the canonic narrative structure[12] is necessarily affected. The actional kernel of the plot bloats up out of proportion, and in this case the succession of panels no longer relates but to an interminable string of incidents, putting the denouement off indefinitely.

The transmediality of suspended narrative must also be taken into account. By transmediality I mean the possibility of "transferring" the specificities of suspended narrative from one medium to another. Thus, whether it is a media feuilleton or saga taken from the contemporary written press or a to-be-continued story from the comics, the exact same method of fragmented production and regular suspension of the narrative can be observed. In this way, it can be said that this particular narrative genre is indeed "transmedial."[13]

8. CONCLUSION

This brief overview of suspended narrative in two separate corpora (media sagas and to-be-continued stories in comics) demonstrates, I hope, how much this transmedial narrative genre deserves to be theorized. Suspended narrative has often been treated with disdain by narratologists who tend to consider it a minor genre, whose fragmentary mode of publication calls into question the unity and coherence specific to those forms of narrative worthy of the name. Yet it allows an enriching reexamination of existing narrative theory and is, unquestionably, a fully legitimate genre that has its rightful place amid the vast array of narrative genres.

Translated from the French by Rodney Coward

---

11. The concept of genericity thus makes it possible to think of a text as participating in several genres rather than belonging to one single genre (see Adam and Heidmann 2006: 25).

12. The canonic structure is a five-part structure composed of the following phases: initial situation—complication—actional kernel—denouement—final situation (see Revaz 2009).

13. The fact that suspended narrative in some way "traverses" the various types of media can be seen not only in the corpus studied in this chapter but also in other types of media productions such as the literary feuilleton or the television series, to mention only the best-known of them.

WORKS CITED

Adam, Jean-Michel. 2011. *Genres de récits. Narrativité et généricité des textes.* Louvain-la-Neuve: L'Harmattan-Academia.

Adam, Jean-Michel, and Ute Heidmann. 2006. "Six propositions pour l'étude de la généricité." *La Licorne* 79: 21–34.

Aristotle. 1932. "Poetics." In *Aristotle in 23 Volumes,* translated by W. H. Fyfe, vol. 23. Cambridge, MA: Harvard University Press. http://www.perseus.tufts.edu/hopper/text?doc=Perseus: text:1999.01.0056.

Baetens, Jan. 1998. *Formes et politiques de la bande dessinée.* Louvain: Peeters.

Baroni, Raphaël. 2007. *La Tension narrative. Suspense, curiosité, surprise.* Paris: Seuil.

Barthes, Roland. 1975. [1966]. "An Introduction to the Structural Analysis of Narrative." *New Literary History* 6, no. 2: 237–72.

Boillat, Alain. 2013. "Récit(s) en fragments: Logiques sérielle et mondaine dans *Little Nemo in Slumberland* de Winsor McCay." *Études de lettres* 3/4: 93–123.

Buzzati, Dino. 2007. [1940]. *The Tartar Steppe.* Translated by Stuart C. Hood. Edinburgh: Canongate Books.

Dionne, Ugo. 2008. *La voie aux chapitres. Poétique de la disposition Romanesque.* Paris: Seuil.

Doyle, Sir Arthur Conan. 2012. [1924]. *Memories and Adventures.* Cambridge: Cambridge University Press.

Dubied, Annik. 2004. *Les dits et les scènes du fait divers.* Geneva: Droz.

Eco, Umberto. 1984. "Narrative Structures in Fleming." In *The Role of the Reader: Explorations in the Semiotics of Texts,* 144–74. Bloomington: Indiana University Press.

Genette, Gérard. 1980. [1972]. *Narrative Discourse: An Essay in Method.* Translated by Jane E. Lewin. Ithaca, NY: Cornell University Press.

———. 1988. [1983]. *Narrative Discourse Revisited.* Translated by Jane E. Lewin. Ithaca, NY: Cornell University Press.

Groensteen, Thierry. 2013. *Comics and Narration.* Translated by Ann Miller. Jackson: University Press of Mississippi.

Kelleter, Frank, ed. 2017. *The Media of Serial Narrative.* Columbus: The Ohio State University Press.

Letourneux, Matthieu. 2010. *Le roman d'aventures, 1870–1930.* Limoges: Presses universitaires de Limoges.

Moirand, Sophie. 2007. *Les discours de la presse quotidienne: Observer, analyser, comprendre.* Paris: Presses universitaires de France.

Monfort, Bruno. 1995. "Sherlock Holmes et le 'plaisir de la non-histoire': Série et discontinuité." *Poétique* 101: 47–67.

O'Sullivan, Sean. 2019. "Six Elements of Serial Narrative." *Narrative* 27, no. 1: 49–64.

Revaz, Françoise. 2009. *Introduction à la narratologie. Action et narration.* Bruxelles: De Boeck.

———. 2017. "L'épisode hebdomadaire des histoires 'à suivre': une forme de chapitre minimal?" In *Pratiques et poétiques du chapitre du 19ème siècle au 21ème siècle,* edited by Claire Colin, Thomas Conrad and Aude Leblond, 135–49. Rennes: Presses universitaires de Rennes.

———. 2018. "Le découpage des histoires à suivre en bandes dessinées: quels types d'unités?" In *Méthodes stylistiques: unités et paliers de pertinence?* edited by Michèle Monte and Philippe Wahl, 297–314. Lyon: Presses universitaires de Lyon.

Revaz, Françoise, and Alain Boillat. 2016. "Intrigue, Suspense, and Sequentiality in Comic Strips: Reading Little Sammy Sneeze." In *Narrative Sequence in Contemporary Narratology,* edited by Raphaël Baroni and Françoise Revaz, 107–29. Columbus: The Ohio State University Press.

Revaz, Françoise, Alain Boillat, Marine Borel, and Raphaël Oesterlé. 2016. *Case, strip, action!, Les feuilletons en bandes dessinées dans les magazines pour la jeunesse (1946–1959)*. CH-Gollion: Infolio.

Schaeffer, Jean-Marie. 2010. "Le traitement cognitif de la narration." In *Narratologies contemporaines: Approches nouvelles pour la théorie et l'analyse du récit*, edited by John Pier and Francis Berthelot, 215–31. Paris: Éditions des Archives Contemporaines.

Weinrich, Harald. 1973. [1964]. *Le temps: le récit et le commentaire*. Translated by Michèle Lacoste. Paris: Seuil.

CHAPTER 6

Discourse Analysis and Narrative Theory

A French Perspective

JOHN PIER

1. FROM STRUCTURE TO DISCOURSE

Structural narratology in France can be dated from Claude Lévi-Strauss's "The Structure of Myth," published in 1955, to Gérard Genette's *Nouveau discours du récit*, which appeared in 1983. During that period, the theory and method of narrative analysis evolved considerably (see Pier 2011, 2017). Later, under the effect of developments such as poststructuralism, deconstructionism, and French Theory, narratology seemed to be eclipsed before reemerging in international research during the 1990s in yet other forms. Where "classical" structural narratology was said to be "text-centered," "postclassical" narratologies, nourished by input from the narrative turn, the growth of interdisciplinarity, and the increasing diversity of narrative objects, has proved to be resolutely "context-oriented." In recent years, narrative theorists have tended either to embrace the lines of continuity between the achievements of structural narratology and the new advances or, on the contrary, to call those accomplishments into question in the light of present-day research.

These developments have all been widely documented, debated, and integrated into ongoing scholarship in a broad array of narratological schools. They, however, are not the concern of this chapter, except in an incidental way. The focus will be on narrative theory from the angle of discourse analysis and, more specifically, on how French discourse analysis, since its inception at the end of the 1960s, has introduced a number of insights, concepts, and analytical practices that deserve to be taken into consideration. Relatively unknown outside the French-speaking scholarly community, the various approaches that have arisen out of French discourse analysis can be associated with structuralism, but this is largely to the extent that they have taken a critical distance from structuralist doctrine in ways that cannot be assimilated into the poststructuralist framework familiar to narrative theorists working in the international mainstream context. This is due in no small measure to the fact that French discourse analysis, particularly in its early stages, was focused on a corpus drawn from political discourse, not narrative.

Discourse analysis lies at the crossroads of the human and social sciences. For this reason, it has been described as "the analysis of language in use" (Brown and Yule 1983: 1) or as "a non-autonomous theory of language" (Toolan 2002: xxiii) and is sometimes referred to as the "discursive turn." Moreover, it has acquired various inflections according to whether it is oriented toward history, anthropology, sociology, psychology, philosophy, or any of a host of other disciplines, including narratology in its literary and other branches. Overall, according to Patrick Charaudeau and Dominique Maingueneau's *Dictionnaire d'analyse du discours,* four orientations can be distinguished in this field: (1) studies that emphasize discourse within the framework of social interaction; (2) studies that focus on situations of language communication and thus on discourse genres; (3) those that seek to link together the functioning of discourse and the production of knowledge along with ideological positioning; and (4) studies that highlight textual organization or identify marks of enunciation (Charaudeau and Maingueneau 2002: 44). The more specifically French tendencies of discourse analysis are the following:

- relatively restricted corpuses, and more particularly corpuses of a historical interest (this applies particularly to early studies in the field);
- an interest not only in the discursive function of language units but also in their properties as linguistic units;
- the privileged role of theories of enunciation;
- the importance granted to interdiscourse; and
- the modes of inscription of the subject in his or her discourse (Maingueneau 1997 [1991]: 24).

"The object of discourse analysis," according to Maingueneau in an important essay, is "*neither textual organization considered in and of itself, nor the situation of communication, but the intrication of a mode of enunciation and a determined social place. Discourse is apprehended here as an activity related* to a *genre* as a *discursive institution*: its interest is to not think of places independently of the enunciations they make possible and that make them possible" (1995: 7–8; emphasis added; see 1997 [1991]: 13).[1] In order to develop the analysis of discourse along these lines, three areas of study are called upon: text linguistics, theories of enunciation, and pragmatics.

As can be seen from the delimitations above, French discourse analysis, because it is geared toward discourses emerging in all social spheres, draws no fast boundary between text and context. In effect, this approach, by its very origins, was context-oriented well before the advent of postclassical narratology, a fact that seems to have escaped the attention of many narrative theorists. This is so even though French discourse analysts began looking more closely at the problems of narrative and literary theory starting in the 1990s.[2] What distinguishes French discourse analysis in its various forms from structuralism, and from structural narratology, is that the focus is no longer on structure or on the structure of text but on discourse as it occurs in context. This orientation entails a number of significant departures from the concepts, principles, and methods that have typically been associated with structuralism and with structural narratology. The mutations that have occurred under the influence of discourse analysis, and that will be taken more fully into consideration here, are the result of research carried out in the areas of text linguistics, the theory of enunciation, discourse genres, and the scene of enunciation.

Before looking into these topics more closely, it is important to take a brief look at the environment in which French discourse analysis emerged. The 1960s are widely hailed as the age of structuralism, and while the impact of this movement cannot be contested, it must be remembered that during those years the so-called Nouvelle critique (not be confused with the Anglo-American New Criticism) was more widely embraced in French academia than structuralism. The Nouvelle critique originated partly from a rejection of the philological approach to literary history that prevailed in French universities from the end of the nineteenth century and partly from the particular interest of literary and academic circles in the individual style of authors. One important source of this emphasis on style is Marcel Proust's *Contre Sainte-Beuve* (a collection of essays published posthumously in 1954), although Leo Spitzer's *Stilstudien* (1928; French translation 1970) was also influential. This development, which was closely aligned with the aesthetics of Romanticism, contrib-

---

1. All translations from the French are my own.
2. For example, Maingueneau's *Pragmatique pour le discours littéraire* (1990) and *Le Contexte de l'oeuvre littéraire* (1993). Already in the mid-1970s some elements of text grammars and enunciative theories began to appear in literary studies. See, for example, Jean-Michel Adam's *Linguistique et discours littéraire* (1976). The same year Maingueneau's *Initiation aux méthodes de l'analyse du discours* appeared.

uted to the rise of the Nouvelle critique, culminating with the appearance of two important publications: *Pourquoi la nouvelle critique. Critique et objectivité* (Doubrovsky 1966; English translation 1973) and *Les Chemins actuels de la critique* (Poulet 1966). The tendencies of the Nouvelle critique were diverse (phenomenology, psychocriticism, genetic structuralism, etc.), but all were united in their rejection of traditional literary history. The dominant school in this current of research was thematic criticism (represented in particular by Jean Starobinski and Jean-Pierre Richard), an approach inspired by the Proustian conception of style and heir to the Romantic conception of the artist.

In principle, as argued by Maingueneau, structuralism should have offered an alternative to the positions held by thematic criticism. However, during the 1960s the "immanent" approach of structural analysis, with its emphasis on the work-in-itself, was believed to complement and buttress the focus of thematic criticism on the structures of the artist's creative consciousness. This parallelism was facilitated by the fact that both structuralism and thematic criticism were rooted in the Romantic understanding of the work as an organic whole. The connection is underscored by Serge Doubrovsky, according to whom, "Unity, wholeness, coherence: I believe that this is the motto common to all the new criticisms or, if you like, their common postulate" (1973 [1966]: 83). At the same time, structuralism, as a linguistic doctrine, was adopted in a piecemeal way by literary scholars, who employed only general concepts such *langue* and *parole,* signifier and signified, paradigmatic versus syntagmatic axes, and so on, often resorting to the categories of traditional grammar while bypassing such developments as transformational grammar, text grammar, text linguistics, and pragmatics. Nevertheless, structuralism did take an essential step by opening the way toward discourse analysis. "By rigorously dissociating literary history and stylistics, context and text, structuralism . . . prepared the conditions for renewal. Unlike most earlier approaches to literary texts, it delved into the nature and modes of organization of texts" (Maingueneau 2004: 26). It is precisely the nature and modes of organization of texts *as discourse* that were then to come into perspective. Discourse analysts took a growing interest in literary texts during the 1990s, but it was not until 2003 that the response to the two publications devoted to the Nouvelle critique appeared: *L'analyse du discours dans les études littéraires* (Amossy and Maingueneau 2003).

2. BEYOND THE SENTENCE

The principal methodological concern of the early discourse analysts had to do with language units beyond the sentence, reaching into the domain of discourse. Two partly complementary but divergent approaches to this problem were available. One, described as "inter-sentential," was initiated by Zellig S. Harris's distributionalism, a method for segmenting texts syntactically into equivalence classes beyond the sentence (Harris 1952). The other, "trans-sentential," is attributed to A. J. Greimas and is based on the logical and semantic rules of isotopy that escape the framework of the sentence (Greimas 1983 [1966]: chap. 6).[3] To be sure, French narratologists did make efforts toward bridging the sentence/discourse gap that are instructive even in today's research environment. A case in point is Roland Barthes's 1966 article "Introduction à l'analyse structurale des récits," in which the author postulates "a relation of homology between sentence and discourse . . . discourse would be a long 'sentence' (whose units would not necessarily be sentences), just as the sentence, allowing for certain specifications, is a small 'discourse.'" Putting forth "an identity between language and literature," he goes on to state that "structurally, narrative partakes of the sentence, just as every constative sentence is, in a certain way, the sketch of a small narrative" (3–4). On this basis, discourse was to be the subject of a "second linguistics," a linguistics that, a few years later, he would dub a "*linguistics of discourse* or *translinguistics* (the term *meta-linguistics,* although preferable, already being taken in a different sense)" (Barthes 2002 [1970]: 611).[4]

These considerations clearly point in the direction of discourse analysis, but they fall short of a satisfactory framework for such analysis. This is due, in part, to the fact that Barthes's proposal fails to distinguish clearly between sentence (a grammatical construction) and enunciate (*énoncé*), the result of an act of enunciation (*énonciation*).[5] As Barthes rightly observed, a discourse is not a sum of sentences: As was to become clear in subsequent years, it was the task of text linguistics to sort these matters out more carefully. For the text linguist, as for the discourse analyst, text breaks down into a *text-structure* and a *text-product* (see Maingueneau 2014: 33–36). Text-structure bears on relations beyond the sentence at the level of microlinguistic cohesion (sometimes called "texture," built up out of anaphors, co-reference, etc.; see Adam 2011: 103–50) and at that of macrostructural coherence (also called

---

3. For a brief history of early French discourse analysis, see Mazière (2010 [2005]).

4. The notion of translinguistics comes from Benveniste (1974 [1969]: 66), to which we shall return below. Shortly after his "Introduction," Barthes began to renounce structuralism in favor of deconstruction, opting instead for a theory of text (see Adam 2001a; Pier 2011: 347–48).

5. The same can be said of Paul Ricoeur when he states that "the structural analysis of narrative can be considered as one of the attempts to extend or transport this [structural] model to linguistic entities beyond the level of the sentence, the sentence being the ultimate entity for the linguist" (1984: 50). In English, both *énoncé* and *énonciation* translate as "utterance." In order to preserve the distinction between the product and the act of enunciating, "enunciate" (the said) and "enunciation" (the saying) will be employed.

"structure" or "compositional structure," consisting of narrative, descriptive, argumentative, explanatory, and dialogical sequences or prototypes together with their combinations; see Adam 2001b [1997]). As for text-product (to be distinguished from *text-archive*—roughly speaking, the signifier), this is the enunciate, in other words, the empirical, observable, and describable trace of a discoursive activity, whether written, oral or visual, consisting of ungrammatical segments as well as of entire books, but also of road signs, operating instructions, political discourses, short stories, films, and so forth—that is, the vast array of speech genres. Moreover, text-product, being an enunciate, is not something that falls out of the sky but is the result of an act of enunciation, defined by Émile Benveniste as "the putting into operation of *la langue* by an individual act of use" (1974 [1970]: 80). From this perspective, the emphasis falls not on the text of the enunciate (the text-product) but on the act of producing an enunciate. It is important to bear in mind that enunciation is not the act of an isolated individual, but that it occurs within the context of interpersonal interaction. Consequently, enunciation must be thought of as co-enunciation involving the participation of more than one enunciator or interlocutor. Interpersonal interaction as it occurs in discourse is analyzed through various linguistic markers including the use of personal pronouns, verb tense, and deictic expressions such as "here," "there," "now," and "then."

The advantages of disentangling text and sentence in this way, and thus of avoiding confusion between grammatical units and structures and the problems associated with enunciation in discourse, are not to be underestimated. Among other things, this calls into question not only the older idea of "a profound unity of language and narrative" in which "character is a noun" and "action a verb" (Todorov 1969: 27), but also the more recent assimilations and distortions resulting from overexpansion of the word "narrative" to cover virtually all forms of discourse.

3. TEXT AND DISCOURSE

Now, these distinctions raise yet another point that calls for commentary and clarification. Following the lead of text linguistics, discourse analysis gives priority to text and discourse rather than to story and discourse, the pair favored by many narratologists. Strictly speaking, the term "story" covers only a limited number of varieties of verbal or other communicative activities. Can a logical demonstration, a military command, a commercial contract, or instructions on how to install a computer program be construed as stories? Clearly there are many forms of discourse circulating in society that can be qualified as stories only marginally, if at all, even though it is the case that such discourses might in some way incorporate narratives without actually being narratives themselves.

This is by no means a mere matter for terminological quibbling, for there is in fact a charged conceptual history behind the standard story/discourse paradigm. It was Tzvetan Todorov who, in "Les catégories du récit littéraire" (1966), proposed the terminology that has become one of the mainstays of classical and postclassical narratology alike. The difficulty with Todorov's proposal is that it superimposes principles taken from the modes of enunciation in French linguistics (*histoire,* characterized by the absence of addresser and addressee, and *discours,* where their presence is marked)[6] onto narrative content and the signifying medium, respectively; this move, in turn, is said to also replace the Russian formalists' principles of *fabula* and *sjuzhet.* Taking things a step farther, in English-language narratology the French and the Russian terms are often presented as equivalent to "story" and "plot." This unhappy mixture of concepts in which *histoire, fabula,* and story, on the one hand, and *discours, sjuzhet,* and plot, on the other, are presented as an apparently homogeneous system has sometimes been diagnosed and occasionally revised (I myself have examined the issues from the standpoint of semiotics; see Pier 2003; Patron 2019 [2015]). Nevertheless, its influence remains widespread, revealing a variety of forms whose parameters are sometimes difficult to define. For example, proposals have been put forth to "export" narratological concepts and categories to disciplines and forms of expression where they may not yield the most pertinent and fruitful results. This has contributed to a "narratological imperialism" (see Phelan 2005) that, for example, has taken on the form of calls for the story/discourse distinction to serve as a basis for interdisciplinary research in fields as diverse as feminist studies and international relations (Dawson 2017). Such undertakings might well be tempered by taking into account the conceptual origins of story and discourse and the fact that narrative is one form of discourse among others.

4. *LANGUE* VERSUS *PAROLE?*

The critical view of structuralist categories taken by discourse analytical approaches also extends to another feature that continues to exert an influence in narratological research, particularly as it has been handed down in

---

6. The fundamentals of these two modes of enunciation are presented in Benveniste (1966: section 5: "L'homme dans la langue"). For a systematic presentation of Benveniste's theory of enunciation, see Ono (2007).

its vulgarized form: Saussure's *langue* and *parole*. In structural narratology, as Gerald Prince has pointed out, these concepts are often used to describe "narrative *langue*" as "the system of rules and norms accounting for the production and understanding of individual narratives," the individual narrative thereby corresponding to "narrative *parole*" (Prince 2003 [1987]: 70).[7] It is worth remembering, however, that Saussure's formulation of *langue* and *parole* is itself problematic and has been the subject of various observations and criticisms. *Langue*, the object of linguistic study, is the abstract "system of signs," a code governed by rules and constraints that are external to the individual but are nonetheless lodged in the minds of the members of the speech community.[8] *Parole* (sometimes called the message) is the material of language and corresponds to an individual and momentary act of will and intelligence; it would thus be "chimerical" to combine *langue* and *parole* from the same point of view, for *parole*, because it escapes the rules of *langue*, is not the object of linguistic study (Saussure 1972 [1915]: 30, 36). Indeed, while Saussure described the sentence as the *syntagm* (words or groups of words ordered through syntagmatic and paradigmatic relations) par excellence, he simultaneously excluded the sentence from *langue*, considering it to be a manifestation of *parole*, characterized by "the liberty of combinations" (172).[9]

Various proposals to remedy this ambivalent situation have been set forth. One example is Noam Chomsky's generative-transformational grammar in which *langue* and *parole* are replaced with the concepts of *competence*, the innate ability of speakers to construct and understand well-formed and ambiguous sentences, and *performance*, sentences realized in situations of communication whose interpretation is dependent on context, psychosocial relations, and so on. These principles have occasionally been adopted by literary theoreticians (for example, Jonathan Culler, in a chapter titled "Literary Competence," states that "linguistics offers an attractive methodological anal-

---

7. According to David Herman, "Barthes identifies for the narratologist the same object of inquiry that (*mutatis mutandis*) Ferdinand de Saussure had specified for the linguist: the system (*la langue*) from which the narrative messages (*la parole*) derives and on the basis of which they can be understood as stories in the first place" (2005: 573). This summary overlooks Barthes's call for a translinguistics.

8. Note that Saussure spoke of system, not of structure. It was Roman Jakobson, Serge Karcevsky, and Nicolas Trubetzkoy who were the first, in 1928, to speak of "structural and functional linguistics" (1930 [1928]). The following year, structure, with the sense of internal relations within a system, was integrated into the ten theses of the Prague Linguistic Circle. For a brief historical account, see "'Structure' en linguistique" (Benveniste 1966 [1962]).

9. Saussurean terminology continues to be influential in more recent narrative theory. In his classification of more than thirty varieties of postclassical narratology, Ansgar Nünning (2003) describes text-centered structural ("classical") narratology as focused on "narrative *langue*" and context-oriented new ("postclassical") narratologies on "narrative *parole*."

ogy: a grammar, as Chomsky says, 'can be regarded as a theory of language,' and the theory of literature of which Frye speaks can be regarded as the 'grammar' or literary competence which readers have assimilated but of which they may not be consciously aware"; Culler 1975: 122). Chomsky's work has also given rise to text grammars (e.g., van Dijk 1972) as well as to narrative grammars (e.g., van Dijk 1973; Prince 1973; Pavel 1985). However, these attempts were hampered by the fact that Chomsky's model is based on the sentence and does not readily apply beyond that limit. For this and other reasons, text grammars gave way to text linguistics which, in the French domain, is born out of the observation that beyond the sentence a new dimension is entered, that of discourse, the analysis of which cannot be satisfactorily carried out using the linguistic categories of the sentence.

5. THE MEDIATING ROLE OF ENUNCIATION
5.1. Benveniste

It was Émile Benveniste who, seizing on the problematic status of the sentence, torn between *langue* and *parole,* advocated a linguistics of discourse or enunciation, separate from a linguistics whose object is *la langue*. As set out in "Les niveaux de l'analyse linguistique" (1966 [1964]), the sentence, whose fundamental property is the predicate, is the upper limit of linguistic analysis. But at the same time it enters a new domain: "The sentence, an infinite creation, variety without limit, is the very life of language. With the sentence, we leave the area of *la langue* as a system of signs and enter another universe, that of language as an instrument of communication, the expression of which is discourse" (Benveniste 1966 [1964]: 129-30). Being a unit of discourse, the sentence is a bearer of sense (it is informed by signification) and reference (it refers to a given situation). With it, the speaker seeks to influence the interlocutor by transmitting information (assertion), requesting information (interrogation), or issuing orders, appeals, and so on (intimation)—none of these three functions being available at the level of *la langue* (130). "L'appareil formel de l'énonciation" (1974 [1970]) develops the argument, stressing that the key to discourse is enunciation, a process in the course of which semanticization of *la langue* takes place within a formal framework. Enunciation involves the act of enunciation itself (which presupposes the implicit or explicit presence of an addressee, a relation to the world, and a pragmatic consensus between the interlocutors); the situation in which the act occurs (each instance of discourse constitutes a center of internal reference); and instruments for realizing enunciation (indices of person, ostension, and temporal forms). Finally, in

"Sémiologie de la langue" (1974 [1969]), Benveniste introduces a third domain, that of *translinguistics*. On the one hand is an intralinguistic analysis comprising, first, a linguistics of system with emphasis on the significance of the sign (semiotics) and, second, a linguistics of enunciation whose focus is the significance of discourse (semantics). On the other hand is the linguistics of discourse, combining the theory of enunciation and the "translinguistics of texts, of works," that is, a metasemantics. This overlapping system, bound together in the middle by the linguistics of enunciation, constitutes a "second-generation" semiology whose methods and instruments may contribute to the development of other branches of general semiology (Benveniste 1974 [1970]: esp. 66). A major reformulation of structuralist doctrine, Benveniste's proposal both departs from Saussure's call for a *linguistique de la parole* and, thanks to the theory of enunciation and translinguistics—a linguistics across sentences—provides a broad outline for the functioning of *parole*, of language, in context. It is also a position that underlies some of the basic features of French discourse analysis.

The consequences resulting from the dual status of the sentence, namely the three domains of analysis identified above, are not a mere technical issue to be noted for the historical record, for they highlight a number of points of broad interest that remain valid for more recent developments in narrative theory. Placing narratology within the parameters of discourse analysis results in a switch of paradigm from the story/discourse pair to text/discourse, as already noted. This is a significant move, for the new frame of reference calls on the resources of text linguistics, on the one hand, and on those of the theory of enunciation, on the other. The system elaborated by Benveniste is centered on the problems of enunciation, not on those of text. And yet, from the standpoint of discourse analysis, the two lines of inquiry are complementary and intersect with one another in various ways. Without going into the detailed inquiry the subject deserves, it can nonetheless be said that intralinguistic analysis provides further specification to the micro- and macro-relations within text-structure, while the analysis of text-product comes within the scope of translinguistics, the semantics of enunciation. This framework marks a fundamental change of emphasis, from *langue* and *parole* to text (as understood by text linguistics) and discourse, the key to which is enunciation, whose traces remain present in the enunciate. One major advantage of the discourse analytical approach to narratology is that this avoids the risks of resolving all types and aspects of discourse into story and thus of narrativizing forms of expression, be they verbal, visual, or auditory, where this may not be warranted or where considerations of another kind may be more germane. Equally important is that with the introduction of enunciation into the analysis of discourse, it is no longer at the level of *la langue* that "the social part of language" is located, "independent of the individual" (Saussure 1972 [1915]: 31, 37), as opposed to *parole* (an individual and momentary, rule-free act), but at the level of discourse. It is in discourse that language in its interpersonal and sociohistorical dimension takes form, not in *la langue*.

As the example of Benveniste shows, the delicate and multifaceted juncture between sentence and discourse raises a number of crucial questions with numerous implications for research across the disciplines. More to the point for present purposes is that through the introduction of enunciation, the relations between text and context as they are commonly thought of in the literary field are reconfigured. Insisting that there is not a "text" around which a "context" is arranged, Maingueneau argues as follows:

> When a work is studied in relation to its system of enunciation rather than being considered a monument transmitted by tradition, the exteriority of context is obviously misleading. A work cannot be conceived of as an arrangement of "contents" making it possible to "express" ideologies or mentalities in a more or less roundabout way. The "content" of a work is in fact traversed by the conditions of its enunciation. Context is not located outside the work in a series of successive envelopes; rather, *the text is the very management of its context*. Works do in fact speak of the world, but their enunciation forms an integral part of the world they are presumed to represent. . . . Literature . . . not only discourses on the world but manages its very presence in this world. (2004: 34–35; emphasis added; see also Maingueneau 2014: 77)

That context is not an "add-on" to text and its structures but that the two are closely bound together through the effects of enunciation goes to the heart of French discourse analysis, which, by its very premises, is context-oriented. So much stands out with the above comments on the complementary criteria of text and discourse, on the one hand, and those of sentence and discourse, on the other, bringing in a set of criteria that sets discourse analysis off from structural narratology. Mainstream narratology, largely unaware of this development, has often taxed structural narratology for its neglect of context, inciting some researchers to advocate "contextualism" as an alternative. Under this hypothesis, "a strictly formalist poetics" must be completed by a "contextualist narratology" (Darby 2001; see also Chatman 1990; Shen 2017): Decontextualized narrative structures (modeled after *la langue*) are, as it were, in need of contextually situated interpretive strategies guided by cues at the discourse level. In his essay outlining the principles of postclassical narratology, David Herman states that "in an integrated approach models for narrative grammar will encompass both a narrative syntax and a narrative pragmatics, both a theory of narrative structure and a theory of narrative processing" (1999: 30, n. 12). Through the lens of discourse analysis, as the arguments above have shown, integration of the various dimensions of discourse, narrative or otherwise, passes through different channels.

5.2. Bakhtin

Another source and important predecessor of French discourse analysis is to be found in Mikhail Bakhtin's contributions to the theory of utterance and speech genres, two subdomains of Bakhtinian dialogism.[10] These contributions are sometimes seen as an extension of Benveniste's translinguistics or linguistics of discourse (e.g., Todorov 1981: 67–93; Barthes 2002 [1970]). However, this is misleading, for although the two researchers did share some common ground on these matters, Bakhtin adopted a specific meaning of the term *metalingvistika* (translated as "translinguistique" by his French commentators, an expression Bakhtin would probably have balked at) to designate his theory of utterance and speech genres within a line of reasoning that he deliberately located outside the established linguistic, philological, and literary disciplines, thus bypassing the usual sense of metalinguistics, an expression normally related to the distinction between object-language and metalanguage. "Metalanguage," he wrote, "is not simply a code; it always has a dialogic relationship to the language it describes and analyzes. The positions of the experimenter and the observer in quantum theory" (Bakhtin 1986: 136). In the West, Bakhtin is generally regarded as a pioneer of what is now called pragmatics, and for this reason his neologism might best be considered to refer to the pragmatics of discourse. The Russian theoretician represents an essential reference for French discourse analysis.

Bakhtin, like Benveniste, considers the sentence technically to be a linguistic unit, not a unit of communication: "We must provisionally pose the problem of the *sentence* as a *unit of language*, as distinct from the *utterance* as a unit of speech communication" (Bakhtin 1986: 73). Closely bound to the question of speech genres (to which I will return), Bakhtin's utterance

---

10. The principal source on these questions is Bakhtin's essay "The Problem of Speech Genres" (1952–53). Also to be mentioned are "The Problem of the Text in Linguistics, Philology, and the Human Sciences: An Experiment in Philosophical Analysis" (1959–61) and "Notes" (1970–71). All are available in Bakhtin (1986). The basic premises of utterance were originally set forth in the 1920s in Voloshinov (1973 [1929]) and in Medvedev and Bakhtin (1978 [1928]), although with a sociological rather than a pragmatic orientation.

is characterized, first, by the change of speakers, forming a link in the chain of communication and thus not coinciding with the sentence. This feature is evidenced by the Russian word for "utterance," *vyskazyvanie,* in which emphasis falls on the beginning and the end of the utterance—a "change of speech subject," not a change of subject matter. The term does not distinguish enunciation (the saying) from the enunciate (the said), the result of an act of saying. Moreover, where Benveniste defines enunciation as "the putting into operation of *la langue* by an individual act of use" (1974 [1970]: 80), Bakhtin, for whom *la langue* concerns all that is repeatable and reproducible in language and utterance what is unique in context (1986: 105), stresses the centrality of the *active responsive attitude* elicited in the addressee by the utterance: "From the very beginning, the speaker expects a response from [the speech participants], an active responsive understanding. The entire utterance is constructed, as it were, in anticipation of encountering this response" (1986: 94). Thus, he asserts, "Every utterance must be regarded primarily as a *response* to preceding utterances of the given sphere" (91; see 68, 82). In this regard, the sentence is neutral, for it is uttered by no one and addressed to no one. Utterances come fused with their contexts—contexts that are themselves mutable.

With these basic features of the utterance a number of others are to be associated. The possibility of responding to an utterance is dependent on its *finalization,* that is, on the semantic exhaustiveness of the theme or sense of the utterance, the speaker's plan or speech will, and the use of typical and compositional generic forms. Another factor is the *relation of the utterance* to the speaker and to the other participants in speech communication. This relation is bound up with semantic content, of course, but also with the expressive tenor of the utterance and the evaluative attitude of the speaker, and it thus plays into compositional and stylistic choices. At the same time, an utterance may anticipate the discourse of another speaker and in some way allude to it. (This factor ties in with reception theory and questions surrounding the implied author and the implied reader.) A further feature of utterance is its *dialogic overtones.* An utterance reverberates with preceding and subsequent utterances and to some degree conceals traces of the utterances of others, thus weakening the boundaries between them, as illustrated most notably by free indirect discourse. Finally, an utterance is addressed to someone, raising the question of its *addressivity.* The interlocutor may be in the immediate vicinity or at a distant location. This may be an individual or a group, but in any case interlocutors are broken down according to the vast and highly diverse gamut of interpersonal and social relations, once again impacting compositional and stylistic choices. Addressivity, without which there is no utterance, is thus an underlying consideration to be taken into account when examining speech genres.

Overall, Bakhtinian utterance as a concrete unit of language is characterized by its wholeness, independently of whether or not it is grammatically well-formed. The whole utterance comprises a thematic (or semantic) content, style (involving lexical, phraseological, and grammatical choices), and particularly compositional structure, the various combinations of which are dependent on the sphere of activity and communication within which a given utterance occurs and the function it fulfills. These factors—none of which are taken into account by the Saussurean *parole*—underlie the formation of speech genres, defined as relatively stable types of utterance: "We speak only in definite speech genres, that is, all our utterances have definite and relatively typical *forms of construction of the whole*" (Bakhtin 1986: 78). Or to put it another way: Without speech genres, and the principles of utterance underlying them, verbal communication would be nearly impossible. Although speech genres exert a normative influence on discourse, they are extremely diverse and, as the features of utterance outlined above show, permeate all aspects of discourse. Speech genres are heterogeneous and culture-sensitive, and they thus present a challenge for any attempt at classification, particularly in the multifarious and more or less unstable primary (simple) genres of unmediated everyday speech, but also in more developed and organized secondary (complex) genres found in artistic, scientific, and sociopolitical forms of discourse, mainly in writing. Primary genres, when they are incorporated into secondary genres, acquire a new status as their relation to the immediate environment is severed.[11]

On the whole, it can be seen from the standpoint of French discourse analysis that Benveniste's translinguistics, by extending the properties of enunciation beyond the sentence to cover the domain of discourse, and Bakhtin's theory of utterance and speech genres, by providing a pragmatic framework for discourse, form an essential complement to text linguistics consisting, as explained above, of text-structure and text-product. Both enunciation ("the putting into operation of *la langue* by an individual act of use") and utterance ("a unit of speech communication") are acts that serve to bridge the gap between text and context, between language as system (*langue*) and language in use (*parole*). Again, discourse analysis, by its underlying premises, is context-oriented and represents, when adopted by narrative theory, a consequential readjustment of or alternative to the story/discourse paradigm and its various avatars.

It stands out from the considerations above that two conceptions of enunciative properties prevail, one "linguistic" (with an emphasis on enunciation),

---

11. My thanks go to Caryl Emerson for her helpful comments on Bakhtin.

the other "discursive" (whose focus is on utterance).[12] These lines of reflection are highly relevant for the mapping out of French discourse analysis to the extent that each exists in a "narrow" and a "broad" form. The former, providing a linguistics of enunciative phenomena, studies enunciative traces such as pronouns, shifters, modalization, evaluative expressions, and so on that refer the enunciate back to its enunciation. The broad form, which includes a linguistics of enunciation, seeks to describe the relations between the enunciate and the various elements that contribute to its constitution and thus coincides with one branch of discourse analysis. In its stronger variety, this form of study corresponds to an enunciative linguistics whose underlying premise is that human language is constituted in the act of enunciation. These various tendencies are generally associated with Benveniste and have been the occasion of many finely honed studies, including analyses of literary texts. However, enunciative phenomena can also be approached from the angle of speech genres, the criteria for which, as demonstrated by Bakhtin, are not strictly linguistic. Thus at the local level, enunciative traces may be indicative of an ideological positioning in a political discourse, of social hierarchy in everyday speech, or of certain sentiments in lyrical poetry. At the global level, the overall framework in which a discourse develops can be examined in terms of the scene of enunciation.

6. SPEECH GENRES IN DISCOURSE ANALYSIS

We will return to the notion of scene of enunciation shortly. First, however, it is necessary to clarify the role of speech genres in discourse analysis, which differs somewhat from Bakhtin's treatment of the subject. Stressing the sociohistorical nature and situational criteria of speech genres that come under the scrutiny of the ethnography of communication and pragmatics, Maingueneau subscribes to many of the characteristics of the Bakhtinian utterance. He also points out the radical expansion of speech genres beyond the traditional triad of lyric, dramatic, and epic and the profound effects of this expansion on how literary genres are perceived (Maingueneau 2004: 178–81).[13] A clear distinction is drawn between discourse types (Bakhtin's "spheres of activity") and speech

---

12. The following synthesis is based on Charaudeau and Maingueneau (2002: 230–31), supported by a large body of research in the field.

13. The study of speech genres is in fact a revival of genres in the sense of ancient rhetoric. In modern times, especially starting with Romanticism, genre theory has been largely restricted to the triad as developed by poetics. See Maingueneau (2014: 112). See also Gérard Genette's proposals for a revision of genre theory as handed down from Aristotle (Genette 1992 [1979]).

genres ("relatively stable types of utterances"), the latter described as "institutions of *parole*": A contract is a genre belonging to the legal discourse type, a sermon is a genre belonging to the religious discourse type, and so forth. There are, of course, subgenres (commercial contracts, the Christmas sermon, etc.), but this raises an additional problem, particularly in the area of literature: Over and above the ambiguous status of autofiction, for instance, when is a biography a work of literature rather than a historical document, or an essay a philosophical argument rather than a work of the imagination?

This is a vast topic that has been written about extensively and that will not be discussed here. Suffice it to say for present purposes that discourse analysis brings in a number of distinctions aimed at refining the category of speech genre. This is done by distinguishing between the different ways speech genres can be viewed. The first has to do with how speech genres relate to spheres of activity. The naturalist novels of Émile Zola are read as a literary genre, but they have also acted as a genre encroaching on the journalistic sphere of activity that produced an impact on social legislation. A second consideration is that some genres are subject to the forces of discursive fields. This is the case of political discourses and religious discourses characterized by different positionings (competing ideologies, doctrines, etc.) marked by shifting enunciative identities. Other areas where enunciative positioning can be observed are the polyphonic novel and in some aspects of implied authorship. Finally, speech genres are closely associated with places of activity: "the office, the schoolroom, the hospital, the street . . . each with numerous genres and subgenres—written/spoken, official/unofficial, work-related or not" (Maingueneau 2014: 64–68). This dimension of genre serves as a reminder of a fundamental tenet of discourse analysis, namely that genre "does not apprehend places independently of the words these places authorize (against sociological reductionism), nor words independently of the places of which they are an integral part (against linguistic reduction)" (Maingueneau 2004: 178).

The centrality of genre in French discourse analysis has resulted in yet further pertinent distinctions.[14] Similarly to Bakhtin's primary and secondary speech genres but taking account of additional factors, Maingueneau differentiates two complementary and asymmetrical "regimes" or "systems," one conversational, the other instituted. In the former, relatively unorganized system, identities and situations remain open-ended and unstable, their contours difficult to circumscribe due to the large number and variety of genres, but also to the perpetually renegotiated relations between discourse and the activities

---

14. The following comments draw mainly on Maingueneau (2004: 181–84, 2014: 114–21). Maingueneau's work in this area dates back to his *Genèses du discours* (1984).

of the immediate environment.[15] In the instituted system of genres, including those of oral discourse (lectures, political speeches, etc.), roles are more narrowly assigned, although there are varying degrees of tension and slippage between these genres and those of the conversational system.

The instituted system of genericity further breaks down into two varieties: routine and auctorial. Routine genres (reports, medical consultations, minutes of the board meeting, etc.) are associated with sociohistorically determined forms of communication in particular situations in which the roles of the participants remain relatively unchanged and the format goes unchallenged. Unlike the genres of the conversational system, whose constraints are local, routine genres tend to deploy global constraints that regulate the entire discourse in a top-down fashion. Some allow for minimal or no deviation from the norm (legal and administrative documents), others for some degree of personal variation (travel guide, televised news broadcast), and yet others are ritualized (television talk shows). For many discourse analysts, routine genres are the preferred object of study, an area in which research of this variety has made significant contributions to the analysis of documents used in the social sciences. Auctorial genres, as the name suggests, emanate from an author or possibly an editor. They are present in works of literature, philosophy, religion, science, journalism, politics, and so on and are often accompanied by a paratext or some other indication as to how they are to be received or negotiated by the public.[16] One of the distinguishing features of auctorial genres, setting them off from the routine genres, is that they are manifested in the form of self-constituting discourses (*discours constituants*). In what does the constituence of such discourses consist?

7. CONSTITUENCE AND SCENE OF ENUNCIATION

In all societies, Maingueneau observes, there exist discourses that lend authority, discourses for "bestowing sense on the acts of the entire community" (2014: 151). In Western societies, such discourses originate in the domains of religion, philosophy, science, and literature, regarded (notwithstanding their historically shifting relations and hierarchies) as "ultimate." Self-constituting, they are "validated by a scene of enunciation which authorizes itself" (Maingue-

---

15. In the conversational regime, there is no close correlation between genre and given situations of discourse. This is even truer in the context of the rapidly changing environment of today's burgeoning communications technologies.

16. On paratextuality—the "undecided zone" between the inside and the outside of the text—see Genette (1997 [1987]) and Lane (1992).

neau 2004: 47); in this way such discourses act as a legitimizing source, the guarantor of numerous auctorial genres. Self-constituting discourses are performative in nature to the extent that they combine the process of *foundation* in and by their enunciation, the determination of *place* associated with a *body of recognized enunciators*, and *memory*.[17] They are constitutive in the sense that they both regulate their own emergence and organize the elements of a given discourse into a textual whole. At the same time, however, the social inscription of these self-constituting discourses is paradoxical, a situation described by Maingueneau as "paratopy." On the one hand, a self-constituting discourse appeals to something beyond itself (religion to the otherworldly, science to reason, etc.), while on the other hand the speaker is faced with the dilemma of managing forms that mark his or her simultaneously belonging and not belonging (Marcel in *À la recherche du temps perdu*). Paratopy indicates not an absence of place (atopy) but rather a difficult negotiation between place and nonplace, a delocalization that forestalls any true constituence.[18]

The problem of self-constituting discourse, characteristic mainly of auctorial genres, is closely related to what Maingueneau calls "scene of enunciation." This term is chosen over "situation of enunciation" (a strictly linguistic concept) and "situation of communication" (employed by sociologists and sociolinguists), since the former is restricted to interaction between the enunciator, the co-enunciator and the non-enunciator, and the latter to factors that are external to enunciation or utterance as act. Scene of enunciation evokes the world of theater (*scène* means "stage"; cf. *mettre en scène*—"to stage") and implies a sort of dramaturgy inherent in language use, thus highlighting the "internal space" of discourse.[19] It is within this space, an instituted space delimited by speech genre, that enunciation occurs and unfolds as a sequence of verbal and nonverbal actions. This opens up a panoply of questions that bear on the pragmatics of discourse. In order to better frame these questions, the scene of enunciation is broken down into three interdependent types of scene.

---

17. Maingueneau relates this triad to the Greek *archeion* of human communities, bringing together the seat of power, a body of magistrates, and public archives (2004: 47). The implicit reference here is to Michel Foucault's *L'archéologie du savoir* (1969), a work often referred to by French discourse analysts, particularly with regard to the notion of discursive formations. For further discussion, see Maingueneau (2014: 81–95).

18. See Maingueneau and Cossutta (1995) and Maingueneau (2004: 46–55, 2014: 149–54); a presentation in English can be found in Maingueneau (1999). For further discussion of paratopy, see Maingueneau (2004: 70–105, 2006: 68–73).

19. See Bakhtin's "unique internal dramatism ... in the utterance" (1986: 96).

7.1. Three Scenes

The first, *global scene,* corresponds to text type or discourse type. Recognizing a book as a literary fiction, a collection of historical studies or a treatise on nuclear physics will trigger different kinds of presuppositions in the reader. Some works are characterized by a dual global scene (e.g., the King James translation of the Bible as both a religious and a literary text). On the other hand, mistaken identity of the global scene can have a considerable impact on how a work is understood and interpreted. This can be seen in Wolfgang Hildesheimer's *Marbot. Eine Biografie* (1981), initially acclaimed as the biography of a forgotten figure of the Romantic era, only to be exposed some years later as a literary fiction (see Cohn 1999).

Generic scene pertains to the sociohistorical conditions of enunciation. This includes, inter alia, the finality of a given genre (the aim of a student research paper in an academic setting is not that of a talk show for late-night television viewers); the linguistic and stylistic resources employed (the lexical choices peculiar to administrative documents as compared to those of popular magazines); and the medium or material support (digital technology has given rise to previously unknown genres such as blogs, chats, and forums, not to mention the hypertext novel inaugurated by Michael Joyce's *afternoon, a story,* in 1987). On being handed a tract in the street, one will need to know whether the global scene is politics or religion before reading further. Sometimes, however, it is a generic choice that must be made: Are Jules Vernes's novels to be read as children's literature or as science fiction?

There are instances in which the scene of enunciation is limited to these two scenes. This is the case mostly of some routine genres such as the publication of acts of parliament (generic scene) that come under the broader text type of law (global scene). The telephone book presents a more extreme example. In such cases, however, the singularity of the text or discourse and its interlocutors is not an issue.

The situation is different with discourses coming within the scope of the auctorial genres. Here, and more emphatically so with literary works, the notion of scenography can be spoken of.[20] This term, normally used in relation to the design of the stage set, refers both to the conditions that make discourse possible and legitimize it and to the product of discourse: To the theatricality of the *scène* (the spatiotemporal framework within which the discourse occurs) is added the dimension of *-graphie* (the process of the dis-

---

20. Also concerned are advertising, political communication, and numerous forms of mass communication.

course's occurrence). In this schema (and in accordance with the idea of the embeddedness of enunciation in context encountered at other points in this chapter), scenography is indissociable from topography and chronography. Scenography, located both upstream and downstream of the work, is not a mere scaffolding or décor for contents, the form of a content, but a true "pivot of enunciation" of discourse (Maingueneau 2004: 201). "To enunciate," writes Maingueneau, "is not only to activate the norms of a pre-existing institution of speech; it is also to construct, on this basis, a singular *mise en scène* of enunciation: a *scenography*" (2014: 129). It is important as well to note that whereas routine genres such as contracts or depositions generally remain unambiguously attached to their global and generic scenes, this is not the case of discourses in which scenography plays a prominent role and acts as the element most likely to retain the reader's or the listener's attention. A realist novel does not require a specific scenography but is free to take the form of a collection of documents and letters, an eyewitness account, a diary, a biography, and so on, with the global and generic scenes forming the background of this enunciation. Scenography is self-constituting in the sense that its emergence, by postulating its own conditions, entails a scene of enunciation that validates itself in the course of this enunciation. To put it another way, "scenography is . . . what comes from discourse and what engenders discourse; it legitimizes an enunciate which, in turn, must legitimize [that scenography] and establish that this scenography from which the word comes is precisely *the* scenography required in order to enunciate as appropriate" (Maingueneau 2004: 193).

7.2 A Scenography

As one of many possible examples of the scene of enunciation with its relations between the global and generic scenes and scenography, we can consider Samuel Richardson's epistolary novel *Pamela; or, Virtue Rewarded* (1740). The letters were originally intended by the author to serve as a compendium of model letters for young people to follow in response to the particular, often practical, circumstances of everyday life; as such, they can be reckoned as a specific type of sample texts among the routine genres.[21] However, in the course of the writing, Richardson decided to introduce an element of morality by turning the letters into a sort of manual for ethical education, one of a

---

21. This characteristic remains in the published work. In one of the prefatory notes to the editor, the letters are praised for "the beautiful Simplicity of Style, and a happy Propriety of Clearness of Expression. . . . This little Book will infallibly be looked upon as the hitherto much-wanted Standard or Pattern for this Kind of Writing" (Richardson 1971 [1740]: 4).

number of distinct generic scenes of this type that prospered in eighteenth-century Protestant England: The heroine's letters to her parents were meant to illustrate how young working class women should resist the wicked designs of their upper-class masters.[22] As for the global scene of *Pamela*, it is a hybrid of religion and ethical philosophy.

Now, the book as we have it is neither a treatise on religion and ethics aimed at ordering a set of concepts nor a code of moral conduct laying down a set of instructions. Rather, it is a collection of letters (together with a number of diary entries) that creates a scenography, complete with a storyline and a cast of characters. There is a palpable disparity between the global and generic scenes and the scenography, which is due in no small part to the fact that the letters are intended for private communication between Pamela and her parents, not for public consumption.[23] In this way, the epistolary scenography adopted by Richardson is also at odds with the ground rules of treatises and codes of conduct (neither of which are narrative genres), for in being withdrawn from public discourse, they lose all raison-d'être. As a consequence, Pamela's letters take on a life of their own and weave a narrative that performatively legitimizes its own enunciation. Upstream, the letters reframe and somewhat subvert the global and generic scenes pertaining to them; downstream, Pamela's private discourse, a "writing to the minute" (in Richardson's phrase), acquires something of the interior dramatic monologue by dint of the reader's intrusion into the communication chain. The term "scenography" seems singularly appropriate here as the controlling voice of an extradiegetic narrator recedes and Pamela's voice takes the stage in a process that foreshadows narrative techniques for the portrayal of consciousness that were to become some of the hallmarks of nineteenth- and twentieth-century narrative fiction.

7.3 Modes of Genericity

From this brief review of Richardson's novel, it can be seen that the relations between generic scene and scenography are multifaceted and have a considerable potential for variety. For the discourse analyst, it is important to situate

---

22. Another prefatory note states: "As to *Instruction* and *Morality*, the Piece is full of both" (Richardson 1971 [1740]: 6). The original title page reads as follows: "*Pamela; or, Virtue Rewarded*. In a series of familiar letters from a beautiful young damsel, to her parents. Now first published in order to cultivate the principles of virtue and religion in the minds of the youth of both sexes" (1). As is well known, the moral message of *Pamela* has long been diversely appreciated. The book remained on the Vatican's *Index* until 1900.

23. On the notion of "overhearing narrative," see García Landa (2004).

these phenomena within the broader context of discourse in all its manifestations. To do so, Maingueneau identifies four modes of genericity characteristic of the instituted genres.[24]

Mode 1 Instituted Genres. Business letters, notarized deeds, and other such routine genres follow an established format that allows for only minimal variation, including in the roles of the participants. The scenographies employed are thus nonindividuated and endogenous. However, documents of this kind can be refunctionalized, as is the case of the official Weekly Bills of Diseases and Deaths incorporated into Daniel Defoe's *A Journal of the Plague Year* (1722).

Mode 2 Instituted Genres. Televised variety shows are routine genres that employ endogenous scenographies allowing a certain leeway for singularizing and original variations, but without calling into question or otherwise violating the norms of the generic scene. Nevertheless, exogenous forms of scenography are possible here, as in Blaise Pascal's *Provinciales* (1656–1657), a religious pamphlet devoted to the disputes between the Jansenists and the Jesuits presented as a series of letters to a Parisian by a provincial author ignorant of the intricacies of the theological debate (see Maingueneau 1998).

Mode 3 Instituted Genres. A radio advertisement can take the form of a song, a dialogue between two customers, or an act of storytelling, its various possible scenographies thus necessarily being exogenous in relation to the relevant generic scene. By contrast, the collage technique employed by John Dos Passos in his trilogy *U. S. A.* (1930–1936), which consists of introducing newspaper clippings into an otherwise conventionally printed text, reproduces an exogenous scenography in the book as a matter of choice.

Mode 4 Instituted Genres. Works such as *Pamela* emerge in a relative generic flux because, at the time of its publication, the English novel was in its formative stage. Due to the tentative and novel relationship between generic scene and scenography, the originality of the scene of enunciation stands out and reinforces the self-constitutive quality of the work's discourse. At the same time, the "Familiar Letters" (a routine genre), whose aim is "to cultivate the principles of virtue and religion," paint a picture that is somewhat at odds with the avowed didactic purpose, for the heroine's moral resistance culminates with the conversion of Mr. B, her social superior, to more noble ways and, in the end, with Pamela's social ascension through marriage. Unlike the instituted genres of modes 1 and 2, those of mode 4 are less bound to the more or less codified discursive activities of the social space, or at any rate take liberties that are not available to those modes.

---

24. The following comments are based on Maingueneau (2004: 181–84, 2014: 133–36).

8. CONCLUSION

The task of narratology is to identify and explore the *differentia specificae* of narrative in all its forms and manifestations. With it, however, this undertaking brings the risk of either isolating narrative from other forms of expression in an attempt to single out what is characteristic of narrative and narrative alone or, in the effort to discern elements of narrative that underlie cultural artefacts generally, to inflate narrative to the point of robbing it of its specificity. With the reminder that all discourse, despite its narrative potential, cannot be framed in terms of narrative or construed as a form of storytelling, discourse analysis offers a way out of this quandary. By broadening its scope to include text and discourse, verbal or otherwise, rather than focusing on story and discourse, discourse analysis provides a means to situate narrative within the varied and fluctuating array of forms of discourse that permeate all domains of social life and cultural and disciplinary pursuits. A crucial step in the elaboration of this framework comes with the shift of emphasis from underlying structure to enunciation, the contextually situated act of language. This not only results in requalification of the relation between *langue* and *parole* but also provides for a transition between sentence and discourse, thus opening the way to translinguistics and at the same time narrowing the gap between text and context. It is in this way that discourse analysis takes account of the linguistic markers of enunciation (translinguistics) as well as of textual organization (text linguistics). Further taken into consideration are speech genres. These are the built-in regulators of enunciation, or utterance as act, that serve to organize discourse compositionally according to the social sphere at hand and thus form a pragmatic condition by which linguistic units are integrated into units of communication.

The configuration of discourse, as it emerges from these perspectives, calls into question positions that have long been entertained, explicitly or implicitly, in the study of discourse in its innumerable varieties. This is the case most notably, for present concerns, of narrative discourse, for within this configuration the opposition between action and representation, between content and form, between text and context, between production and reception, no longer seems tenable. Rather than isolating contents from their modes of transmission, discourse analysis underscores the inextricable interaction of these dimensions (see Maingueneau 2004: 49).

Indeed, when narrative is viewed through the lens of discourse analysis, the intersection of constituence, auctoriality, and scene of enunciation takes on particular salience. The convergence of these three dimensions of discourse coincides to no negligible degree with world-building, authorship, and scenography of narrative in its prolific manifestations.

WORKS CITED

Adam, Jean-Michel. 1976. *Linguistique et discours littéraire. Théorie et pratique des textes.* Paris: Larousse.

———. 2001a. "Barthes en 1970: de la translinguistique à la déconstruction." In *Littérature et sciences humaines*, edited by A. Boissinot et al., 125–48. Paris: Les Belles Lettres & Université de Cergy-Pontoise.

———. 2001b. [1997]. *Les textes: types et prototypes. Récit, description, argumentation, explication et dialogue.* Paris: Nathan.

———. 2011. *Genres de récits. Narrativité et généricité des textes.* Louvain-la-Neuve: Harmattan-Academia.

Amossy, Ruth, and Dominique Maingueneau, eds. 2003. *L'analyse du discours dans les études littéraires.* Toulouse: Presses universitaires du Mirail.

Bakhtin, M. M. 1986. *Speech Genres and Other Late Essays.* Edited by Caryl Emerson and Michael Holquist. Translated by Vern W. McGee. Austin: University of Texas Press.

Barthes, Roland. 1966. "Introduction à l'analyse structurale des récits." *Communications* 8: 1–27.

———. 2002. [1970]. "La linguistique du discours." In *Œuvres complètes*, III, edited by Éric Marty, 611–16. Paris: Seuil.

Benveniste, Émile. 1966. *Problèmes de linguistique générale.* Paris: Gallimard.

———. 1966. [1962]. "'Structure' en linguistique." In *Problèmes de linguistique générale*, 91–98. Paris: Gallimard.

———. 1966. [1962]. "Les niveaux de l'analyse linguistique." In *Problèmes de linguistique générale*, 119–31. Paris: Gallimard.

———. 1974. [1969]. "Sémiologie de la langue." In *Problèmes de linguistique générale*, II, 43–66. Paris: Gallimard.

———. 1974. [1970]. "L'appareil formel de l'énonciation." In *Problèmes de linguistique générale*, II, 79–88. Paris: Gallimard.

Brown, Gillian, and George Yule. 1983. *Discourse Analysis.* Cambridge: Cambridge University Press.

Charauedeau, Patrick, and Dominique Maingueneau, eds. 2002. *Dictionnaire d'analyse du discours.* Paris: Seuil.

Chatman, Seymour. 1990. "What We Can Learn from Contextualist Narratology." *Poetics Today* 11, no. 2: 309–28.

Cohn, Dorrit. 1999. "Breaking the Code of Fictional Biography: Wolfgang Hildesheimer's *Marbot*." In *The Distinction of Fiction*, 75–95. Baltimore: The Johns Hopkins University Press.

Culler, Jonathan. 1975. *Structuralist Poetics: Structuralism, Linguistics, and the Study of Literature.* Ithaca, NY: Cornell University Press.

Darby, David. 2001. "Form and Context: An Essay in the History of Narratology." *Poetics Today* 22, no. 4: 829–52.

Dawson, Paul. 2017. "How Many 'Turns' Does it Take to Change a Discipline? Narratology and the Interdisciplinary Rhetoric of the Narrative Turn." In *Emerging Vectors of Narratology*, edited by Per Krogh Hansen, John Pier, Philippe Roussin, and Wolf Schmid, 405–43. Berlin: De Gruyter.

Doubrovsky, Serge. 1973. [1966]. *New Criticism in France.* Translated by Derek Coltman. Chicago: The University of Chicago Press.

Foucault, Michel. 1969. *L'archéologie du savoir.* Paris: Gallimard.

García Landa, José Ángel. 2004. "Overhearing Narrative." In *The Dynamics of Narrative Form: Studies in Anglo-American Narratology*, edited by John Pier, 191–214. Berlin: Walter de Gruyter.

Genette, Gérard. 1988. [1983]. *Narrative Discourse Revisited.* Translated by Jane E. Lewin. Ithaca, NY: Cornell University Press.

———. 1992. [1979]. *The Architext: An Introduction.* Translated by Jane E. Lewin. Berkeley: University of California Press.

———. 1997. [1987]. *Paratexts: Thresholds of Interpretation.* Translated by Jane E. Lewin. Cambridge: Cambridge University Press.

Greimas, Algirdas Julien. 1983. [1966]. *Structural Semantics: An Attempt at Method.* Translated by Danielle McDowell et al. Lincoln: University of Nebraska Press.

Harris, Zellig S. 1952. "Discourse Analysis." *Language* 28: 1–30.

Herman, David. 1999. "Introduction: Narratologies." In *Narratologies: New Perspectives in Narrative Analysis,* 1–30. Columbus: The Ohio State University Press.

———. 2005. "Structuralist Narratology." In *Routledge Encyclopedia of Narrative Theory,* edited by David Herman, Manfred Jahn, and Marie-Laure Ryan, 571–76. London: Routledge.

Jakobson, Roman, Serge Karcevsky, and Nicolas Trubotzkoy. 1930 [1928]. "Quelles sont les méthodes les mieux approrpriées à un exposé complet et pratique de la phonologie d'une langue quelconque?" In *Actes du 1er Congrès International des Linguistes du 10–15 avril, 1928,* 33–36. Leiden.

Lane, Philippe. 1992. *La périphérie du texte.* Paris: Nathan.

Lévi-Strauss, Claude. 1955. "The Structural Study of Myth." *Journal of American Folklore* 78: 428–44.

Maingueneau, Dominique. 1976. *Initiation aux méthodes de l'analyse du discours.* Paris: Hachette.

———. 1984. *Genèses du discours.* Liège: Mardaga.

———. 1990. *Pragmatique pour le discours littéraire.* Paris: Dunod.

———. 1993. *Le Contexte de l'oeuvre littéraire.* Paris: Dunod.

———. 1995. "Présentation." *Langages* 117: 5–12.

———. 1997. [1991]. *Analyse du discours.* Paris: Hachette.

———. 1998. "Scénographie épistolaire et débat public." In *La lettre entre reel et fiction,* 55–71. Paris: SEDES.

———. 1999. "Analysing Self-Constituting Discourses." *Discourse Studies* 1, no. 2: 175–200.

———. 2004. *Le discours littéraire. Paratopie et scène d'énonciation.* Paris: Armand Colin.

———. 2006. *Contre Saint Proust, ou la fin de la Littérature.* Paris: Belin.

———. 2014. *Discours et analyse du discours.* Paris: Armand Colin.

Maingueneau, Dominique, and Frédéric Cossutta. 1995. "L'analyse des discours constituants." *Langages* 117: 112–25.

Mazière, Francine. 2010. [2005]. *L'analyse du discours. Histoire et pratiques.* 2nd ed. Paris: Presses universitaires de France.

Medvedev, P. N., and M. M. Bakhtin. 1978. [1928]. *The Formal Method in Literary Scholarship: A Critical Introduction to Sociological Poetics.* Translated by Albert J. White. Baltimore: The Johns Hopkins University Press.

Nünning, Ansgar. 2003. "Narratology or Narratologies? Taking Stock of Recent Developments." In *What Is Narratology? Questions and Answers Regarding the Status of a Theory,* edited by Tom Kindt and Hans-Harald Müller, 239–75. Berlin: Walter de Gruyter.

Ono, Ayako. 2007. *La notion d'énonciation chez Émile Benveniste.* Limoges: Lambert-Lucas.

Patron, Sylvie. 2019. [2015]. "Homonymy in Genette, or the Reception of the *History/Discourse* (*Histoire/Discours*) Opposition in Theories of Fictional Narrative." In *The Death of the Narrator and Other Essays,* 30–44. Trier: Wissenschaftlicher Verlag Trier.

Pavel, Thomas. 1985. *The Poetics of Plot: The Case of English Renaissance Drama*. Minneapolis: University of Minnesota Press.

Phelan, James. 2005. "Who's Here? Thoughts on Narrative Identity and Narrative Imperialism." *Narrative* 13, no. 3: 205–10.

Pier, John. 2003. "On the Semiotic Parameters of Narrative: A Critique of Story and Discourse." In *What Is Narratology? Questions and Answers Regarding the Status of a Theory*, edited by Tom Kindt and Hans-Harald Müller, 73–97. Berlin: Walter de Gruyter.

———. 2011. "Is There a French Postclassical Narratology?" In *Current Trends in Narratology*, edited by Greta Olson, 336–67. Berlin: De Gruyter.

———. 2017. "Von der französischen strukturalistischen Erzähltheorie zur nordamerikanischen postklassischen Narratologie." In *Grundthemen der Literaturwissenschaft: Erzählen*, edited by Martin Huber and Wolf Schmid, 59–87. Berlin: De Gruyter.

Poulet, Georges. 1966. *Les Chemins actuels de la critique*. Paris: Plon.

Prince, Gerald. 1973. *A Grammar of Stories*. The Hague: Mouton.

———. 2003. [1987]. *Dictionary of Narratology*. Revised ed. Lincoln: University of Nebraska Press.

Richardson, Samuel. 1971. [1740]. *Pamela; or, Virtue Rewarded*. Edited by T. C. Duncan Eaves and Ben D. Kimpel. Boston: Houghton Mifflin Company.

Ricoeur, Paul. 1984. *Temps et récit II. La configuration du temps dans le récit de fiction*. Paris: Seuil.

Saussure, Ferdinand de. 1972. [1915]. *Cours de linguistique générale*. Edited by Charles Bally and Albert Sechehaye. Paris: Payot.

Shen, Dan. 2017. "'Contextualized Poetics' and Contextualized Rhetoric: Consolidation or Subversion?" In *Emerging Vectors of Narratology*, edited by Per Krogh Hansen, John Pier, Philippe Roussin, and Wolf Schmid, 3–24. Berlin: De Gruyter.

Spitzer, Leo. 1970. [1928]. *Études de style*. Translated from German and English by Éliane Kaufholz, Alain Coulon, and Michel Foucault. Preceded by Jean Starobinski: "Leo Spitzer et la lecture stylistique." Paris: Gallimard.

Todorov, Tzvetan. 1966. "Les catégories du récit littéraire." *Communications* 8: 125–51.

———. 1969. *Grammaire du "Décaméron."* The Hague: Mouton.

———. 1981. *Mikhaïl Bakhtine: le principe dialogique suivi de Écrits du Cercle de Bakhtine*. Paris: Seuil.

Toolan, Michael. 2002. "General Introduction." In *Critical Discourse Analysis: Critical Concepts in Linguistics*, vol. 1, xxi–xxvi. London: Routledge.

van Dijk, Teun A. 1972. *Some Aspects of Text Grammars: A Study in Theoretical Linguistics and Poetics*. The Hague: Mouton.

———. 1973. "Grammaires textuelles et grammaires narratives." In *Sémiotique narrative et textuelle*, edited by Claude Chabrol, 177–207. Paris: Larousse.

Voloshinov, V. N. 1973. [1929]. *Marxism and the Philosophy of Language*. Translated by Ladislav Matejka and I. R. Titunik. Cambridge, MA: Harvard University Press.

CHAPTER 7

Regimes of Immanence, between Narratology and Narrativity

DENIS BERTRAND

1. INTRODUCTION

The notion of narrativity experienced its hour of glory in Greimassian semiotics to such an extent that it was sometimes considered emblematic of the discipline itself.[1] Today, such close identification between the two seems outdated because the analytical concepts of narrativity now appear to form an uncontested part of this theory, at least for those researchers who lay claim to it. Without attempting to promote a "return to the sources," there are nonetheless two reasons to reconsider the status of this concept, one circumstantial, the other theoretical. The first feeds into the second, allowing us to reexamine the foundations of narrativity within the global scope of the principles that

---

This chapter is based on the inaugural lecture of the Paris Semiotics Seminar (Universities of Limoges, Paris 4 and Paris 8), delivered on November 6, 2013 and titled "Les régimes d'immanence, entre narratologie et narrativité." It was originally published in Spanish under the title "Los regimenes de inmanencia, entre narratologia y narratividad," in Alessandro Zinna and Luisa Ruiz Moreno, eds., "La inmanencia en cuestión, III," *Tópicos del Seminario. Revista de semiótica*, XVII, 33, Benemérita Universidad Autónoma de Puebla, June, 2015, pp. 163–88 (translated by Juan Miguel G. Dothas). We wish to thank the editors of this journal for their authorization to publish the essay in English.

    1. The first didactic presentation of semiotics was published by Joseph Courtés in 1976: *Introduction à la sémiotique narrative et discursive*. See also Denis Bertrand, *Précis de sémiotique littéraire* (2000) and Therese Budniakiewicz, *Fundamentals of Story Logic: Introduction to Greimassian Semiotics* (1992).

provide semiotics with its status as a science of language, at the forefront of which is the principle of immanence.

The circumstance at the origin of the ideas examined in this chapter is the astonishing resurgence of narratology in debates currently taking place in France in the human sciences. It has long been the case in the English-speaking countries that, notwithstanding a considerable body of research in the literary disciplines, the practice and study of narrative are coupled with promotional discourse, both in politics and in marketing. This phenomenon has now resurfaced in the human sciences in France with the success of "storytelling," a term that might be paraphrased "narrative matters." Coming from the US, the notion was introduced in France through Christian Salmon's *Storytelling. La machine à fabriquer des histoires et à formater des esprits* (2007; English translation 2010). Observing that the narrative paradigm has come to "replace rational reasoning" in numerous social, economic, and political fields, Salmon comments on the triumph of this paradigm in a debate that had already caused a stir in the language sciences during the 1970s. This debate opposed two competing models said to lie at the heart of the intelligibility and efficacy of discourse: the *narrative model* coming out of semiology, and the *argumentation model* coming from rhetoric. The success of storytelling, according to the dust jacket of Salmon's book, amounts to "an incredible holdup of human imagination." The word "storytelling," now wholly a part of the French language, is on the lips of every columnist and communications consultant.

On the international scale, the resurgence of narratology has been accompanied with academic research programs and of international meetings devoted to narrative. To give only one example, the conference "Narrative Matters," the theme of which was "Narrative Knowing / Récit et Savoir," was organized in June 2014 by the University of Paris Diderot and The American University of Paris. The participants in this conference addressed the role of narrative in a wide variety of disciplines, including psychology, psychanalysis, sociology, anthropology, history, philosophy, the language sciences, literary studies, feminist studies, gender studies, education, medicine, health and social action, biology, law, religious sciences, computer sciences, and visual studies. The aim was to reflect on "the question of the sometimes controversial epistemological powers of narrative." All in all, it sought to take stock of the preeminence of narrative over argumentation from the perspective of cognition. Narrative, understood as an immediate, natural, and spontaneous given of discourse, casts its shadow—or its light—over all fields of knowledge. Interestingly, one of the main theoretical references at this conference was Donald Polkinghorne's *Narrative Knowing and the Human Sciences* (1988). This book puts forth an argument in favor of what was later to be known as "cognitive narratology." According to the author, "the core of the argument I make in this book is that narrative is a scheme by means of which human beings give meaning to their experience of temporality and personal actions.... Narrative meanings provide a framework for understanding the past events of one's life and for planning future actions" (Polkinghorne 1988: 11). It is noteworthy that this thesis is also defended by Paul Ricoeur in his three-volume *Temps et récit* (1983–1985; English translation 1984–1988). Ricoeur, as is well known, confers on narrative the phenomenological function of bestowing form, legibility, and orientation on the myriad happenings that occur in daily life, without which experience remains an unordered jumble of perceptions. Narrative provides temporality and memory with a structure that renders happenings intelligible. The essential function of narrative is thus to provide a "synthesis of the heterogeneous" by triggering, thanks to its configurations, the constitutive power of narrative in order to "refigure" lived experience in the aporia of time and thus make experience intelligible through the organizing power of narrative discourse.

Another reason for reexamining the issues, of a theoretical nature and relatively independent of the one described above, also inspires this study. This involves the connection that narrativity in the semiotic sense—located upstream of narratology—entertains with the problem of immanence, at the same time highlighting the particular status of narrativity. Given the resurgence of research in narrative theory, one might ponder the absence in French research since the 1960s and '70s (aside from the writings of Paul Ricoeur) of any direct or indirect reference in narrative theory to the link between narrativity in the semiotic sense and immanence that was once present in the work of Roland Barthes, Tzvetan Todorov, Gérard Genette, and especially Algirdas Julien Greimas. The latter was in fact the only one to integrate the "structural analysis of narrative" into an overall theoretical system for the analysis of discourse meaning. On reexamining Greimas's reference work (written together with Joseph Courtés), *Sémiotique. Dictionnaire raisonné de la théorie du langage* (1979; English translation 1982), one cannot but be struck by the transversal and nearly invasive presence of narrativity in many of the entries, even in those that at first sight seem to have little to do with narrative. Such is the case, for example, of the entry "Immanence," where the categories *immanence / transcendence* are used to describe the contrasting statuses of the actants *subject* (hero) and *sender* (the instance of authority that mandates the hero and sanctions his actions).

This absence of reference to French studies devoted to narrativity and the narratology of the 1960s and '70s, to semiotics (Greimas et al), and to semiology (Barthes et al), is hardly to be wondered at. Semiotics is in no way the proprietor of narrative theory and is not entitled to claim precedence over it. The problem can be approached in terms of the sociology and history of the human and social sciences and involve studying the ways ideas circulate in these disciplines. Here, however, the issues will be looked at from the inside, from a conceptual point of view. Obscuring the relation between narrativity and immanence calls for an attempt to understand how a discipline that is underpinned by the narrative hypothesis is ignored to such a degree by present-day research. What has narrative semiotics done to allow its contribution, which in my opinion is decisive, to lose sight of this broad understanding of narrative? And why is it that this fundamental dimension of the theory of language seems to have been abandoned not only by semioticians but also by narratologists to such an extent that it no longer appears except in introductory textbooks?

These questions are worth looking at more closely. Essentially, the answer can be found by examining the passage from *narratology*, a discipline that deals with the generic variations of narrative, to *narrativity*, which is central to the semiotic conception of discourse meaning. At one time a key concept, narrativity, which is integral to the principle of semiotic immanence, has since faded from view. How did this state of affairs come about? How is it that narrativity has ceased to be theoretically, conceptually, and concretely productive? One of the reasons for this transformation may well lie in the principle of immanence, and even more so in a certain radicalization of this principle. This, in any case, is the hypothesis I wish to develop here.

First of all, it will be necessary to look again at the problem of the shift away from narratology in the strict sense to an "extended" or even "generalized" narrativity by referring to a decisive contribution on this topic, marking a true bifurcation at the theoretical level: the introduction to Greimas's book *Du Sens II* (1983). The second point to be examined is the particular relation between narrative structures and the principle of immanence, with the former demonstrating the pertinence of the latter in at least one of its acceptances. Another point is the considerable effort by a number of semioticians devoted to breaking free from the shackles of immanence, either through the radical critique by Jean-Claude Coquet or through its extension and pluralization, as proposed by Jacques Fontanille in the form of "semiotic practices." Taking leave of the "principle of immanence" and looking more closely at the "plane of immanence" and the implications of this new concept, I will then take up the approach to this difficult question developed by Gilles Deleuze and Félix Guattari in a chapter entitled "The Plane of Immanence" of their book

Qu'est-ce que la philosophie? (1991; English translation 1994). Analysis of this approach will lead the way to a more open concept by replacing "principle" and "plane" with "regimes of immanence." For a concrete and exemplary case of the plurality of regimes, narrativity in the sense it is understood here (but that has been left out of account by present-day studies) will be examined in Cervantes's *Don Quixote*. This novel, a critical monument for narratologists, forces us, due to the intriguing enunciative pluralization of narrative positions, to acknowledge the presence of narrativity not only in the "said" of discourse but also in its "saying."

2. FROM NARRATOLOGY IN THE STRICT SENSE TO GENERALIZED NARRATIVITY

Nowhere in Greimas and Courtés's *Dictionary* can there be found an entry "Narratology." On the other hand, the entries "Narrative program," "Narrative trajectory," and "Narrative schema" as well as entries relating to action ("Actant," "Actor," "Subject," "Sender," etc.) and the modes or modalities of structuring action, all capped off with the entry "Narrativity," take up several dozen pages. Furthermore, these terms spread out in a true conceptual web over a considerable number of other entries. Indeed, during the late 1970s these concepts formed the radiating heart of Greimas's semiotic theory.

In the entry "Narrativity," it is stated as follows: "Narrativity has . . . gradually appeared progressively as the very organizing principle of all discourse, both narrative (identified, in the first instance, as figurative) and nonnarrative" (Greimas and Courtés 1982 [1979]: 209). Further on the authors observe that "deep narrative structures . . . can account for the appearance and development of all (not only verbal) signification [and] can also assume not only the narrative performances but also articulate . . . the different forms of discursive competence. These semiotic structures . . . or semio-narrative [structures]," they conclude, "are in our view the depository of fundamental signifying forms" (210). In addition to the internal structures of enunciated discourse (the "said") are the structures of discursive competence and performance at the enunciative level, the level of "saying." On this conception, enunciation, in Émile Benveniste's sense as the founding act of the subject, also arises out of the diversity of its interactions, and thus out of generalized narrativity or "the organizing principle of all discourse." Clearly, then, narrativity relates to other entries of the *Dictionary* that cover all dimensions of meaningful activity to one degree or another: diegesis, enunciation, narrative trajectory, and fundamental syntax as well as, though less directly, "modality" insofar as the status and identity of the actant result from modal determinations.[2]

While the *Dictionary* sets out the main lines of narrativity, it is in the broad synthesis provided by the introduction to *Du Sens II* that a major theoretical turn in semiotics is achieved: Semiotics splits off from narratology, while the notion of narrativity is left to hypertrophy. In the end, the concept of narrativity is weakened while semiotics, during the 1970s, turned resolutely toward what was called at the time the "all modal." This vast movement was seen by Greimas, in historical terms, as scientific progress—progress that appeared, first, with the reformulation of Vladimir Propp's *functions* as actantial relations and the "canonic succession of events" in the form of the narrative schema. Progress also occurred with the passage from the structure of actants to the open-ended modal mechanism that underlies each actantial identity, effectively pushing this actantial identity as such into the background. There was progress yet again with the extension of the scope of modality, reserved up to then to subjects, in such a way as to include the modalization of objects (as desirable, detestable, remarkable, etc.) with repercussions on the state of the subject, thus opening up to modulations of a passional nature. Progress, finally, took place with the rise of a universe of sense into which modality is integrated, where each broad sphere of individual and social meanings is bound to a basic modal determination: The passional is based on wanting (*vouloir*), the legal on duty (*devoir*), rhetoric and persuasiveness on knowing (*savoir*), and manipulation and domination on power (*pouvoir*). These various dimensions of scientific progress come about by exploiting the autonomy, finally mastered, of syntax and its operations. All in all, an edifice of remarkable coherence is set up—coherence, since this architecture is firmly rooted in the principle of immanence through its key concept: relation, a logical principle that is deployed in the process of narrativity.[3] But this is a narrativity that ultimately became a victim of its own success.

From this construction there resulted a crisis in the very concept on which the construction is based. Narrative syntax split off from the set of discourses

---

2. For the semiotician, the actant is defined by its modal composition. More precisely, this means that the actant emerges from a mixture of wanting (*vouloir*), knowing (*savoir*), believing (*croire*), duty (*devoir*), and power (*pouvoir*) that determines being (*être*) and doing (*faire*)—each of these modalities with its own form of negation. Modality serves to modify a predicate: "Paul drinks" → "Paul can/must/wants to drink." These modalities are open-ended so that the identity of the actant evolves in the course of the narration.

3. Relation is understood here in the sense of "relation between terms" (hierarchy, contrariety, contradiction, complementarity, etc.). It is derived from the Saussurean postulate of "difference" or "differential relation," a principle that opens up the possibility of sense in the universe of language: Sense exists only in and through difference.

out of which it was born to become the analytical model that supposedly underlies all forms of discourse—even the generation of meaning and extending so far as perception of the natural world. A sound is interpreted as a *threat*, a look as a *promise*, a gesture as a *sign of hostility*. The world is perceived through the filter of narrative. Such a generalization led Greimas, in his introduction, to a somewhat demystifying observation: "All discourse is thus 'narrative.' Narrativity is thus emptied of its meaning" (1983a: 18). This conclusion carries over to a final consideration of a more general epistemological nature: "It is as though certain instrumental concepts, having exhausted their heuristic value, a new project—the construction of a modal semiotic syntax capable of creating its own problematics and of defining new semiotic objects—were already there, after some ten years of collective effort, ready to take over" (18). As one illustration among others of this movement toward the fading away of narrative is the observation by Per Aage Brandt, in his discussion of the modal basis of cognitive semiotics, according to which, "For the enunciator, modal integration is intended to signify the mental representation of a dynamic situation," a process described a few lines further on as a "micro-drama" (Brandt 2014). The term "narrativity," however, falls out of use. It has done its duty.

Now, this state of affairs raises a question: Can it be said that the discursive and cultural universe of narrative, with its extremely diverse generic varieties, its particular forms of writing and functions of persuasion, has been pushed aside? Has exploration of this "region below ideas"—which, according to Maurice Merleau-Ponty (1996: 217), explains the "irreplaceable nature" of narrative—been irrevocably abandoned? Whatever the case, it does not appear that semioticians, since the time of the modal turn, have sought to restore the world of narrative studies or that they have been involved in narratological research. This is highly regrettable, for there are a considerable number of topics that, in the light of subsequent advances in semiotic theory, might very well be looked at anew. Let us take the apparently trivial example of a sentence by the controversial contemporary novelist Michel Houellebecq, examined through the semiotic approach, both somatic and passional: the sense of "fatigue" brought about by the invasive use of commas and the endless postponement of the final period, thus delaying to the utmost the tiresome inchoative moment of a new sentence. This example suggests that a phenomenologically based semiotics may very well be in a position to renew its ties with narrative inquiry while at the same time restoring the "stylistic" surface of writing, a consequence of authorial practice itself. However, the abandonment of narrative seems to be the price to pay for the search for new semiotic objects, drawn on by the logic of "progress."

3. THE QUESTION OF IMMANENCE AT THE CROSSROADS OF NARRATOLOGY AND NARRATIVITY

Narratology, thanks to the diversity of its types and forms, inevitably opens up to the external side of discourse and the effects, both individually, through writing and reading in act (consider Proust's theory of novel reading as part of his practice of novel writing), and collectively and socially when, for example, it comes to examining the modal question of knowing who takes form in discourse and who generates its effects in various sociocultural fields. In sum, narratology is incorporated into what Jean-François Bordron and I have called "the pragmatic environs" (*entour pragmatique*) of semiotic systems in their discursive realization.[4] By the same token, narratology summons up the question of the pertinence of the principle of immanence.

In *La quête du sens. Le langage en question* (1997), Jean-Claude Coquet, for whom immanence is a bête noire, describes the principle in this way: "Phenomena such as events, states of affairs, perceptions, movements, etc., reduced to abstract terms, enter into a closed system of relations" (2); "language is an abstract object where only the relations between terms count" (109–10).[5] Since the time of Louis Hjelmslev, in the 1930s, immanence has in fact stood as "the foundation of linguistics." This postulate is clearly taken over in Greimas and Courtés's *Dictionary* with the following deontic and quasi-legal formulation: "Since the object of linguistics is form (or natural language in the Saussurean sense), any recourse to extra-linguistic facts must be excluded, because it breaks down the homogeneity of the description" (1982 [1979]: 151).

Now, the structures of narrativity are admirable achievements of an immanentist approach to meaning and stand as proof of its pertinence, productiveness, and efficacy. These structures include actantiality, modality, and aspectuality together with their syntagmatic deployments in narrative programs and schemas as well as their "enrichment" at the various levels of conversion of the generative trajectory including, inter alia, the passage from actant to actor by way of "thematic roles." They open the way to constituting

---

4. The subtitle of the 2013–2014 Paris Semiotics Seminar, "Principe d'immanence et entour pragmatique" (see note 1 in this chapter), was commented on as follows in our introductory text: "The pragmatic environs of semiotic systems may prompt one to revise or even to bracket this principle of immanence, long acknowledged to be essential. A number of orientations that have emerged in the human sciences these past years, by setting forth themes with a direct take on lived meaning, even seem to be in a position to move their disciplinary borders."

5. See also Coquet (2007), particularly the chapters titled "Le 'ça pense' et les deux niveaux du principe de réalité: phusis et logos" (40–56); "Deux paradigmes de la sémiotique européenne: la narrativité et la discursivité" (167–83).

a formal grammar of discourse, making it possible, for example, "to proceed ... with calculations of unequal modal competence by two subjects faced with an object of value which, differently evaluated, include modal attributions of that object" (Greimas 1983a: 11–12). It is this same logic of immanence that, as already mentioned, governs semiotic construction in a cascade going from bifurcation to bifurcation or from conversion to conversion of modal totalization. This then makes it possible to incorporate the semiotics of suffering (*pâtir*) into the semiotics of acting (*agir*) under a homogeneous conceptual mechanism. And yet, it is this same logic of immanence that has caused some semioticians, carried away by the generalization of narrativity and its abstraction, to lose sight of the universe of narrative discourses as such. This is a heavy price to pay.

4. FROM THE "PRINCIPLE OF IMMANENCE" TO "PLANES OF IMMANENCE"

It would be interesting to reconstitute the history of how other semioticians have sought to escape the straitjacket of immanence, or at least loosen it a bit. The most radical position is no doubt the one taken up by Jean-Claude Coquet, who rejects the notion in the name of the "reality principle." He opposes somatic predicates, coming from *phúsis* (nature), by which expression is given to one's "take" (*prise*) on the world, and cognitive predicates, coming from *lógos*, which are merely a "second take" (*reprise*) on the immediacy of contact with things and beings. "*Somatic predicates* (or reality predicates)," Coquet argues, "say the perceivable whereas *cognitive predicates* describe the world. '*To say*' is not '*to describe*' ['*Dire*' n'est pas '*décrire*']" (2011: 102). However, on closer examination of the instruments of analysis he proposes, particularly the actantial status of the non-subject, setting off the "perceiving body" from the body of the subject and logical assumption off from judgment, it can be observed that what opposes the two, from the modal perspective, in fact comes from the immanentist approach. This being the case, there is some doubt as to the complex entanglement, in Coquet's development, of the two principles, immanence and reality. Nevertheless, the prospects for new insights arising out of this approach in terms of analysis and emphasis in several fields of the human sciences are particularly fruitful. The semiotics of enunciative instances developed by Coquet make it possible to achieve a better grasp of the full range of psychopathological discourses, to seize the subtle articulations of literary expression and to better understand artistic experience—in a word, to better navigate one's way through the array of fields where the subjectivity of the perceiving subject comes directly into play.

Also to be mentioned is Jacques Fontanille, whose book *Pratiques sémiotiques* (2008) outlines a position that differs profoundly from Coquet's. While Fontanille seeks release from the stranglehold of the text as an "all-signifying whole," closed in on itself, so as to take account of the "practices" by which it is enveloped, this in no way involves rejecting the principle of immanence. On the contrary, Fontanille seeks to expand this principle and to open it up by incorporating pertinent levels of meaningful experience in its broadest sense. These levels of pertinence can be converted into so many "planes of immanence" fitting into one another like Russian dolls. It is in this way that sense experience, both iconic and figurative, gives rise to pertinent distinctions, understood as the expression of signs—first plane of immanence. The sign is then converted into another experience, that of an oriented and intentional composition of figures resulting in the signifying totality of the text-as-utterance (*texte-énoncé*), itself characterized by pertinent distinctions—second plane of immanence. Thus, from sign to text-as-utterance, from text-as-utterance to object (its medium of inscription), from object to the scene of praxis as an open but circumscribed process with the interactions this implies; from the scene of praxis to strategies with their experiences of management, accommodation, and adjustment; and finally, from strategies to forms of life that introduce stylization and the axiological investments of subjects—this extraordinary and elaborate scaffolding is laid out by Fontanille in accordance with a hierarchy of planes of immanence (Fontanille 2008: 17–36 et passim). Each plane has its own set of concepts and rules together with its modes of integration from one plane to another. Semiotics is thus released from the restrictive closure of the text, opening up to the global and lived "reality" of meaning in situ without going against its founding principles: The closure of the all-signifying whole is expanded into successive layers, bound together by connectors of logical implication. Fontanille's hypothesis for the pluralization of planes of immanence is highly attractive. Of course, it needs to be evaluated not only through concrete analyses (Fontanille provides numerous examples) but also and especially within the context of interdisciplinary relations. This is because in one way or another each level comes up against concerns, objects, and concepts that can also be found in other fields of study.

In any case, the pluralization of planes of immanence, and in particular the relations set up between the various planes with their rigorous distribution of analytical concepts, opens the way to an approach that looks at this same problem under the expression "foliated plane of immanence" (*plan d'immanence feuilleté*). This notion, coming from the chapter "Plane of Immanence" in Deleuze and Guattari's *What Is Philosophy?*, is also designated with the novel term "planomen" (Deleuze and Guattari 1994 [1991]: 35). This is a demanding text, brimming with ideas, whose methods of inquiry and definition cast a new light on immanence, broadening both its linguistic and its semiotic meanings and at the same time offering a fresh look at the relation between narrativity and immanence.

Deleuze and Guattari define the plane of immanence in a nearly structural way through the relation of solidarity and difference it maintains with concepts in the field of philosophy. Concepts, according to them, are isolated entities and do not adapt easily to one another: "Their edges do not match up." What allows concepts to "take" (in the sense of hardening plaster) and to form a coherent and unified whole is their "plane of consistency or, more accurately, the plane of immanence of concepts, the planomen" (Deleuze and Guattari 1994 [1991]: 35). But in another way, this formulation ties up with the requirement of "interdefinition" of concepts insisted on by semiotics and so rigorously claimed by Greimas, starting with *Sémantique structurale* (1966; English translation 1983) and extending through Greimas and Courtés's *Dictionary* to Greimas and Fontanille's *Sémiotique des passions. Des états des choses aux états d'âme* (1991; English translation 1993). This other way is spelled out by Deleuze and Guattari in a series of figurative definitions making use of comparison, metaphor, and catachresis drawn from areas of experience as varied as organic life, technical processes, the four elements, geography—all of them far removed from any form of taxonomy in a dazzling disarray of spheres of existence. Here are a few of these definitions:

> Concepts are the archipelago or skeletal frame, a spinal column rather than a skull, whereas the plane [of immanence] is the breath that suffuses the separate parts. . . . Concepts are concrete assemblages, like the configurations of a machine, but the plane is the abstract machine of which these assemblages are the working parts. Concepts are events, but the plane is the horizon of events, the reservoir or reserve of purely conceptual events. . . . [The plane is] the absolute horizon, independent of any observer. . . . Concepts pave, occupy, or populate the plane bit by bit, whereas the plane itself is the indivisible milieu in which concepts are distributed without breaking up its continuity or integrity. . . . The only regions of the plane are concepts themselves, but the plane is all that holds them together. . . . It is the plane that secures conceptual linkages with ever increasing connections. (Deleuze and Guattari 1994 [1991]: 42)

More abstractly, and perhaps more enlighteningly for those who are familiar with the generative trajectory and with approaches involving interdefinition and the tensive relations between durational and terminative processes, Deleuze and Guattari explain that "the elements of the plane are *diagrammatic features,* whereas concepts are *intensive features.* The former are movements of the infinite, whereas the latter are intensive ordinates of these movements" (1994 [1991]: 39–40).

Unlike the monosemic rigor of linguistic definition and the architecture of semiotic modeling, these figurative characterizations form a network of highly polysemic images. The figurative dimension of language is of course a vector that evokes the senses. However, when it renders everything to the senses, the figurative dimension causes meaning to become elusive. Meaning overflows the image whose limits, due to the plurality of its fields of application in the natural world, become indeterminate. In the profusion of representations it occasions, the figurative both intensifies and dilutes. What now are the consequences of this situation for the plane of immanence? One is that immanence is inescapably subject to fluctuations, to intense variations. The plane of immanence modulates and stretches; it is elastic and recursive.

5. TOWARD REGIMES OF IMMANENCE

One can very well subscribe to the principle of semiotic immanence thanks to its efficacy in terms of well-reasoned coherence and analytical usefulness, while at the same time conceding that meaningful "leftovers" may remain inaccessible. Indeed, it is this very efficacy that underlies the principle of pertinence. At the same time, one cannot fail to take account of the modulations of immanence that take on various forms of appearance and the different ways these modulations are perceived. As pointed out by Deleuze and Guattari, concepts such as those being debated here (modality, actant, subject, etc.) owe their existence to the fact that they are "constructed . . . in an intuition explicit to them: a field, a plane, and a ground that must not be confused with them but shelter their seeds and the personae who cultivate them. Constructivism requires every creation to be a construction on a plane that gives it an autonomous existence" (1994 [1991]: 7). From this point of view, the "plane of immanence" is clearly set off from the "principle of immanence" in that it is not so much the result of a theoretical decision, thereby laying down the conditions of analysis, as it is a condition for the very existence of the concept: The principle of immanence, both in isolation and in the network it forms with other concepts, is totally dependent on the plane of immanence and is even consubstantial with it. Even when it is overshadowed by other features or apparently ignored or refused, or when it remains imperceptible in the heterogeneity of several interspersed or rival planes, the plane is something that "must be regarded as prephilosophical. It is presupposed not in the way that one concept may refer to others but in the way that concepts themselves refer to a nonconceptual understanding" (40). It exerts its influence in the underpinnings of the discourse that describes, analyzes, conceptualizes. It is thus the task of analysis to disentangle the strands of this plane, be it only gropingly, by trial and error: The plane serves as a sort of grid held up against non-sense. To escape this quandary, it is of course possible to have recourse to transcendence (the unsayable, the sublime, etc.), but this only leads to the resurgence of the figure of the Sender and thus back to narrativity . . . and immanence.

It is on this basis that we can speak of "regimes of immanence." Unlike the *principle* of immanence that underlies a deontic modality (prescribing a conceptual order) and *planes* of immanence along which epistemic modalities are distributed (setting out an undercoat of hypotheses and certainties), *regimes* of immanence refer to modalities of veridiction governed by apparentness (*paraître*). The term "regime" (from Latin *regimen*: guidance, government), because it is highly polysemic, is open-ended, particularly in French, where it appears in expressions as diverse as *régime politique, régime alimentaire* (diet), *plein régime* (full capacity), *régime de croisière* (running speed), *régime fiscal* (tax system), and *régime matrimonial* (antenuptial agreement). Overall, "regimes of immanence" designates the ordering of concepts and thus forms an essential source of veridiction. As noted by Deleuze and Guattari, "the plane is surrounded by illusions," illusions that envelop the plane as "mirages of thought" (49), causing apparentness to merge with quasi-being. The authors even refer here to the Nietzschean typology: illusion of transcendence, illusion of universals, illusion of the eternal (when it is forgotten that concepts must be created), illusion of abstraction (when the figural source of concepts—"army of metaphors"—is taken into account), and illusion of discursivity (when propositions are confused with concepts), to which the illusion of communication can obviously be added. The latter two types of illusion concern particularly semioticians who back discourse meaning up with concepts relating to intelligibility and communicability.

Against this backdrop, it is now possible to return to what it is that anchors narrativity in such an open-ended understanding of immanence. Might it be that narrativity is but another name for immanence, given that the bonds between them make them inherent to one another? This is what is hinted at by the numerous narrative overtures in the series of images listed above: From each of these images there emerges a scene that unfolds in a potential narrative. It would thus be worthwhile to seek out, within the epistemes, the principal regimes of immanence that intersect through the conceptual constructions of narrative. Without attempting to go fully into this matter here, it is nonetheless possible to get an idea of the relations between immanence and narrativity based on a particularly rich example: Cervantes's *Don Quixote*. To what regimes of immanence does the writing of Cervantes, a narrator par excellence and meta-narrator of his own narrative, obey?

6. *DON QUIXOTE*, OR: IS IT POSSIBLE TO ESCAPE NARRATIVITY?

The regimes of immanence in *Don Quixote* are twofold, at a minimum. One operates in the narratological sense, the other on the basis of narrativity. According to this hypothesis, one is structured by the narrative "said" (*le dit*), the other by the "saying" (*le dire*) of the narrative.

Cervantes's novel, with its 126 chapters in two volumes, is a gold mine for the narratologist. In it, innumerable chivalric romances are caught up in an elaborate *mise en abyme*, enriching the story of the hero and his squire. Alongside this are the story of the niece and the governess, stories about the priest and the barber, about the innkeeper and the population of "normal" people who, when they meet or tell stories to each other, prove to be about as caught up in narrative folly as the hero of the novel. What interests us here is that the regimes of immanence of these characters, namely all the reasons they have to believe in their deeds and movements, in their reality, and their illusions, are intertwined. Moreover, the motivating forces and dynamics of the numerous embedded narratives, uttered by equally numerous narrators borrowing in prose or in verse from all the narrative genres available at the time, go so far as a critical and learned metadiscourse by a church canon on the chivalric romance, alternately denounced and praised (see vol. 1, chaps. 47 and 48). This effervescence of narration relates back to the canonical narrative schema. The standard sequences of this schema stand out at one point early on in the novel in the form of "the oddest fancy that ever entered a madman's brain":

> He [don Quixote] believed that it was necessary, both for his own honor and for the service of the state, that he should become a knight-errant, roaming through the world with his horse and armor in quest of adventures and practicing all that had been performed by the knights-errant of whom he had read. He would follow their life, redressing all manner of wrongs and exposing himself to continual dangers, and at last, after concluding his enterprises, he would win everlasting honor and renown. (Cervantes 1957 [1605/1615]: 59)

This passage can be easily analyzed through the steps of the narrative schema:[6]

1. qualifying test: modeling of the subject through his belief ("He believed that it was necessary"), his preparatory programs ("his horse and armor"), definition of the quest ("quest of adventures");
2. decisive test: "redressing all manner of wrongs and exposing himself to continual dangers"; and
3. glorifying test: "he would win everlasting honor and renown."

This corresponds wholly to the Proppian schema, a model that was subsequently to be refined by semioticians into three sequences that are general in scope, covering three dimensions of signification governed by narrativity: manipulation (to cause to believe), the act of doing, and sanction (evaluation of the doing and recognition).

Alongside this first, multiform world of the narrative, another narrative universe is woven that is much more complex and every bit as multiple. This is the universe of narrative enunciation. Its dominant trait is that it derides the narrative, mocking the narrative saying and disqualifying it. How can the voice that triggers this festival of illusion be characterized? First of all, this is a voice that can be ascribed to no one. *Don Quixote* is the narration of a narrator who both conceals and repudiates himself. He denies his enunciative position by passing it, like a hot potato, from enunciator to enunciator. From the enunciative perspective, his discourse is structured in a fractal manner: The enunciator dives endlessly into a recursive machinery of speech in action. The prologue, which the author confesses he is unable to write, is taken over by a kindly friend who dictates to him the methods of plagiarism, which amounts to a delegation of enunciation—enunciation to the second degree. This stands out in the second part of *Don Quixote* where the manuscript, having been lost in the climax of a fight (the story about the mighty fight with the "gallant Biscayan"), is no longer the Spanish text but a translation of old notebooks, written in Arabic by "Sidi Ahmed Benengeli, Arab historian," found at the market in Toledo. The "I" of the enunciator, displaced by a deictic shift, pops up here and there as though by accident; usually—for this is a dialogic novel—the narrative *parole* is delegated by all possible means to Another, any other whatsoever. In addition, the editorial reality, starting with the second part, mixes in with fictional reality. In 1614, the year prior to publication of the continued account of Don Quixote's adventures (the first volume of which dates from 1605), there appeared in Tarragona a forged work under the same title,

---

6. See Greimas and Courtés (1982 [1979]: 203–6).

marketed as the second volume of the famous knight's adventures. Appealing to his reader in the prologue to the real second volume, "the author" (if indeed it is he) declares: "You would like me to call him an ass, a fool, and a bully, but I have no intention of doing so. Let his sin be his punishment—let him eat it with his bread, and there let it be" (Cervantes 1957 [1605/1615]: 525). The "author" goes on to incorporate the plagiarized character into the narration of the new adventures, with Don Quixote meeting the readers of the very fiction he came from or refusing to go to one city or another because his stand-in had already sojourned there.

This dizzying *mise en abyme* of enunciation—metadiscursive through and through—generates a new regime of immanence. This is an enunciative plane of enunciation whose object is not the said (*le dit* or "the enunciated") but the saying (*le dire* or enunciation)—saying together with the narrative constraints that are peculiar to it. This equivocation goes on, pitting enunciation against narrative, the inexorable purveyor of illusions. Don Quixote is the first victim of these illusions, but the other characters are also victimized, as is the author himself. This enunciative equivocation can continue only by consenting, against all odds, to the immanent constraints of narrativity. The regime of immanence at issue here consists in making no illusions about illusion. By its very recursiveness, this is a regime of immanence that triggers the infernal circle of a narrative illusionism from which there is no escape.

The point I wish to make is that *Don Quixote*, within the novelistic genre, inaugurates a critical reflection on the very constitution of the novel. Subsequently, Sterne's *Tristram Shandy,* Diderot's *Jacques le Fataliste,* Gide's *Les faux monnayeurs,* Fowles's *The French Lieutenant's Woman,* Perec's *La vie mode d'emploi,* and Calvino's *Si una notte d'inverno un viaggiatore,* to name only a few works, are so many milestones in the long series of meta-narrative writing that asserts itself as yet another mark of the generic specificity of the novel: a genre that highlights and calls into question, within its writing, the very narrative illusion it deploys. To put it another way, the meta-novel highlights the narrativization of enunciation: The narrator, or even the author, inserts him- or herself into the narrative framework and becomes, at the level of enunciation and interaction with the reader, a character in the full sense of the word, endowed with a thematic identity, a hierarchical series of programs of action, confrontations with antagonists, and so on. Within this broader context, however, the particular feature of *Don Quixote* is that enunciative narrativization is inscribed within a more global denunciation of narrative illusion, an illusion that leads its hero to folly and its reader to a dizzying state of uncertainty. Narrativization of this type thus comes to be an act of resistance by narrativity: Over and above and even against all forms of narrative, narrativity determines the conditions of the intelligibility of discourse, generating rules that are general in scope. It would appear, then, that narrativity emerges from a more fundamental "grammar" than the implementation of any given narration.

In the end, *Don Quixote,* despite the enunciative pluralization of its narrative positions—or rather due to these multiple positions—is subject to the demands of narrativity that lie at the heart of enunciation itself, a condition for the very possibility of narrative utterance. Consequently, the novel as meta-novel, with its underlying conceptual system, is organized through two separate regimes of immanence. One is the technical level of narrative with its narrative schemas, consisting of purely stereotypical products arising from custom and the culture of stories. The other regime is located on what Deleuze and Guattari call the "plane of aesthetic composition." This is the plane where material is at work, the plane where enunciative material occurs and renders the complex of sensations perceivable, making the text expressive.[7] Such is the phenomenon that occurs in Cervantes's novel with narrative enunciation. It extends from the critique of narratology to the irreducibility of narrativity. It can be observed that the technical composition of narration leads back to the material that is the act of its enunciation, its verbal utterance, and that enunciation is the seat of sensation and feeling. Narrative always splits open, confronted with the chaos of indetermination, rummaging about in search upstream of the determination of forms. It is, then, the gesture of writing and narrating (translating, copying, plagiarizing, pluralizing the simulacra of *parole,* causing narrative forms to stammer) that is confronted with the implacable narrative constraints of meaning.

7. CONCLUSION

To wind up these reflections on the intermingling of narratology and narrativity against the undulating backdrop of immanence, I would like to summarize the argument in favor of the notion of regimes of immanence. This notion is distinct from the principle of immanence, which is unique and coercive due to its deontic substratum. It also differs from the pluralized planes of

---

7. See Deleuze and Guattari (1994 [1991]: 195–96): "There is only a single plane in the sense that art includes no other plane than that of aesthetic composition: in fact, the technical plane is necessarily covered up by or absorbed by the aesthetic plane of composition. It is on this condition that matter becomes expressive: either the compound of sensations is realized in the material, or the material passes into the compound, but always in such a way as to be situated on a specifically aesthetic plane of composition."

immanence bearing on the evolution of disciplines through the coexistence of planes subject to epistemic modulations. As for regimes of immanence, also in the plural, they take form against a background of veridiction by intermingling, as seen in the writing of *Don Quixote*, the dual illusionism of the narrative seductions of the said (pertaining to narratology) and the perceivable constraints of the saying (pertaining to narrativity).

I thus part ways, but in appearance only, with immanence as a theoretical and methodological requirement. I see it as an irreducible constraint, assumed or ignored, linked to the very production of concepts and figures—in other words, to enunciative activity itself. This results in a cautious opening up and modulation: Despite illusionism with regard to supposed truth, regimes of immanence assume conceptual spheres that, at various levels and along different scales, seek to bring out the unperceived in meaning with the use of new analytical instruments. Regarding the relations between narratology and narrativity, it has been possible to observe, through the example of *Don Quixote*, a going back and forth between the said and the saying where saying—enunciation in act and body delving into the depths of itself, up to the limit of the possible—is paradoxically stymied by the screen of narrativity.

Translated from the French by John Pier

WORKS CITED

Bertrand, Denis. 2000. *Précis de sémiotique littéraire*. Paris: Nathan.

Brandt, Per Aage. 2014. "Sens et modalité—dans la perspective d'une sémiotique cognitive." In *La négation, le négatif, la négativité*, edited by Denis Bertrand, Jean-François Bordron, and Verónica Estay-Stange. *Actes Sémiotiques*, no. 117. http://epublications.unilim.fr/revues/as/.

Budniakiewicz, Therese. 1992. *Fundamentals of Story Logic: Introduction to Greimassian Semiotics*. Amsterdam: John Benjamins.

Cervantes Saavedra, Miguel de. 1957. [1605/1615]. *Don Quixote de la Mancha*. Translated with an introduction by Walter Starkie. New York: New American Library.

Coquet, Jean-Claude. 1997. *La quête du sens. Le langage en question*. París: Presses universitaires de France.

———. 2007. *Phusis et Logos. Une phénoménologie du langage*. Saint-Denis: Presses universitaires de Vincennes.

———. 2011. "Les prédicats somatiques." In *Comment dire le sensible?* edited by Denis Bertrand and Jean-Claude Coquet, *Littérature* 163: 102–7.

Courtés, Joseph. 1976. *Introduction à la sémiotique narrative et discursive*. Paris: Hachette.

Deleuze, Gilles, and Félix Guattari. 1994. [1991]. *What Is Philosophy?* Translated by Tomlinson and Graham Burchell. New York: Columbia University Press.

Fontanille, Jacques. 2008. *Pratiques sémiotiques*. Paris: Presses universitaires de France.

Greimas, Algirdas Julien. 1983a. "Introduction." In *Du sens II. Essais sémiotiques*, 7–18. Paris: Seuil.

———. 1983b. [1966]. *Structural Semantics: An Attempt at Method.* Translated by Danielle McDowell et al. Lincoln: University of Nebraska Press.

Greimas, Algirdas Julien, and Joseph Courtés. 1982. [1979]. *Semiotics and Language: An Analytical Dictionary.* Translated by Larry Crist et al. Bloomington: Indiana University Press.

Greimas, Algirdas Julien, and Jacques Fontanille. 1993. [1991]. *The Semiotics of Passions: From States of Affairs to States of Feeling.* Translated by Paul Perron and Frank Collins. Foreword by Paul Perron and Paolo Fabbri. Minneapolis: University of Minnesota Press.

Merleau-Ponty, Maurice. 1996. *Notes de cours (1958–1959 et 1960–1961).* Preface by C. Lefort. Posthumous edition edited by S. Ménasé. Paris: Gallimard.

Polkinghorne, Donald. 1988. *Narrative Knowing and the Human Sciences.* New York: State University of New York.

Ricoeur, Paul. 1984–1988. [1983–1985]. *Time and Narrative,* 3 volumes. Translated by Kathleen McLaughlin and David Pellauer. Chicago: The University of Chicago Press.

Salmon, Christian. 2010. [2007]. *Storytelling: Bewitching the Modern Mind.* Translated by David Macey. London: Verso.

CHAPTER 8

Fiction, Expanded and Updated

OLIVIER CAÏRA

1. INTRODUCTION: THE NOTEBOOK EXPERIMENT

What do we call fiction in everyday life? As a sociologist, I began by asking a few people this simple question. Their task was not to draw up a list of what came to their mind at the moment, but to record in a notebook what parts of the next twenty-four or forty-eight hours could be considered a fictional experience.

The result was both puzzling and intellectually challenging. Of course, these people had read novels, short stories, and comics; they had seen movies, TV serials, and sometimes theatrical productions. But they also mentioned computer games, mathematical exercises, philosophical examples, jokes, *Dungeons & Dragons*, chess, live action role-playing games, improvisational theater, and more.

More interestingly, expressions like "radio ad," "personal website," "rock song," and "contemporary art exhibition" came with question marks, and some people asked me whether these objects were fictional or not. Since I was studying fiction, I was supposed to provide them with a clear definition of the term. This chapter is an answer to their question, fifteen years later.

The "notebook experiment" put into relief five dimensions of the theory of fiction:

1. The range of works and experiences that people call "fiction" today is significantly wider than the range of examples discussed in academic research. So we may need an expanded definition of fiction.
2. These records include many simulation games and some abstract games like chess, Tetris, or Sudoku. Some are computer-based, others are tabletop games. What they have in common is a logical-mathematical "engine." So we may want our definition to reunite two long-standing philosophical traditions: fiction based on mimesis and logical-mathematical fiction.
3. Since our contemporaries can fill their notebooks with relative ease in this experiment, perhaps we can still "sort out fact from fiction" despite what Marie-Laure Ryan (1997, 2006) calls the "doctrine of panfictionality." Therefore, our expanded and updated definition of fiction must reflect two aspects of our day-to-day experience: *why* we keep thinking that fiction is a specific form of communication and *how* we can identify and handle this specificity.
4. Given that social actors sometimes resort to question marks to frame their experience of fiction, our definition should also accommodate different levels of personal evaluation and social consensus about what can or cannot be called "fiction."
5. When conflict arises about the fictionality of a work or an experience, what concepts can we use beneath and beyond the "fictional contract"? These conflicts can be described as an interplay between pragmatic instructions—borrowed from the frame theory—and Gilles Deleuze's notions of contract and institution.

My conclusion will show how contemporary narratology can gain further insight into the nature of fictionality from this sociological definition of fiction.

2. EXPANDING THE RANGE OF FICTIONAL OBJECTS

Intellectual debate is largely built on examples. Typical ones provide a common basis for discussion between theorists: It suffices to mention Sherlock Holmes's address, Mr. Pickwick's morning routine, or Anna Karenina's tragic fate to remind any scholarly reader that you will be discussing David Lewis's (1978), Thomas Pavel's (1986), or Colin Radford's (1975) works. Atypical ones deserve detailed examination and thus become a benchmark for comparing different theories. Wolfgang Hildesheimer's imaginary biography, *Sir Andrew Marbot* (1981), became the "typical atypical" example of problematic fictionality. It has been studied thoroughly by many scholars, including Jean-Marie Schaeffer (2010 [1999]), Dorrit Cohn (1999), Marie-Laure Ryan (1999), and Richard Saint-Gelais (2001).

In the best case, typical and atypical examples ensure cumulative progress or help to understand intellectual dissent. In the worst case, they become tools of academic conservatism. But more fundamentally, they are beacons—sometimes fences—that draw the symbolic perimeter of legitimate discussion. The notebook experiment shows a huge discrepancy between the perimeter of theoretical debate and the range of everyday-life fictional experiences. This expansion raises major issues in both narratology and the theory of fiction.

First, the link between fiction and narrative becomes far more complex in this new landscape. Many theorists take for granted that fiction is a particular case of narrative (e.g., Lewis 1978; Ricoeur 1984 [1983]; 1985 [1984]; Walton 1990; Currie 1990; Lamarque and Olsen 1994). This assumption can generate two Procrustean biases. In the first case, fiction is cut out to fit the bed of narrative, thanks to a narrow choice of examples, mainly from novels, plays, and classic movies. In the second case, narrative is unduly stretched to include objects of low or dubious narrativity, such as abstract games. Janet Murray's lines on Tetris as "a perfect enactment of the overtasked lives of Americans in the 1990s" (Murray 2017 [1997]: 178; see also Eskelinen 2001) perfectly illustrate this drift. If we admit that fiction and narrative have nothing more in common than a remarkable historical conjunction, we can begin to question the relationship between the fictional framing of various forms of human communication and the more or less narrative organization of their content.

For example, since the turn of the millennium, board and video games have become more narrative than ever, but they still are not narratives, as many ludologists have argued (Juul 2001; Eskelinen 2001; Frasca 2003). Instead of seeing fiction as a subspecies of narrative, we can study the varying degrees of narrativity in different areas of fictional expression. Espen J. Aarseth calls quest games "post-narrative discourse" precisely to "explain why they are mistaken for narratives and also be better placed to rescue those aspects of narratology that continue to be of use in our analysis" (2004: 375). Quest games are based on a diegesis and a plot. They require professional scriptwriting and provide high levels of tellability; nevertheless, they are meant to be *played*, not told or shown. To echo Aarseth's words, we may call "pre-narrative discourse" the many static descriptions of fictional landscapes, characters, institutions, or objects that are designed to stimulate immersion and narrative imagination. The documents that studio staffs call "bibles" in various fields such as television, video games, comics, or tabletop role-playing games are both clearly fictional and pre-narrative.

Second issue: *How* can scholars study this wider field of fictional experiences? Many of them remain based on *works,* on material devices that can be kept and reproduced. But we can no longer ignore the importance of fictional *performances,* which require recording, observation, or participation. Unfortunately, fieldwork remains a "minority report" in the contemporary debate on fiction: It is accepted as long as its results concur with mainstream theories based on particular works or corpus analysis. When the ethnographer notices something unusual or unexpected (e.g., the fact that scriptwriters rarely use "forking paths" devices in interactive fiction, or that fans buy and create more and more *non-narrative* content about their favorite fictional universes), statements drawn from field-based research tend to remain marginal in the theoretical discussion.

This leads to the third issue: interactivity. Many games have entered our expanded field of fictional experience. Thanks to theorists like Aarseth (1997), Schaeffer (2010 [1999]), and Ryan (2001, 2006), video games and text-based adventures are now seen as legitimate fictional works. The bad news is that another Procrustean process is taking place. On the one hand, interactive fiction is commonly reduced to its digital side at the expense of body- and natural-language-based practices like improvisational theater and tabletop or live action role-playing games. On the other hand, the Procrustean bed of fictional experience is unduly occupied by works alone at the expense of performances, which brings us back to the issue of ethnographic material. This focus on the scripted and reproducible part of interactive fiction makes us miss an essential point: the ability to surprise and to be surprised through improvisation, a key feature of interactivity. What would we think if musicologists studied jazz only as a form of recorded music?

3. NONMIMETIC FICTION AND SIMULATION GAMES

The fourth issue requires special comment. In our enlarged landscape of fictional objects, many are digital, oral, theatrical, or pen-and-paper simulation games: Their textual, bodily, or audiovisual representation is based on a logical-mathematical "engine," a set of abstract rules used to simulate perception and action within their diegesis. Further away from traditional mimetic works, abstract games like checkers, poker, craps, backgammon, J. H. Conway's "Game of Life," and Tetris are also mentioned as fictional experiences in the notebook experiment.

The fictionality of these nonmimetic games is not a problem in itself, since they perfectly match the long-standing definition of mathematical fiction:

They are autonomous axiomatics, systems that were not designed to model a part of the physical or social world. The problem lies not in these objects, but in the way that scholars deal with them in today's mainstream theory of fiction. The classical approach, inspired by Aristotle's *Poetics* and Plato's *Republic*, is to regard mimesis as a necessary feature of any fiction. This assumption reveals a frequent confusion between the *semiotic* aspect and the *pragmatic* status of fictional communication. Like narrativity, mimesis is historically the most common manifestation of fictionality, but it is not the only one.

Ironically, Aristotle and Plato were also the fathers of the philosophy of axiomatic fiction (Cléro 2004). For centuries, mimetic and axiomatic traditions have evolved separately, probably because nobody imagined that there could be any link between Platonic polyhedrons or non-Euclidian geometry, on the one hand, and literary or theatrical representations, on the other. This link became obvious in the mid-1970s when *Dungeons & Dragons* players began to throw eight-, twelve-, and twenty-sided dice for their fictional character to kill monsters, pick locks, or cast spells (Caïra 2007). During the same decade, computer scientists started to take an interest in interactive fiction (Montfort 2003), while live action role-playing games societies began springing up in many Western countries (Kapp 2013). They were all asking the same question: How can abstract rules simulate mimetic worlds and processes?

There are no clear-cut boundaries between "purely" mimetic fiction and simulation games (see, for example, Georges Perec's novels or Peter Greenaway's films) or between "purely" abstract systems and simulation games (chess or Cluedo can be viewed as both). Hence, the expanded field of fiction we are dealing with can best be illustrated by a continuum between two poles, as shown in Figure 1.

It must be stressed that we can no longer shoehorn the definition of fiction into a theory of mimesis and ignore the long-standing philosophy of mathematical fiction, for the recent emergence of simulation games encourages us to unify the field. It is therefore important to consider fiction not only as a medium-free phenomenon (Walton 1990; Ryan 2006), but also as a "mode-free" object independent of representation (Caïra 2011). Narrative mimetic fiction is the dominant case, but narrativity and mimesis are not necessary conditions for defining fiction. Fiction does not depend on any particular mode of communication, be it mimetic or axiomatic, analogic or digital.

At the same time, unity does not mean uniformity. Mimetic and axiomatic fictions remain fundamentally distinct poles in this continuum, so that it remains possible to study literary fiction without any notion of mathematical fictions. The most interesting part of this continuum is its middle, where the two systems coexist. Gonzalo Frasca used the neologism "simiotics" to

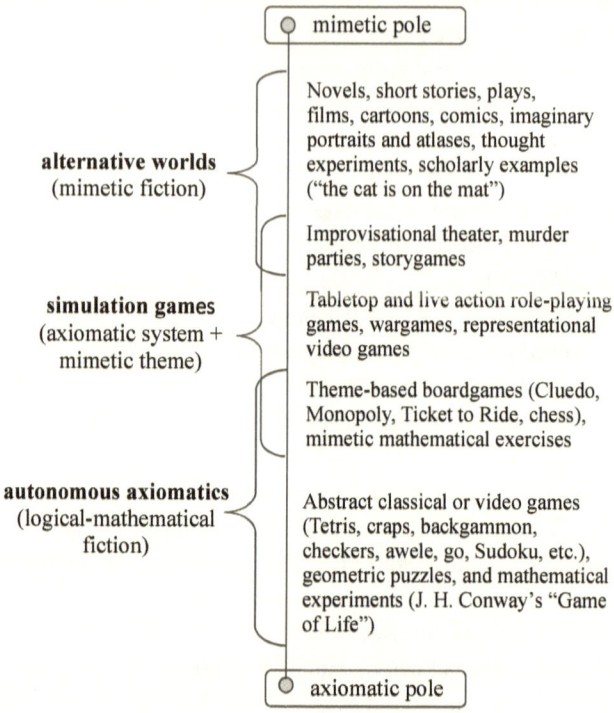

FIGURE 1. Expanded field of fiction

describe specifically how simulations produce meaning (Frasca 2001). My point becomes sociologically clear when I interview scriptwriters, computer scientists, or designers who work on these simiotic fictions: They all stress the need to develop skills in both poles and to entertain a dialogue with experts of the two modes.

4. FICTIONAL AS OPPOSED TO DOCUMENTARY COMMUNICATION

Now that the links binding fiction, narrative, and mimesis together are cut, let us put forward a definition of fiction. What all the above-listed objects have in common is not a set of formal features. Despite the efforts made by literary theorists (e.g., Hamburger 1973 [1957]), there is no "language of fiction" (MacDonald 1954), no "distinction of fiction" (Cohn 1999) that would provide a clear-cut boundary for the various objects we are trying to encompass. By contrast, Hamburger's and Cohn's works are extremely helpful when it comes to determining how we identify "clues" or "signposts" of fictionality in cultural fields we are familiar with, although none of them is reliable enough to build a definition on (see Genette 1993 [1991]). If a message involves imaginary beings, the use of verbs of inner action, or the expression of a fictive *Ich-Origo*, we will probably use these clues to define it as fictional. But sometimes we also find these features in documentary communication. Furthermore, many works are deemed fictional even though they provide none of these clues.

The opposition between fiction and reality is also irrelevant, as many discussions on the ontological status of fictional beings have shown (e.g., Pavel 1986). John R. Searle was probably the first theorist to "locate" fictionality outside the ontological background and the formal features of the message. When commenting on a passage from Iris Murdoch's novel *The Red and the Green*, Searle points out that

> such a proposition may or may not be true, but Miss Murdoch has no commitment whatever as regards its truth. Furthermore, as she is not committed to its truth, she is not committed to being able to provide evidence for its truth. Again, there may or may not be evidence for the truth of such a proposition, and she may or may not have evidence. (1979 [1975]: 62–63)

The most important expression here is "may or may not": Searle emphasizes the freedom offered to interactants in fictional communication. They *may or may not* use existent beings, places, and events; they *may or may not* make historically or logically true statements. The difference between documentary and fictional communication is not a semantic matter of truthfulness, but a pragmatic matter of commitment. This is precisely where the link between sociology and the theory of fiction becomes clear: The various ways in which people are committed to a message they utter (and consequently the various ways in which they are supposed to be able "to provide evidence for its truth") are historical and sociological objects.

In "The Logical Status of Fictional Discourse," Searle achieved a major breakthrough toward a definition of fiction. However, his frame of reference remained dependent on speech act theory, which made it difficult for him to deal with nonliterary forms of fiction. Moreover, he insisted on the reader's different expectations toward fictional and nonfictional discourse, but he did not provide any indication as to *how* the reader can distinguish fiction from nonfiction in the first place. In his article, the difference is given as self-evident: the first passage is labeled "non-fiction" because it is taken "at random" from a newspaper; the second is labeled "fiction" because it comes from a novel.

Jean-Marie Schaeffer (2010 [1999]), who insisted on the particular cognitive treatment of fictional messages, used the expression "pragmatic frame" (*cadre pragmatique*) to describe how a communicational device can be established as a fictional device. Dealing with "devices" rather than with "texts" allows Schaeffer's theory to encompass many forms of fictional works and experiences. My point is that framing is not only a cognitive operation but also a social one.

5. DEFINING FICTION

Since Gregory Bateson introduced it in his influential article "A Theory of Play and Fantasy" (2000 [1955]), framing has become a major concept in the psychology and, through Goffman's *Frame Analysis* (1974), the sociology of experience. Framing is a familiar but complex operation that puts into relief both the strengths and weaknesses of Hamburger's and Searle's definitions of fiction. As Searle argued, fictionality is clearly not "located" in the message or in its diegesis but is established by social categories and institutions that, for example, distinguish between a newspaper article and a novel (see also Menoud 2005). Nevertheless, in the absence of explicit categorization, we analyze the messages we receive in order to decide whether they are fictional or not. Searle and Hamburger were both right because these are the two sides of a typical framing process.

Indeed, Bateson defined the psychological frame as an intermediary notion between the physical piece of wood that separates a picture from the wall behind it and the imaginary line used by mathematicians to mark "sets" off from one another:

> The first step in defining a psychological frame might be to say that it is (or delimits) a class or set of messages (or meaningful actions). . . . In many instances, the frame is consciously recognized and even represented in vocabulary ("play," "movie," "interview," "job," "language," etc.). In other cases, there may be no explicit verbal reference to the frame, and the subject may have no consciousness of it. (2000 [1955]: 187)

On this basis, the framing process can be shortened or simplified by an explicit instruction: "This work (or experience) is fiction"; or by referring to a category of fictional works or experiences: "This work is a novel" or "This experience is a role-playing game." But we also use implicit framing techniques: If we say or write "The cat is on the mat," an academic audience or reader will instantly categorize this proposition as a fictional example (although our neighbor might look for a real cat on a real mat).

Why do we use frames? A frame is not a simple set of contextual information. Bateson defined it as a "premise system" that applies to the communication process:

> Any message, which either explicitly or implicitly defines a frame, *ipso facto* gives the receiver instructions or aids in his attempt to understand the messages included within the frame. . . . Every metacommunicative or metalinguistic message defines, either explicitly or implicitly, the set of messages about which it communicates, *i.e.*, every metacommunicative message is or defines a psychological frame. (2000 [1955]: 188)

Fictionality is one of these premises. The message "This is fiction" works as a metacommunicative Searlian instruction, saying: "Expect no commitment to the truth of any message within this frame." Fictional framing lifts the burden of proof that weighs upon documentary communication. Thus, fiction is not a frame in and of itself, but fictionality is a cognitive and pragmatic property that can be applied to any work or segment of experience. This definition is medium-free and "mode-free": It encompasses the whole range of works and experiences between the mimetic and the axiomatic poles. It also leaves open the question of who—or what—is in charge of framing the communication process. It can be the word "novel" printed on a book cover or a friend saying "Imagine for a minute that. . . ." Frame theory does not imply one-way communication: It helps describe group interaction as well as the text-reader relationship.

Naturally, the burden of proof differs according to the mimetic/axiomatic polarity I discussed earlier. In the field of mimetic communication, taking a documentary stance is a matter of cross-checking and collation of multiple versions. This is what we expect from serious journalism. As Marie-Laure Ryan wrote: "Fictional texts are automatically true to their reference world, but nonfictional texts must establish their truth in competition with other texts that describe the same world" (2006: 51). In the evaluation of an axiomatic system, "documentarity" becomes a question of isomorphism between the logical-mathematical engine and the empirical data it is supposed to model (Hofstadter 1980: 57). This is what we expect from science.

As a fundamental means of artistic expression, scientific speculation, and technical training, fiction is better characterized by the lifting of a pragmatic burden than in terms of what it *should* be. This definition is not prescriptive because no theorist can forecast how fictional communication may evolve with time. It would also be a mistake to assign fictional communication any particular function, since the uses of fiction vary greatly from one culture to another (see Lavocat and Duprat 2010).

6. THE SIMPLICITY AND COMPLEXITY OF FICTIONAL FRAMING

At an individual level, it seems that the more explicit a framing message is, the smoother communication gets. But as Erving Goffman showed in *Frame Analysis* (1974), complications arise both at the micro- and macro-sociological levels. Indeed, the fictionality of works and experiences can become a significant and controversial issue, be it political, financial, religious, or otherwise.

Since we cannot expect the message "This is fiction" to appear explicitly in every work or experience we deal with, it is useful to distinguish two sorts of framing practices: top-down and bottom-up framing.

Top-down framing is technically simple, but rhetorically dubious. Pragmatically, we can identify an individual or institutional "voice" saying explicitly: "This work or experience is fiction." The frame is clearly established, so that nobody should ignore or challenge it. In face-to-face interaction, this clarification is often motivated by fear of misunderstanding (e.g., with children or foreigners). On a sociological level, the more explicit a framing instruction is, the more suspicious it becomes. If a writer or a studio feels the need to point out that "this is a work of fiction," this is mainly because this work "may" rather than "may not" contain controversial references to documentary versions of the world. Cultural history provides numerous examples of *romans, poèmes, pièces de théâtre,* and *films à clef*. These works allow at least one consistent interpretation in which the veil of fictionality is lifted so that the receiver can identify real-life characters, institutions, places, and events.

Top-down framing is a clever way to enjoy the best of both worlds: the defensiveness of fiction and the more or less disguised accuracy of documentary. It can be used to avoid censorship, social disapproval, or lawsuits from the people depicted and their relatives. Attorney John T. Aquino showed how Hollywood studios began to use the famous "All persons fictitious" disclaimer after the *Rasputin and the Empress* (1932) trial. Russian Princess Irina and Prince Felix Yusupov sued MGM for libel in London because the movie insinuated that the prince killed Rasputin after the monk had raped the princess. Lord Justice Scrutton openly advised the American studio to learn from the British book industry:

> Part of the defence in the action seems really to be: "It is quite true that the defendant said that this is a story of fact, but it is really all fiction." We ought to have used, if we described it properly, the formula which is now put at the beginning of most novels: "All circumstances in this novel are imaginary, and none of the characters in it are real." (quoted in Aquino 2005: 184)

Hollywood studios followed this advice, and this disclaimer became an extraordinary legal shield for the industry, even when real names were used and when the movie was marketed as "based on a true story."

Since the beginning of the twenty-first century, the video game industry has begun to display similar disclaimers every time new software is released. This is especially the case for games set in urban, contemporary contexts. The disclaimer allows the studio to make direct or indirect references to real-life persons, institutions, places, or events without risking prosecution. In the *Grand Theft Auto* franchise, your character can drink a soda named Sprunk, wear Zip jeans, listen to Weasel News, and visit the giant Statue of Happiness in the waters off Liberty City, but any similarity with reality would be purely coincidental (Caïra 2010). Fictionality had to be made explicit when studios began to release video games *à clef*.

Bottom-up framing is a different process. In many cases, works or segments of experience are not declared fictional, but we manage to frame them as such because they seem to exclude any documentary interpretation or because they seem to belong to a well-known genre of fiction. Once again, if we consider "The cat is on the mat," we clearly understand that our bottom-up framing of this sentence as fictional is based on past readings in logic, linguistics, and philosophy. If uttered indiscriminately, the phrase will lead anyone else to actually look for a cat and a mat: By default, it will be framed as documentary.

Before we look at examples of bottom-up framing, we must remember the question marks in the notebook experiment: Are a "radio ad," a "personal website," a "rock song," or a "contemporary art exhibition" fictional or not? Do we really care? People are not generally as obsessed with concepts and categories as scholars tend to be. The distinction between fictional and documentary frames is a fascinating one, but it is only relevant when questions arise. Our societies do not generally deem it useful to decide whether art exhibitions or rock songs are fictional or not. In particular cases, though, the question may arise. Sandrine Morsillo (2012) studied several exhibitions whose fictionality was controversial. In 2011, a rock song, Dire Straits' *Money for Nothing* (1985), was examined in terms of fictionality when the Canadian Broadcast Standards Council censored its second verse, which contains the word "faggot." In defense of the song, it became necessary to argue that this homophobic word was uttered by a fictional character, a frustrated warehouse worker who could be seen in the song's video clip.

If most Hollywood movies are explicitly labeled as fictional, uncertainty about framing has sometimes triggered success or controversy in film history. Framed as a documentary about the rescue of a film crew in the Amazon rain forest, Ruggero Deodato's *Cannibal Holocaust* (1980) was mistaken for a snuff movie. Deodato knew how to manipulate framing information: He and his crew stipulated by contract that none of the actors who played one of the characters that died in the narrative would appear publicly for one year following the film's release. The onscreen killing of several animals reinforced viewers' uncertainty as to the pragmatic status of *Cannibal Holocaust* (Charredib 2012). Similar techniques resulting in confusion between fictional and documentary films were used before and after the release of *The Blair Witch Project* in 1999 (Caïra 2005: 212–14).

Radio and television are particularly interesting media in terms of bottom-up framing because we often turn them on while a program is being broadcast. In the absence of explicit framing instructions, the receiver will collect clues in order to determine whether this program is fiction or not. Audiences who followed Orson Welles's 1938 radio drama *The War of the Worlds* from the beginning knew for sure that this work was an adaptation of H. G. Wells's novel. But listeners who had missed the speaker's introductory sentences could easily confuse Welles's fake news flashes with real ones. On December 13, 2006, the French-speaking Belgian television (RTBF) announced that the Flemish parliament had unilaterally declared Flanders independent. A strange framing message appeared on a black screen for a few seconds: "Ceci n'est peut-être pas une fiction." ("This may not be fiction."). Anchorman François de Brigode then presented several news flashes and interviews about demonstrations for and against secession, various consequences of the dissolution of Belgium, and the evacuation of the royal family. After thirty minutes, an onscreen message saying "This is fiction" was displayed until the end of the program. In both cases, CBS and the RTBF had to make public apologies, which shows how dubious framing can raise macro-social tensions.

7. BENEATH AND BEYOND THE FICTIONAL CONTRACT

If too implicit or too explicit, the framing instruction becomes sociologically problematic. Literary tradition and speech act theory have accustomed us to approaching fiction in terms of contract and felicity conditions. When entering a fictional frame, we are supposed to accept its "terms of use," and fortunately this is how it happens most of the time: We receive or interact with a work without questioning the fictional frame. Although it looks like a contractual situation, I prefer to consider it differently. "This is fiction" is, like most framing messages, an *instruction*. If—and only if—accepted or unchallenged, can it be seen as a contract. Otherwise, we enter the field of controversial frame analysis. Erving Goffman's work constantly reminds us that social actors can be strategists and that pragmatics is not only the study of consensual communication. Fiction sometimes becomes a battlefield.

On a micro-sociological level, the framing instruction can be rejected: The receiver may refuse to acknowledge the fictionality of a message, for instance, because it is identified as a disguised documentary, and consequently the burden of proof should weigh on its sender. On a macro-sociological level, the instruction may be rejected by individuals but upheld by law, by case law, or simply by collective a priori judgments. Indeed, explicit fictional frames can consolidate into cultural categories and institutions. In his famous essay on masochism, Gilles Deleuze stressed the difference between contract and institution:

> The contract presupposes in principle the free consent of the contracting parties and determines between them a system of reciprocal rights and duties; it cannot affect a third party and is valid for a limited period. Institutions, by contrast, determine a long-term state of affairs which is both involuntary and inalienable; it establishes a power or an authority which takes effect on a third party. (1971 [1967]: 76–77)

This distinction is particularly important in cases of libel, defamation, or invasion of privacy. When real persons find themselves or their relatives portrayed in a work, it may be hard for them to consider it fictional. Here are three examples (which space does not permit me to fully describe):

1. A Japanese student sued her South Korean friend Yu Miri mainly because of the graphic description of her facial tumor Miri gave in her first novel, *The Fish Swimming in the Stone* (1994). The court forbade its publication

in book form, and the Supreme Court of Japan confirmed this decision in 2002 (Oura 2010).
2. The families of Billy Tyne, captain of the *Andrea Gail*, and other crewmen sued Warner Bros. after the release of Wolfgang Petersen's *The Perfect Storm* (2000), a movie "based on a true story" about the loss of the swordfish ship. They claimed that Tyne (George Clooney) was depicted "as having piloted the Andrea Gail in an unprofessional, unseaworthy, and incompetent manner, and as having suffered a self-imposed death, abandoning his crew and any hope of survival" (Aquino 2005: 55). The Florida Supreme Court dismissed the plaintiff's action.
3. Some of the twenty villagers of Lussaud attacked and insulted French writer Pierre Jourde and his family after the publication of *Pays Perdu* (2003), a narrative in which they could identify every member of their small community, depicted in a negative light. The Aurillac Court sentenced them to fines and suspended prison terms (Caïra 2011: 161–65).

The theory of fiction should take account of the distinction between contract and institution: Is the instruction "This is fiction" only valid between contracting parties, or can it apply to a third party? This is not just a legal question. In his article on controversial fictions in Japan, Yasusuke Oura wrote:

> Is the reading "contract" that fragile? Indeed, nobody is naive enough to believe that it suffices to affirm the fictionality of a work somewhere in the text or the paratext to get rid of all referential issues.... We literary theorists probably tend to assume too easily that writers act in good faith. Fiction—or rather its alleged harmlessness—can cover up dark intentions: slander, vengeance, conspiracy, etc. There is no lack of historical examples. (2010: 179; my translation)

8. CONCLUSION: ENRICHING NARRATOLOGY

Fiction is both a pragmatic and a cognitive phenomenon. A fictional frame lifts the burden of proof that weighs on communication within it. By extension, we call "fictions" the works, beings, and experiences created within fictional frames. As a sociologist and as a narratologist, I needed a definition of fiction that would encompass the various works and experiences I deal with in my fieldwork. This definition, based on frame theory, can help answer three questions: "Is it fiction?"; "Why is it fiction?"; and "How do we know/decide whether it is fiction?"

To cover an expanded and updated range of objects, this definition is based on Occam's principle of parsimony. It is not a scornful or aggressive decision to exclude narrative, language, medium, and mimesis from it. It is a scientific choice that makes it possible to reintroduce these concepts once fiction has been defined independently from them, and therefore to enrich the debate with philosophers, anthropologists, sociologists, psychologists, ludologists, and media theorists.

More specifically, narratology and the sociology of fictional frames have a lot to learn from each other for at least four reasons:

1. Our expanded landscape of fiction can help map out the processes of extension and adaptation of successful fictional universes. Not all fictional works and experiences are narratives, but many raise issues of narrativity, scriptwriting techniques, and narrative tension (Baroni 2007). The problematic articulation between traditional storytelling and digital programming is clearly identified in the middle of the mimetic/axiomatic axis.
2. Among these objects, simulation games should not be reduced to video games, as is often the case in narratology. Although tabletop role-playing games, verbal or pen-and-paper storygames, and other practices based on analogic modes of expression are less visible, they provide rich material for the study of interactive storytelling.
3. The notion of frame should encourage narratologists to study small-group configurations and shared narrative authority beyond the traditional one-way communication models. Improvisational theater and tabletop games like *Once Upon a Time* (1993) or *Fiasco* (2009) are good examples of collective narration based on simple rules.
4. Frame theory is also useful for the study of embedded frames and metalepsis, in documentary as well as in fictional works. Uncertainty about framing often stems from complex narrative designs, as close studies of works like Hildesheimer's *Sir Andrew Marbot* (Schaeffer 2010 [1999]) or Deodato's *Cannibal Holocaust* (Charredib 2012) reveal.

It is necessary both to provide a robust conceptual definition of fiction and to acknowledge the fuzziness of its applications. The distinction between fiction and nonfiction has never been as unclear as it is nowadays, with the proliferation of hybrid forms of expression such as autofictions, fictionalized myths, docufictions, factions, fictional encyclopedias, mockumentaries, hoaxes, reality shows, and so on. "Hybridizing Fiction and Non-Fiction" (Ryan 2006: 42) is possible because frames are subject to historical change, strategic manipulation, and social judgment.

WORKS CITED

Aarseth, Espen J. 1997. *Cybertext: Perspectives on Ergodic Literature.* Baltimore: The Johns Hopkins University Press.

———. 2004. "Quest Games as Post-Narrative Discourse." In *Narrative across Media: The Languages of Storytelling,* edited by Marie-Laure Ryan, 361–76. Lincoln: University of Nebraska Press.

Aquino, John T. 2005. *Truth and Lives on Film.* Jefferson, MO: McFarland & Co.

Baroni, Raphaël. 2007. *La tension narrative. Suspense, curiosité et surprise.* Paris: Seuil.

Bateson, Gregory. 2000. [1955]. "A Theory of Play and Fantasy." In *Steps to an Ecology of the Mind,* 170–93. Chicago: University of Chicago Press.

Caïra, Olivier. 2005. *Hollywood face à la censure.* Paris: CNRS Éditions.

———. 2007. *Jeux de rôle: Les forges de la fiction.* Paris: CNRS Éditions.

———. 2010. "Fiction et mondialisation." In *Fiction et cultures,* edited by Françoise Lavocat and Anne Duprat, 281–91. Paris: SFLGC.

———. 2011. *Définir la fiction. Du roman au jeu d'échecs.* Paris: Éditions de l'EHESS.

Charredib, Karim. 2012. "Vraisemblance, Jeu & Anthropophagie: Débrouiller *Cannibal Holocaust.*" In *Fictions & médias, intermédialités dans les fictions artistiques,* edited by Bernard Guelton, 91–105. Paris: Publications de la Sorbonne.

Cléro, Jean-Pierre. 2004. *Les raisons de la fiction: les philosophes et les mathématiques.* Paris: Armand Colin.

Cohn, Dorrit. 1999. "Breaking the Code of Fictional Biography: Wolfgang Hildesheimer's *Marbot.*" In *The Distinction of Fiction,* 79–95. Baltimore: The Johns Hopkins University Press.

Currie, Gregory. 1990. *The Nature of Fiction.* Cambridge: Cambridge University Press.

Deleuze, Gilles. 1971. [1967]. *Masochism: Coldness and Cruelty.* Translated by Jean McNeil. New York: Zone Books.

Eskelinen, Markku. 2001. "The Gaming Situation." *Game Studies* 1. http://www.gamestudies.org/0101/eskelinen/.

Frasca, Gonzalo. 2001. "Video Games of the Oppressed." Master's thesis, Georgia Institute of Technology.

———. 2003. "Simulation versus Narrative: Introduction to Ludology." In *The Video Game Theory Reader,* edited by Mark J. P. Wolf and Bernard Perron, 221–35. New York: Routledge.

Genette, Gérard. 1993. [1991]. *Fiction and Diction.* Translated by Catherine Porter. Ithaca, NY: Cornell University Press.

Goffman, Erving. 1974. *Frame Analysis: An Essay on the Organization of Experience.* Cambridge, MA: Harvard University Press.

Hamburger, Käte. 1973. [1957]. *The Logic of Literature.* Translated by Marilynn J. Rose. Bloomington: Indiana University Press.

Hofstadter, Douglas. 1980. *Gödel, Escher, Bach: An Eternal Golden Braid.* New York: Vintage Books.

Juul, Jesper. 2001. "Games Telling Stories: A Brief Note on Games and Narratives." *Game Studies* 1. http://www.gamestudies.org/0101/juul-gts/.

Kapp, Sébastien. 2013. "L'immersion fictionnelle collaborative: une étude de la posture d'engagement dans les jeux de rôles grandeur nature." Doctoral thesis, Paris: EHESS; Brussels: ULB.

Lamarque, Peter, and Stein Haugom Olsen. 1994. *Truth, Fiction and Literature*. Oxford: Clarendon Press.

Lavocat, Françoise, and Anne Duprat, eds. 2010. *Fiction et cultures*. Paris: SFLGC.

Lewis, David. 1978. "Truth in Fiction." *American Philosophical Quarterly* 15: 37–46.

MacDonald, Margaret. 1954. "The Language of Fiction." *Aristotelian Society*, supplemental vol. 28: 165–96.

Menoud, Lorenzo. 2005. *Qu'est-ce que la fiction?* Paris: Vrin.

Monfort, Nick. 2003. *Twisty Little Passages: An Approach to Interactive Fiction*. Cambridge, MA: The MIT Press.

Morsillo, Sandrine. 2012. "Des fictions d'expositions." In *Fictions & médias, intermédialités dans les fictions artistiques*, edited by Bernard Guelton, 75–90. Paris: Publications de la Sorbonne.

Murray, Janet. 2017. [1997]. *Hamlet on the Holodeck: The Future of Narrative in Cyberspace*. Updated ed. Cambridge, MA: The MIT Press.

Oura, Yasusuke. 2010. "Procès de la fiction, procès de la littérature: sur quelques cas au Japon." In *Fiction et cultures*, edited by Françoise Lavocat and Anne Duprat, 176–95. Paris: SFLGC.

Pavel, Thomas. 1986. *Fictional Worlds*. Cambridge, MA: Harvard University Press.

Radford, Colin. 1975. "How Can We Be Moved by the Fate of Anna Karenina?" *Proceedings of the Aristotelian Society*, supplemental vol. 49: 67–80.

Ricoeur, Paul. 1984. [1983]. *Time and Narrative*, volume 1. Translated by Kathleen McLaughlin and David Pellauer. Chicago: University of Chicago Press.

———. 1985. [1984]. *Time and Narrative*, volume 2. Translated by Kathleen McLaughlin and David Pellauer. Chicago: University of Chicago Press.

Ryan, Marie-Laure. 1997. "Postmodernism and the Doctrine of Panfictionality." *Narrative* 5, no. 2: 165–87.

———. 1999. "Frontière de la fiction: digitale ou analogique?" *Fabula*. https://www.fabula.org/forum/colloque99.php.

———. 2001. *Narrative as Virtual Reality: Immersion and Interactivity in Literature and Electronic Media*. Baltimore: The Johns Hopkins University Press.

———. 2006. *Avatars of Story*. Minneapolis: University of Minnesota Press.

Saint-Gelais, Richard. 2001. "L'effet de non-fiction: Fragments d'une enquête." *Fabula*. https://www.fabula.org /effet/interventions/16.php.

Schaeffer, Jean-Marie. 2010. [1999]. *Why Fiction?* Translated by Dorrit Cohn. Lincoln: University of Nebraska Press.

Searle, John R. 1979. [1975]. "The Logical Status of Fictional Discourse." In *Expression and Meaning*, 58–75. Cambridge: Cambridge University Press.

Walton, Kendall L. 1990. *Mimesis as Make-Believe*. Cambridge, MA: Harvard University Press.

CHAPTER 9

Narratology and the Test of Greek Myths

The Poetic Birth of a Colonial City

CLAUDE CALAME

As a short and methodological prelude, the semio-narratological approach to myths and particularly to Greek myths proposed here must be contrasted to our modern way of making and writing history. Here, for the purpose of demonstration, the history of a flourishing colonial city in ancient Greece, Cyrene, on the Mediterranean coast of northern Libya, will be taken as an example.

Contemporary archaeologists and historians agree: The development of Greek Cyrene began in the second half of the seventh century BCE. The presence on that site of objects dating from Late Helladic III A and B (corresponding for us to the end of the fourteenth century BCE) suggests even more remote contacts between Greece and the Mediterranean coast of Africa. However, nothing indicates, before the middle of the archaic period, the development there of a city in the Greek sense of the word and concept.[1] Such, at any

---

The study offered here is a partial version, focused on a mythical and poetic narrative by the Greek poet Pindar, of the chapter "Narrating the Foundation of a City: The Symbolic Birth of Cyrene," which appeared in: Edmunds, Lowell, ed.. *Approaches to Greek Myth*. Second Edition. pp. 281–352. © 1990, 2014 Johns Hopkins University Press. Adapted and reprinted with permission of Johns Hopkins University Press. The original translation is by Susan Maslan and Samuel Schmidt.

1. Note, however, that these same rare objects have once again raised the possible validity of the most ancient date attributed by Eusebius to Cyrene's colonization, that is to say, 1336 BCE (as opposed to 761 and 632); see *Chronicon* VII 52.18, 87.16–9, and 96.19 Helm. This thesis was rejected in its time on the basis of less substantial documentation assembled by Chamoux (1952: 69–91).

rate, is the interpretation proposed by archaeology and by documentary history in an effort to reconstruct a chronology in keeping with our sense of history, based on the traces left by the passage of time—an arithmetic time with a double orientation: one that sketches out an accumulation of years after the supposed birth of our own civilization's founding hero, the other extending back before that date.[2] Nothing is more foreign, however, to the Greek way of viewing what constitutes for us the temporal ordering in time of a historical past and the ordering in discourse of the succession of human actions at the origin of a founding event.

Self-evident proof of this perspective can be found in the multiplicity of events and human actions that an ancient Greek poet would have been most likely to place at the (temporal) origin of the city whose rulers, his contemporaries, he praises: Apollo's rape of the nymph Cyrene and celebration on the Libyan coast of his union with this young lion huntress in the time of the gods; occupation of the site by the sons of Antenor, accompanied by Helen, following the destruction of Troy; and transfer of a clod of Libyan earth by a son of Poseidon to another son of the same god and its coming to ground at Thera (Santorini) so as to return, metaphorically, to its land of origin in the colonial expedition of Battus, Cyrene's "historical" founder, seventeen generations later, in the time of men. In this third version of the poetic narrative of the foundation of Cyrene offers a first chronological reckoning, but no indication is given about the number of generations separating Battus's colonizing act, in "historical" time, from the time and circumstances of its narration.

Despite this lack of chronological detail, the poetic performances of the narrated events and actions in this indeterminate past are amenable to precise dating. I have summarized above, in order, the narratives contained in the Ninth, Fifth, and Fourth *Pythian Odes* of Pindar. Belonging to the poetic form of the epinician, these poems were composed to celebrate an athletic victory at the Panhellenic games. The first ode sings of the victory obtained at the hoplite race during the twenty-eighth Pythian Games by Telesicrates of Cyrene in the year 474 BCE; it was probably performed in Cyrene at the time of festivities marking the return home of the athlete. The second ode celebrates the success in the chariot race of the brother-in-law of Arcesilas the Fourth, King of Cyrene, on the occasion of the thirty-first Pythiad, in 462; it was sung in honor of the king's charioteer near the Garden of Aphrodite, per-

---

2. This "arithmetic" time, oriented within the perspective of Christian culture, enters into the larger category of "chronical time" (*temps chronique*), as defined by Benveniste (1974) [1970]). Ricoeur 1988 [1985]: 104–26) takes this notion up, calling it "calendar time" (*temps calendaire*). Neither of these authors, however, analyzes the material aspect of the time of physical events; nor do they consider the orientation of chronical time toward the present—essential to understand the pragmatics of historical discourse (see Calame 2009b [2006]: 14–24).

haps at the festival of the Carneia. A great civic and cultic ritual, the Carneia were celebrated in honor of Apollo, the god founder of the colonial city. As for the last of these odes, composed on the occasion of the same chariot victory, it was performed in the king's palace itself, most probably during a banquet celebrating this most prestigious of agonistic and Panhellenic victories.[3]

This projection of founding events into a chronologically indeterminate past seems to constitute the touchstone of what we know as myth. By fixing the ephemeral present into atemporal permanence, these primordial, exemplary events provide us with an ideal means of entry into what, in my view, is the basis of mythological narrative, and thus into a fruitful analysis of poetic narratives requiring a semio-narratological approach.

After reviewing the "indigenous" Greek conception of narratives that, to us moderns, are myths, a brief definition of the analytical and semio-narrative approach will be provided within the perspective of a pragmatically oriented narratology. I will then go on to study the narrative development of Pindar's Fourth *Pythian*. The highly developed account by the poet of Thebes of the "mythical" foundation of the colonial city Cyrene in Libya, related to the legend of the Argonauts, will be examined from three points of view: in its very complex temporal development; in its enunciative and pragmatic dimension; and in the various semantic registers that emerge out of its syntax.

1. MYTH AND NARRATIVE FORMS

Actually, what we call myth has no existence in itself, nor does it correspond to any universal cultural reality. In essence, myth is a concept invented by modern anthropology out of uncertainties gradually recognized by the Greeks themselves as to the historical reality of certain episodes in their own tradition. To this tradition the epithets "legendary" and "historic" are equally applicable: For the Greeks, the credibility of a narrative lies not so much in its congruence with factual, historical truth as it does in a judgment about the moral coherence and verisimilitude of a given narrative. It is true that the Greeks invented a concept called "the mythic" (*muthodes*), but as far as myth is concerned, their concept differed from the definition accepted by the *communis opinio* of modern anthropologists. Thus, what we call myth has neither essence nor reality apart from a purely Eurocentric perspective; it does not correspond to a (primitive) mode of human thought. Each culture possesses

---

3. On the Ninth *Pythian*, see Carey (1981: 65–66, 93); on the Fifth *Pythian*, see Currie (2005: 254–56); on the Fourth, see Giannini (1979: 35–36) and Gentili, Bernardini, Cingano, and Giannini (1995: 103–11) as a probable citharodic performance.

its own genre taxonomy for the narratives of its historic-legendary tradition.[4] In the central Himalayas, for example, the Pahari culture possesses a rich oral tradition. But even within the local taxonomy, the criteria of classification fail to present any kind of homogeneity: They refer, variously, to the content of the songs or to the different occasions of their being recited (see Gaboriau 1974).[5] Decisive are not only the context of performance of the narrative we consider as being a myth in particular historical, institutional, religious, and cultural circumstances, but also the generally poetic form assumed by narrative and its narration.

In ancient Greece, myth did not exist, except as a general notion of the mythic or the fictional that developed toward the end of the fifth century along with the kind of politico-military, anthropological history exemplified by Thucydides. What seems to us to belong to the legendary history of Greece is actually made up of a number of narratives, the contents of which set them off from one another, thus preventing them from being assigned to homogeneous categories such as the category of myth: stories of a reigning family in the form of genealogies; narratives dealing with the founding of cities (*ktíseis*); local stories centering on a particular event; biographies of heroically magnified "historical characters."[6] Our knowledge of these "historical" genres depends on fragmentary products coming out of the movement to rewrite a coherent legendary past, a movement whose traces can be made out in the fifth century. It can be seen, for instance, in Acusilaus of Argos's attempt to inscribe the legends of the Trojan War and of Heracles in the perspective of a single genealogical line centered on Argos, thus originating out of a theo-cosmogony. Consisting of a rewriting in prose of a history first told in Homeric diction, these stories were titled *Genealogiai* or *Historiai* by the ancients. They told about *tà arkhaîa or tà palaiá*, "the things of old," and about *tà patrôia*, "the history of the ancestors": Nothing here has to do with *muthoi*, a word that referred in classical Greece to developed discourses sometimes relying on a narrative argument and meant to be efficacious.[7] Thucydides himself, in his *arkhaiología*, tells about the events before the Persian Wars and the

---

4. See, for example, Sternberg (1987) for the ancient Hebrews.

5. The situation in archaic Greece is very similar with regard to poetic forms of oral performance (see Calame 1974). For a critical view on the modern concept of myth, see Calame (2011a: 19–57, 2015: 23–76).

6. See, in this connection, the reflections of Lasserre (1976). Strangely, the author omits local genealogical history from his list, a history that is well represented, for the archaic period, by the *Corinthiaca* of Eumelus of Corinth (see Pausanias 2.1.1. *Corinthiaca* frags. 1 and 4 Bernabé).

7. On the systematization of genealogies, see Fowler (2006); on Acusilaos, see especially Calame (2008).

Peloponnesian War, mentioning the first attempts to control the Aegean Sea with their protagonists: first the king of Crete, Minos or Pelops, and then the leaders of the Trojan War such as Agamemnon or Achilles—all heroic figures presented as historical persons.

Moving back in time from the classical to the preclassical epoch, one becomes aware that legendary history does not exist as a specific genre. It generally gets confused with poetic forms that are distinguished by the manner of execution. For example, a long narration in sung verse meant for a citharodic performance tells of the destruction of Troy in the *Iliou Persis* by Stesichorus, not to mention the numerous heroic narratives embedded in the different forms of archaic lyric (or rather, melic) poetry to illustrate the proposal of a poet composing and narrating for a given ritual and social occasion.[8]

In large measure, the fifth century continued to pay tribute to these different modes and forms of configuring history. Be it melic verse, as for Pindar, *logos* in prose, as for Herodotus, or the so-called Oath of the founders[9] or poems in epic form, as for Apollonius Rhodius, the narrative of the founding of the great Greek colony of Libya exists for us solely in the broadest variety of discursive, and generally poetic, forms intended for a particular situation of enunciation within a broader historical, social, religious, and cultural context.

2. A SEMIO-NARRATIVE APPROACH OPEN TO PRAGMATICS

The variety and complexity of enunciative situations in the narratives of Cyrene's founding provide compelling evidence in support of the semio-narrative approach proposed and discussed here. This approach focuses on the logic of the narrative and semantic network set within the context of pragmatic constraints. It involves a conception of pragmatics that lies between two poles: the conception of pragmatics current in the English-speaking world, which, to put it concisely, links the meaning of texts to their context and linguistic acts to speech acts, and the structural conception, which, based on the principle of the "immanence" of text, confines pragmatics to the cognitive dimension of communication. Here, preference is given not to a purely structural narratology but to a pragmatically based narratology that takes into

---

8. Stesichorus frags. 196–205 and S 88–132 Page-Davies. On the role of myth in melic poetry, see, for instance, Gentili (1984: 153–202) and Calame (2009c) with critical remarks on the application of the "lyric" mode to the poems of action which belong to the broad Greek category of *mélos*; see also Calame (2019 [1998]).

9. See Calame (2009b [2006]: 149–75) on the Cyrenaean decree making a double use of the legend in the foundation of Cyrene by Battus.

account the enunciative dimension of narrative in which meaning emerges from the social and cultural context of production and performance of the discourse.

When considering elaborate poetic texts, it is necessary to first retrace the thread of a narrative development that is constantly interrupted, confused, or diverted because of particular generic conditions or as a result of its own internal logic. This is especially the case with Pindar, a master of analepsis, prolepsis, rupture, condensation, retrospective digression, and the subtle allusive stroke.[10] But beyond reconstituting the logic of narrative action and the causality linking together the individual acts that make it up, it is essential to take account of the values brought into play—values that are inscribed in the succession of actions with their protagonists, whether affirmed or denied by them, and transformed into new values: not only the syntax of the poetic narrative we typically call "myth" but also the semantics of Pindar's narrative and, through its enunciative apparatus, the pragmatic features that are closely linked to the situation of enunciation.

The pragmatic semio-narrative reading of a poem by Pindar proposed here requires a few methodological and theoretical explanations. As far as the semantics and surface discursive structures of narrative are concerned, it is essential to pay attention to the different figures embedded in the protagonists of the narrative action, in their actions, and in the space where they act. By *figures* I mean those concrete semantic elements taken from the "natural," social, and cultural world in order to give a semantic profile to the actors of the narration, their actions, and the spaces in which they develop, giving rise during the course of the narrative's development to its "reality effect" (Roland Barthes). By taking on the form of actors, actions, and spatial trajectories (*parcours*), *these* figures develop along the syntactic dimension (*axe syntagmatique*) laid out by the linear unfolding of the story. In general, this unfolding can be analyzed according to the structural and "canonic schema" of narrative, which involves four phases: (1) manipulation (prompted by a condition of lack), (2) competence, (3) performance, and (4) sanction (return to a state of narrative equilibrium). These phases constitute the causal and temporal logic underlying the development of narrative. It means that, broadly speaking, in a situation of difficulty and lack, the "sender" (*destinateur*) will give the "subject" of the narrative action (the hero) (*manipulation*) the *competence* for a *performance* (a trial [*épreuve*]) that will then be rewarded (*sanction*). All in all, the canonic narrative schema represents, in the semio-narrative system elaborated by Algirdas J. Greimas and his pupils, what is generally thought

---

10. On Pindar's narrative technique as forms of plays on time, see Hurst (1985).

of as plot. Current research holds that plot must be understood in terms of "narrative tension."[11]

When taking into account the syntactic and semantic dimensions of narrative together with its pragmatics in the analysis of poetic form, it is particularly important to distinguish, with Greimas, between the syntactic positions in the narrative (*actants* such as the sender or the subject) and the generally anthropomorphic figures (*actors*) that assume these different narrative roles.[12]

Moreover, recurrence in the text of semantic elements based in cultural representations and embedded in the narrative action and their actors generates figurative "isotopies," that is, semantic registers that assure the semantic and logical coherence of narrative and poetic discourse, often in a thread of subtle metaphorical plays.

As for semio-narrative structures, the deepest level of semantic construction and syntactic schematization, it will be seen in Pindar's narrative poem how the themes that directly underlie the reiterations produce isotopies. On this basis, theme is understood as the most abstract semantic level where the interpreter can identify the concepts underlying the choice, in the natural and social world, of surface figures based on cultural representations. It is at this level that a (poetic and "poietic") discourse becomes the location of a culturally and ideologically determined construction calling for interpretation of an anthropological and symbolical order. Discourse, being dependent on a certain historical and cultural paradigm, demands of the modern reader a true effort of transcultural translation.[13]

These tentative expressions of the meaning production process through narrative syntax and semantic organization can never take on any value in themselves, for they are modern and interpretive reconstructions. It is invariably necessary to relate such meaning production to the conditions of per-

---

11. On these concepts, see the corresponding entries in Greimas and Courtés (1982 [1979], 1986). On narrative tension, see Baroni (2007: 7–47). For a discussion on "narrative divergences and tensions" in the complex narrative thread of *Pythian* 4, see section 4 in this chapter.

12. Among the critiques of these concepts are those by Rastier (1987: 117–19, 172–75, 177–211). I agree with Rastier that the distinction between "figurative" and "thematic" isotopies is of little practical use. I also reject any hierarchy of isotopies, as their metaphorical reciprocities prevent this. Without entering into the subtle distinctions adopted by Rastier, the notion of "generic isotopy," based on the reiteration of general traits like "animal" or "human," is replaced by that of "thematic isotopy." On the other hand, "theme" is retained even though, not manifested on the textual surface, it is reconstructed by the interpreter. Themes form the basis of the particular semantic orientation of each text.

13. For the (poetic) pragmatics of Greek myths, see Calame (2007). See also my study of 2004 (with the other contributions published in the special issue of *Arethusa* 37) and Calame (2009a: 39–66). Relying on enunciation, semantics, and pragmatics, the narratological approach proposed here is quite different from the structural approaches found in the contributions edited by Grethlein and Rengakos (2009).

formance of what has been transmitted to us as text. Syntactic and semantic analysis cannot take place without pragmatics, that is to say, without reference to the conditions of the production and reception of meaning. In conjunction with semio-narrative study, the analysis of discourse shows that narrative meaning is inferred particularly through the marks and strategies of enunciation inherent in a given discourse itself. The figures and values that the text sets into play, and that semio-narrative analysis attempts to track down in their articulation, are pertinent only in relation to the interpretive community to which the narrative was originally and concretely addressed. Thus we cannot accept the supposed structural closure of the text (and its "world"), for a text necessarily refers, through discourse, to the world in which it is produced (discourse = text + context, to be schematic). In the case of narration of the foundation of Cyrene, with its different versions (in the form of an epinicion or poem of praise [Pindar], a *lógos* of inquiry [Herodotus], a learned epic poem [Apollonius Rhodius], a literary hymn [Callimachus]), each discourse, by staging the past of a cultural community, is a case of symbolic representation developed by a creative poet from the perspective of a specific situation expressing a variety of political, social, religious, and cultural meanings and functions. Whether historical or legendary, the narratively, semantically, and poetically constructed past is always a function of the present.

From the point of view of the relationship of the narrative poem with the present enunciative situation, it is useful to refer to the distinction, in what Émile Benveniste calls the "formal apparatus of enunciation," between "story" or "narrative" (*histoire* or *récit*) and "discourse" (*discours*). Linguistically, "story" is characterized by the use of third-person pronouns; the aorist, *imparfait*, and preterit verb tenses; and deictic expressions designating spatial or temporal distance: This corresponds to the *énoncé* (the enunciate). The other level of expression is marked by the use of first- and second-person pronouns (singular and plural); verbs in the present, future, and perfect tenses; and deictic expressions referring to "now" and "here": This is the *énonciation* (act of enunciation). What is constructed in the discourse on the enunciative level (e.g., the authorial figure or mask of authority corresponding to the poetic "I") must be distinguished from the historical performer of the text. This is the case, in Pindar's epinicians, of the actantial position of the poetic "I"; it refers to a *persona poetica* corresponding both to the person of the poet and to the performer of his composition, generally a choral group of young men. From the enunciative point of view, this takes the form of "choral delegation" (the poet's voice) at the discourse level and results in enunciative polyphony.[14]

---

14. See in particular Benveniste (1971 [1959], 1974 [1970]). These enunciative criteria are employed in the analysis of ancient Greek poetry by Calame (1995 [1986]: 3–26, 2004).

In light of these considerations, the following reading does not treat the legend or myth of founding as an abstract narrative entity or a narrative summary of mythography. Rather, it seeks to map out the poetic development of Pindar's narrative through the narrative, semantic, and enunciative forms in which it is realized as song and ritual performance.[15]

3. A COMPLEX NARRATIVE AND TEMPORAL ARIADNE'S THREAD: PINDAR'S FOURTH *PYTHIAN*

To illustrate how semantic and cultural content are organized by a complex narrative syntax and conveyed through a particular poetic form with its pragmatics of enunciation in a ritualized performance, I will follow one of the versions of the legendary foundation of the Greek colonial city Cyrene as recreated and staged by Pindar for the singular occasion already mentioned. Actually, the long Fourth *Pythian* is a highly developed narrative—an exception to what we know of Pindaric production. Here is the beginning of the epinicion in the English translation by William H. Race (1997):

> Today, Muse, you must stand beside a man who is a
>   friend, the king of Kyrene with its fine horses,
>   so that while Arkesilas is celebrating
> you may swell the breeze of hymns
>   owed to Leto's children and to Pytho,
> where long ago [pote] the priestess who sits beside the golden
> eagles of Zeus prophesied when Apollo was not away   5
> that Battos would be the colonizer
> of fruit-bearing Libya, and that
> he should at once leave the holy island to found a city
> of fine chariots on the white breast of a hill,
> and to fulfill in the seventeenth generation that word
>   spoken in Thera by Medea,   10
>   which (she . . .) had once [pote] breathed forth
> from her immortal mouth. Such were her words
> to the semigods who sailed with spear-bearing Jason:
> "Hear me, sons of great-hearted men and gods,
> I declare that one day [pote] from this sea-beaten land [i.e., Thera]
>   the daughter of Epaphos [i.e., Libya]

---

15. For an analysis of Greek myths along these lines, see Calame (2007, 2009).

will have planted within her a root of famous cities 15
at the foundations of Zeus Ammon.
In place of short-finned dolphins
   they will take swift horses
and instead of oars they will ply reins
   and chariots that run like a storm.
This sign will bring it to pass that Thera
will become the mother-city of great cities—the token 20
which Euphamos once [*pote*] received at the outflow
of Lake Tritonis ...

At the outset, this Pindaric narration centers on the occasion of its recitation: the celebration of Arcesilas the Fourth, the current king of Cyrene (temporally marked by the first word of the ode: *sámeron*, "today," corresponding to a first temporal level, T1). There is also a mention at the outset of Apollo, the narrative sender of the king's action (the narrative manipulation), and of the Muse as the sender of the poetic persona (the subject of the poetic action beginning "here and now"). The implicit poetic "I" calls on the Muse as "you" in order to celebrate the king Arcesilas in a banquet with music, *hic et nunc*, also with songs addressed to Artemis and Apollo as well as to Pytho.

Then, however, the extraordinary Pindaric time machine is set in motion, and quickly the audience is transferred from the *discours* to the *récit*. Through the spatial adverb *entha* (line 4), the mention of Delphi transports us from the present of the performance of the song to a past time when the priestess of Apollo, under the control of Zeus, designated Battus of Thera (our Santorini) as founder of Cyrene (the narrative action unfolds in the same place, but in the aorist with protagonists designated in the third person) (see Hurst 1983). The oracular speech is addressed in an indeterminate past (*pote*, line 4, T2) to the one who is destined to go to "fruit-bearing (*karpophoros*) Libya" (line 6). Thus Apollo, through the mediation of the Pythia, is set in relation to the hero-founder Battus. Whether ode or oracle, in the present or in the past, a speech of divine origin, spoken by an inspired mediator, brings together the human actor and the divinity who guides his action.

The victory won by the chariot of the current king Arcesilas then completes a narrative program at a moment of narrative sanction. The meaning of this victory is in some way inverted because, once materialized in the poem, it is conceived as an honor paid to Apollo as sender of a victorious action at the level of the discourse. In contrast, at the level of the "story" (*récit*), Battus finds himself at the beginning of a trial into which he has been enlisted by that same god. This is the initial phase in the narrative program according to the canonic narrative schema: manipulation of Battus by Apollo by which he is endowed with a heroic competence leading to the performance of the founding act. The narrative constructed by Pindar thus seems, in its logic, to make the heroic story of Battus, founder of Cyrene, the narrative beginning of the present story of the contemporary king of the city. However, the temporal structure of the semio-narrative action is more complicated and will develop, as we will see, on no fewer than five temporal and spatial levels, from the present to the most remote "mythical" past, in different spaces:

- T1: time of the performance of the song (Arcesilas IV)—Cyrene
- T2: time of the founding action (Battus)—Thera, then Cyrene
- T3: time of a potential narrative program (Danaeans)—Sparta, then Libya
- T4: time of the prophecy to the Argonauts (Medea)—Thera
- T5: time of the main manipulation (Euphemos)—Libya

Sanction appears at T1 and manipulation at T2 so that the narrative is still not yet complete. Pindar then goes back seventeen generations before the founding act of Battus (T4). Again, it is through the mediation of divinely inspired speech that the narration finally begins to develop in a prediction articulated through the immortal mouth of Medea, seized with a prophetic delirium that seems sourceless. When putting in at Thera, an island in the Aegean sea, Medea speaks to the demigod Argonauts. Her first narrative utterance refers to the route that will later be followed by Battus from Thera to Libya (T2). However, this utterance situates the spatial trajectory (*parcours*) at an entirely distinct figurative level in that the utterance brings non-anthropomorphic actors into the scene: a clod of earth and a sea wave. From the insular Thera, Libya will give root to future cities consecrated to Zeus Ammon. Here one learns, through an implicit reference to the agonal occasion of the poem (the Pythian victory of the chariot of Arcesilas IV in T1), that Theran colonists, instead of seafarers, are destined to become tamers of horses and drivers of chariots.

Medea, the queen of the Kolchians, will finally enunciate the performance phase of the main narrative, along with the narrative transformation it signals. At her temporal level (T4), she prophesizes to the future founders of Cyrene under the lead of Battus (T2) more or less the same future that Tiresias foresees for Odysseus during his encounter with the Homeric hero in the Underworld: that the Homeric hero will return to his city to restore order and will journey by foot until the oar he is carrying is mistaken for a winnowing fan. A sacrifice to Poseidon will then mark Odysseus's leave-taking from the sea's domain and the beginning of a period of earthly abundance in the midst of his own people. For the descendants of Battus, this prophecy results in a transition from mastery of the waves to mastery of horses. Even on land, then, we remain in the privileged domain of Poseidon, who controls the savage forces of the horses as well as those of the sea and those of the earth itself.[16]

To complete this narrative transformation, a chronological reckoning is activated by mention of the seventeen generations that separate Medea's prediction from the founding act of Battus. But this chronological reference point is carefully effaced by the repetition of *pote,* "once upon a time," in lines 10 and 14: Both the speech of the woman inspired by Aietes and the founding event she announces are located in an indeterminate past (superposition of T2 and T4).

Indeterminate as it might be, this past nevertheless begins to take on the form of a succession of events. Could Thera be considered the capital of a colony? The opportunity arises for Medea to recall an essential precedent, not contemporary with the colonists but further back in time, in connection (as we will see) with the clod of earth from Libya that will be transferred back, metaphorically, to Libyan soil in Cyrene. Once again in an indeterminate past (*pote,* line 20), the narrative action is referred back to its non-anthropomorphic foundation (at an even more remote temporal level, T5); the heroic action discovers at last its beginning, anticipating from afar the manipulation whose object will be Battus the founder (in T2).

Pindaric narration, however, fulfills the canonic schema only in terms of its most formal aspect. First, in place of the condition of lack that generally drives every narrative plot by inserting it into a causal sequence, the narrative of Medea creates a situation of paradox. Attempting to reach the Mediterranean Sea from the river Ocean, the Argonauts have just pulled their vessel for twelve days "across the back of a barren land." They come to the mouth of Lake Triton, that body of water in the interior; Jason's "chariot"—from "beam" (*doru,* line 27), which by synecdoche can mean both ship and chariot—then acquires its maritime character again, and its "bridle" is used once again as an anchor.[17] In this way, the thematic categories of navigation and equitation are mingled, although they are carefully distinguished in the later phase of the narrative. In this singular situation (*pote,* line 20, T5), Triton-Poseidon appears alone to the Argonauts:

---

16. Homer, *Odyssey* 11.119–37 (see 23.266–84). See the commentary by Hansen (1977). On Poseidon's modes of intervention in marine and equine domains, see Detienne and Vernant (1974: 176–200, 221–41).

17. The function of dominating the savage forces of the horse assumed by the bit is well defined by Detienne and Vernant (1974: 183–91).

>   (...)—the token   20
> which Euphamos once [*pote*] received at the outflow
> of Lake Tritonis, when he descended from the prow
> and accepted earth proffered as a guest-present by a god
> in the guise of a man—and father Zeus, son of Kronos
> pealed for him an auspicious thunderclap—   25
> when he came upon us jangling the bonze-jawed
> anchor, swift Argo's bridle,
> against the ship. Before that, we had drawn up
> the sea-faring bark from Ocean in accordance
> with my instructions, and for twelve days   30
> had been carrying it across desolate stretches of land.
> At that point the solitary god approached us,
> having assumed the radiant face of respectful man,
>   and he began with the friendly words
> which generous men first utter when offering dinner   35
> to strangers upon their arrival.

In the absence of a true condition of initial lack, the meaning of the manipulation phase of the narrative as a whole remains hidden at first. Assuming a mortal shape, Poseidon gives Euphemus, the first of the Argonauts to disembark on the shore of Lake Triton, a handful of earth (T5) as a "gift of hospitality" (*xeinia*, line 22; *xenion*, line 35). It may be observed that the words of hospitality accompanying this gift are explicitly assimilated by Pindar into those uttered at the banquet offered to a foreigner (lines 29–34). It is precisely at a banquet that Arcesilas the Fourth receives Pindar's song (line 2). The original *xenion* (gift) that Euphemus receives from the hands of Poseidon is thus nothing other than the prefiguration of the hymn that the king of Cyrene, his descendant, receives from the poet—a subtle interference between story and discourse (*récit* and *discours*).

Should this be read as a simple act of welcome? Not at all, for the gift is accompanied by a clap of thunder sent by Zeus himself. Described as *aisios* (line 23), thus responding to the will of destiny, the sign from Zeus marks, within the narrative frame of the Argonauts' expedition, the point of departure for a new narrative action. The new subject of the narrative action will not be the Argonauts as a group but Euphemus, king of the holy city of Taenarum, *anax* (master, line 45), and *hērōs* (hero, line 36), for he is the son of Europa and Poseidon, the one "who masters horses" (*hipparkhos*, line 45), the child born in the center of continental Greece near Cephisus but who reigns over the extreme reaches of the Peloponnesus. It is thus definitely to his equal that the god Poseidon, who takes the form of Eurypylus, speaks. Eurypylus himself, the scholia tell us, is the incarnation of Triton, but he is principally another son of Poseidon, of the god who, Pindar says, embraces the earth and has the power to shake it (*gaiaokhos, ennosidas,* line 33).[18]

Insofar as it does not arise from a condition of lack and is consequently not the object of a query, the miraculous clod of earth appears as a spontaneous gift, without causal provocation. If the doubly divine intervention could be said to institute this gesture of hospitality as the manipulation phase of narrative action, this first step leads to a competence and then to a performance, neither of which is realized. As envisaged in Medea's prophecy, the same narrative program would have led Euphemus, on his return to Taenarum, to throw the clod of earth into the mouth of Hades, which was believed to open near the cape of the same name. By the fourth generation (T3), the descendants of Euphemus of Taenarum, along with Danaeans emigrating from Sparta, Argos, and Mycenae, would have taken possession (*ke . . . labe,* in the unreal mode; 47–49) of the Libyan continent.[19]

4. NARRATIVE DIVERGENCES AND TENSIONS

Against this program, uttered in the unreal mode (T3), Medea sets in motion the program that will be substituted for it in reality, even though some features of this program appear to be negative at first sight. Euphemus, as it turns out, has just lost control of the clod of earth, whose guardians let it fall into the sea instead of bringing it to the mouth of Hades. But this in no way prevents the divine gift from undergoing a change of status: In coming to ground on the island of Thera, where Medea and the Argonauts are presently to be found (*en tāide nasōi,* "upon this island," line 42, T4), it is promised as the possible "indestructible seed" of Libya. However, in order for the realization and the sanction of this transformation to take place as performance, the intervention of an anthropomorphic actor is indispensable.

Thanks to the intervention of such an actor, the negative narrative program, activated by the coming-to-ground of the clod and replacing of the unrealized program, will not delay in taking on a positive inflexion. This nar-

---

18. See the ancient commentary in the scholion on Pindar, *Pythian* 4.61 (II, p. 105, 20–4 Drachmann); see also ad 4.51 (104.17–8 (from here on, scholiasts will be cited in this abridged form), where Eurypylus is presented as indigenous king of Cyrene (see below).

19. According to scholion ad 4.85 (109.4–9), the emigration of the Danaeans, originating from Sparta, Argos, and Mycenae, is brought about by the return of the Heraclids, usually associated with the "Dorian invasion" (see Giannini 1979: 41, n. 30).

rative reorientation is perfectly marked at the temporal level. Granted, the miraculous clod of earth arrives at Thera "out of season" (*prin horas,* line 43), but "now" (*nun,* line 50), at the moment of Medea's prediction (T4), an anthropomorphic actor will take the destiny of the divine gift back into his hands so as to inflect its course. On reaching Lemnus, a point that Pindar locates, contrary to subsequent tradition, at the end of the Argonauts' expedition, Euphemus and his companions will unite with the women of the island.[20] And in anticipation of the seventeen generations that will pass after the time of Medea's prophetic utterance (T4), one learns that the *genos* born of this fleeting union will emigrate to Thera, "in this island" (line 52 takes up line 43). It is there that the future lord (*despotas,* line 53) of Libya will be engendered. Through Medea's voice (T4), the narrative performance resulting from Apollo's manipulation of Battus (line 5, T2), and from the manipulation of Poseidon (line 37, T5) finally reaches a complete temporal and spatial convergence.

The reorientation of the unfolding of the narrative program has as its corollary not only the temporal deviation indicated above but, more importantly, a displacement in the line of descent of Cyrene's founding hero. Battus is not the direct, legitimate descendant of Euphemus, since his ancestor was born of an extramarital union between the king of Taenarum and a woman from another country. Added to this genealogical displacement, there occurs a change in sender of the heroic action: It is no longer Poseidon but rather Apollo who, according to the oracular words, is destined to guide Battus toward those regions of the Nile reigned over by Zeus, son of Cronus (lines 55–56).

Medea's Theran prediction (T4) is located spatially and chronologically at the center of the narrative. The phase of Euphemus's manipulation by Poseidon (T5) and of his failed performance thus occurs before the time of the prediction and at another place. The clod of Libyan earth is lost at that time and subsequently reappears at Thera, in the very place of Medea's prophecy. Starting from this point, and extending into the future, the bastard race engendered from the passion of Euphemus and the Lemnian woman is guided from Lemnus to Thera, leading it back to its abandoned origin. Hence, the second phase of manipulation, already mentioned: Apollo presents to Battus, a descendant of Euphemus, the oracle that will permit the seed to return to Libya, where it will bear fruit. At the realization of this performance, nothing is lacking to complete the narrative program but the phase of sanction.

---

20. Scholion ad 4.455b (160.25–9) attributes to the Lemnian woman with whom Euphemus unites the name of Lamache or Malache. It will be noted that the scholiast designates Euphemus with the term *archegos,* which is equally applicable to the author of the act of founding a *genos* as to the oecist of a colonial city (Casewitz 1985: 246–48).

Medea the vaticinator is no longer in a position to prophesy the sanction of the narrative action, but rather the object of the narration enunciated by the poem itself. Taking up the narrative perspective of the sorceress again, the one who sings the ode twice carries on and completes the narrative until the time of the utterance and thus of the performance of the song (T1).

First, in an address to Battus, the son of Polymnestus, the narrator insists on the manipulation phase of the hero Theran's colonial undertaking by showing that the oracular order from Apollo is the object of a triple repetition. Given in response to a question on an entirely different subject (the stammering that afflicts the future founder), this oracle is additionally said to be "spontaneous" (*automatos*, line 60), making Battus a predestined king (*pepromenon*, line 61). As for the sanction of Battus's colonizing act, it is not yet made explicit in these lines. However, the narrator places this event during the prosperous times of Arcesilas, who lives "now" (*nun*, line 64[21]), at the time of the poem's recitation (T1), eight generations later. The action of the king of Cyrene is also favored by the Delphic god. This is explained in the following lines:

> O blessed son of Polymnastos, it was you
> whom the oracle, in accordance with that speech, exalted   60
> through the spontaneous cry of the Delphic Bee,
> who thrice bade you hail and revealed you to be
> the destined king of Kyrene,
> when you were asking what requital would come
> from the gods for your stammering voice.
> Yes, indeed, now in later time as well,
> the eighth generation of those sons flourishes in Arkesilas,   65
> to whom Apollo and Pytho granted glory ...

The narrative of the foundation of Cyrene is then interrupted by the longest narrative attested in a poem by Pindar: a passage devoted to the adventures of the Argonauts. Mention of the king Arcesilas (T1), the addressee of the poem, is taken up again toward the end of the poem (line 250) in a direct address, at the discourse level. It is repeated at the exact moment when the unfolding of actions of which the Argonauts are protagonists (T4) begins to become confused with the events leading up to the founding of Cyrene (T2): their diversion by way of the Ocean (and thus by way of Libya) and lingering with the Lemnian women who, we learn, have killed their husbands (line

---

21. This *nun* seems to pick up again the *nun* that, in line 50 (Medea's prediction), designates the moment of birth of the race of Battus and thus of Arcesilas.

252). In the end, the union of the Greek heroes with these homicidal women is fortunate, because from it will be born the privileged "race" of Euphemus, destined to rediscover Libyan ground: from Lemnus to Lacedemonia, whence they will adopt Spartan culture; from there to Calliste-Thera, which they will colonize; and finally, through the intervention of Apollo, to Libya, where they will administer with prudent intelligence (*mētin*, line 262) "the divine city of Cyrene." The narrative finishes by rediscovering its own logic, with its spatial trajectory. With a final address to Arcesilas (line 298), it turns back to the place and time of the sung performance of the epinician composed by Pindar (T1): Damophilos "would tell, Arkesilas, what a spring of ambrosial verses he found, when he was recently a guest at Thebes." From the *récit* with its complex and multilevel temporality and spatiality we return, at the end of the poem, to the "here and now" of the *discours*.

5. A SEMANTIC LABYRINTH: ISOTOPIES AND METAPHORS

The complexity of semantic development in the Fourth *Pythian* loses nothing in comparison to that of its complex syntactic and temporal articulation. The interlacing of recurrent isotopic figures, which assures their semantic coherence, is so dense that a commentary on the entire poem would require a book-length study in itself. The various semantic strata within the narrative tissue of the Fourth *Pythian* depend intimately on the enunciative voices that support them. Actually, Charles Segal (1986) has devoted an entire monograph to this Pindaric poem, emphasizing the skillful polyphony that interlaces the voice of the narrator addressing *hic et nunc* to king Arcesilas IV of Cyrene the prophetic words of Medea reported in direct discourse and the oracles of Apollo relayed by the voice of the Pythia and cited indirectly, not to mention the individual voices of the Argonauts, protagonists of the narrative, to whom Pindar willingly gives the floor, such as Mopsus the soothsayer of Zeus. All of these voices are prophetic in a context in which the clod of Libyan earth itself becomes an oracular portent (*ornis*, line 19).[22]

On the other hand, attention has yet to be paid to the hierarchical relations that, from the perspective of the legend of Cyrene, orchestrate the three voices mentioned above. These take shape, at first, through mediation of the narrative's temporal organization. The first, Medea's prophecy (T4), inspired (*anepseuse*, line 11) perhaps by Aphrodite (see lines 216–19), occurs in the *pote*,

---

22. See in particular Segal (1986: 27, 30–51, 136–45, 171, 183). These views show a welcome convergence with those I develop here.

"once upon a time," the furthest back in time as far as enunciation is concerned. Seventeen generations later (T2), one finds the oracles of the Pythia inspired by the god of Delphi. Finally, in the "today" (*sameron*, line 1) of the poem's execution (T1), the voice of the narrator is relayed to Arcesilas's side by the Muse.

Most important here is undoubtedly the spatial arrangement of these different voices. I have already referred to the central position assumed in the narrative itself by Thera, the location of Medea's prediction. To this we can now add Delphi, the explicit origin of the Apollonian oracles. Yet it is up to the voice of the poet, from Thebes onward (line 222), and through the mediation of the Muse, to set Delphi and then Thera in relation with Cyrene. The spatial order of the different voices supporting the utterance of the poem ends by inverting the temporal organization of these same voices. The original voice is also the most decentralized voice and the most recent one that can designate, after Thebes, the hitherto uncharted course between Thera, Delphi, and the land of Libya. To the temporal mark "today," which opens the poem, there responds the spatial mark that concludes it, closing the work upon itself to create a ring-shaped structure: *Thebai*. Thebes is the source of ambrosial songs (line 299), that is to say, songs of divine origin.[23] From the enunciative "here" and "now," referring to the *hic and nunc* of the performance of the poem at Cyrene, we thus come back to the space of its composition at the end of a long and intricate double narrative.

5.1. Productivity of the Soil and "Mother" City

Having considered the narrative's modes of utterance and the homologies that organize its space, time, and shared reference to divine inspiration, we move on to the actual tissue of utterances woven by these voices. Before teasing out the complex spatial image that the narrative constructs, we will try to define the isotopies that arrange its contents. We know that in classical Greece, as in other societies, the moment of matrimonial union is readily compared to labor. The metaphorical relation is frequently between a field made fertile by being plowed and sown and the essential goal of the Greek institution of marriage: the production of handsome children, themselves conceived, in a vegetal image, as offspring or as new shoots. As for agricultural activity, and particularly grain-centered culture, this serves as a metaphorical expression for the

---

23. On the springs that give forth water of divine origin, by which the poet calms the poetic thirst of his patron, see Gianotti (1975: 110–14). On the prophecy of Medea, see Athanassaki (2003: 101–5).

achievement of civilization. Agriculture and the production of grain were at the center of the Greek representation of social life, while political activity was the birthright of offspring born of legal marriage between citizens.[24]

Pindar articulates the semantic values of the narrative of founding Cyrene and civilizing Cyrenaica precisely upon these three semantic levels and lines—agricultural production, foundation of a family, and the development of civic life—according to a vegetal isotopy and a doubled human isotopy. The poem plays all the while on the reciprocal metaphorical relations of these three semantic lines. The clod that Euphemus receives from the hands of Eurypylus-Poseidon as a gift of hospitality was originally a handful of earth (*gaia*, line 26). But at the very moment when it is presented to Euphemus, it becomes a fragment of "plowed earth" (*aroura*, line 34), only to be transformed into a "divine clod" (*bōlax daimonia*, line 37) when the hero sets foot on the ground of Libya to receive it. Incidentally, this encounter with the human incarnation of Poseidon occurs after the Argonauts' long journey across a region of earth (*gaia*, line 26) that is entirely barren. Arriving in Thera, the clod becomes the "indestructible seed" of Libya (*sperma aphthiton*, line 43). Then, Medea's prediction evokes two complementary images of the clod's return to its land of origin: The return is conceived as an act of transplantation (*phuteuesthai*, line 15) by Libye, granddaughter of Zeus, and also as the pulling of a root (*rhiza*, line 15) from the "land battered by floods" (*haliplaktos ge*, line 14) that Thera represents. This root is destined to produce the trunk for numerous cities on ground already prepared for its coming, the land consecrated to Zeus Ammon (*themethla*, line 16, implies in its etymology the founding act expressed by the verb *tithenai*). However, the gardener for this transplantation would appear to be Battus, the future master of these plains covered with clouds and rain (line 52), the fertile territory (*pion*, line 56) controlled by the son of Cronus.

In the same way as the plays on time, the metaphor drawn from the fecundation of the earth contributes to the conjoining of two acts—the two narrative performances that, at the poem's beginning, distinguish their respective phases of manipulation. At the beginning of the ode, Libya was already seen as a "productive" land (*karpophoros*, line 6), and within this frame the hill forming the acropolis of Cyrene could be defined as a breast (*mastos*, line 8).[25] Having served as relay for the fecund clod, Thera can henceforth serve, in the proper sense of *matropolis* (line 20), as the "mother city." Both simultaneously

---

24. These representations of the foundations of civilization have been analyzed in particular by Vernant (1974: 48–53).

25. It will be noticed that to this nurturing *mastos* there corresponds the *omphalos* of Delphi, center of a "well-wooded mother" (74), that is, a fertile earth.

and metaphorically, the fecundation of the soil thus results from and produces nurturing cities.

Nevertheless, this manipulation of earth is unable, in its strictly feminine character, to fully accomplish the act of founding a city. The absent masculine principle will be supplied by the *genos* of Battus by way of the narrative displacement described above. This *genos,* conceived in the bed of foreign women (*allodapai,* line 50), is reinterpreted at the end of the poem, where it changes into a "predestined seed" (*sperma moiridion,* the term *sperma* being a correction by Hermann), planted in "foreign fields" (*arourai allodapai,* line 254). In turn, Euphemus's "race" takes on a plantlike sprouting (*phuteuthen,* line 256).[26] Its action bears as much on the administration of the divine city of Cyrene as it does on the mastery and fecundation of Libya's well-watered plains, which are made to "swell" (line 260) by the god's benediction. In the end, Euphemus's offspring will take over control of both the city's political activity and the agricultural production of its *chōra.*[27] The success of this transplantation stands out at the very moment Pindar's poem is performed: Its blossoming (*thallei,* line 5) is attributed to Arcesilas the Fourth, offspring (*meros*) of Battus, thus to the eighth generation.

Even so, the imbrication of these three metaphorical levels and lines through the Pindaric narrative (agricultural production, foundation of a family, development of civic life), no one of which is hierarchically superior to another, fails to account sufficiently for the specificity of the founding of a colonial city. Still missing is a properly cosmogonic dimension. The spatial trajectories (*parcours*), followed respectively by the clod (the feminine element) and by the race of Euphemus (the masculine element), with clear-cut gender roles, are particularly important in this respect.

The clod of earth issues from the shore of the Libyan Lake Triton. Actually, one of the numerous versions of the birth of Athena locates the event on the shores of Lake Triton (Tritogeneia is one who is "born of the earth"; *gēgenēs*).[28] But this terrain—propitious for chthonic births—is not in itself sufficient to ensure that fertility of the clod, a gift of hospitality from the god Poseidon.

---

26. Segal (1986: 68–71) has shown the ties that align the metaphorical labor of Battus's ancestor with that undertaken by Jason to capture the Golden Fleece (lines 224–30). Note, too, that Segal is sensitive to the "citizen" isotopy that runs through the entire ode (see 7, 19–20, 56, 260, 272), but that he neglects its "terrestrial" counterpart.

27. Segal (1986: 81–82) has been sensitive as well to the "citizen" isotopy that runs through the entire ode (see 7, 19–20, 56, 260, 272), but he neglects its "terrestrial" counterpart.

28. Herodotus 4.179, 188; Diodorus of Sicily 3.70.2 as well as scholion ad 4.36a (102.7–11) and scholion to Apollonius of Rhodes 4.1311 (313.140 Wendel); see also Diodorus of Sicily (5.70.4, 5.72.3). Athena is born from the umbilical cord of Zeus fallen near the river Triton in Crete at a spot called, ever since, *omphalos* (see Callimachus, *Hymn to Zeus* 42–47).

Its first destination, as we have seen, is one of the extremities of the Greek continent, the Peloponnesian Cape Taenarum with its mouth of Hades (line 44) and the sanctuary of Poseidon associated with it. Through this opening, explicitly associated with "extremities," Heracles is said to have dragged Cerberus into the light of day.[29]

In any case, through the neglect of Euphemus and his guards, the clod of Libya disappears into the sea instead of being swallowed up into the bowels of the earth. It is received by an island, a bit of anchored earth in the vast stretches of the sea. The mediating role played by Thera is marked as much by its geographical position midway between Libya and the Peloponnesus as by its hybrid status as an island, a status that many Greek insular lands, particularly Delos and Rhodes, share with Thera.

5.2. A "Myth" of Autochthony

It is likely that the word "autochthony" has sprung into the mind of readers of this essay. For these islands, though, it is a strange autochthony, for they themselves undergo autochthonous births that generally benefit the founding heroes of continental lands or places (*chorai*). And again, it is a question of birth out of the ocean depths, not out of the bowels of the earth.

We know, for example, the double myth of Athenian autochthony. The first king of Attica, Cecrops, is not only born from the earth (this is the fate of any number of primordial beings) but issues from the earth belonging to the city over which he will extend his sovereignty. Like Triton, he is *diphuēs*, a being half-man, half-serpent. As with the other colonizing heroes, his intervention signifies a change of name for the land over which he reigns: "Acte" becomes "Cecropia" before bearing the name "Attica." But more importantly, the autochthonous birth of Cecrops coincides with the moment the gods reapportion the Greek cities among themselves, the honors (*timai*) of Zeus, from which each receives in turn a share of the honors. Hence, the famous struggle between Athena and Poseidon. Thanks to the olive tree, Athena is able to extend her power over Attica, while Poseidon claims the same control by inverting the gesture of founding islands: Under the blow of the god's trident,

---

29. On Heracles and Cerberus, see Euripides, *Hercules Furens* 23–25, 612–21, 1275–278, among others. See also Pausanias 2.35.10 as well as 3.25.5, who, to nurture his skepticism in regard to the cavern he visits at Cape Taenarum with its path of communication to Hades, cites the attempt at a rationalizing explanation by Hecataeus *FrGHist* 1 frag. 27.

the sea rises up in the center of Athens, on the rock of the Acropolis.³⁰ As in primordial Libya, early Attica is marked by a mixture of earth and water. Here we would have to add the second legendary birth from the earth founding the claim of the Athenians of the classical period for autochthony. Future king of Athens as Erechtheus, Erichthonios is born from the soil of Attica fecundated by the seed of Hephaistos: The god ejaculated before reaching the flying Athena, the virgin goddess with whom he was in love and whom he tried to rape.³¹

There are, then, autochthony myths whereby continental cities give root to their inhabitants on the ground of the motherland. But there also exist "marine" autochthony myths that aim to give terrestrial roots to islands floating at sea before causing continental peoples, capable of founding human civilization, to emigrate there. While Santorini occupies an intermediate geographical position between the continent and Libya, and while its foundation by Theras confers upon it, in all likelihood, the status of a hybrid autochthony (like Delos or Rhodes), Libya itself assumes an even more marginal position, exemplifying a third class of possible representations of autochthony. Centered on Lake Triton and placed under the control of Poseidon, Libya is indeed truly neither earth nor sea. To acquire an "autochthonous" value, its roots would most fittingly originate on the outside, in the bowels of the continent, near Cape Taenarum. But in an additional confusion of separate categories, the Libyan earth comes to ground on the island of Thera, and only there can it acquire the generative force of a germ; this also is the moment when human actors can intervene in a positive way.

Autochthony, therefore, cannot be realized without anthropomorphic actors. Of course, even before its arrival in Thera, the piece of Libyan earth

---

30. A propos of Cecrops, see notably Aristophanes, *Wasps* 438, and Philochorus *FrGHist* 328 frag. 93, *Marmor Parium FrGHist* 239 A 1, and so on. For the dispute between Poseidon and Athena, see Herodotus 8.55, Plutarch, *Themistocles* 19, Pausanias 1.26.5, 8.10.4, and so on. If the double nature of Cecrops (half-man, half-serpent) attaches this figure to the earth, that of Triton (half-man, half-dolphin) attaches him to the sea, as does his descent from Poseidon and Amphitrite (see Hesiod, *Theogony* 930–31, Apollonius of Rhodes 4.1602–19, etc.). Libye herself is termed *autokhthōn* (Herodotus 4.45.3). In relation to the birth from the earth expressed by the concept *of gēgenēs*, autochthony has the added implication of residence on the ground where one was born (see Rosivach 1987; more recent bibliographies can be found in Calame 2009a [2000]: 142–49, 2011a).

31. On Erichthonius, born from the seed of Hephaestus scattered on the ground of Attica without having touched Athena the *parthenos*, see Apollodorus 3.14.6 as well as Homer (*Iliad* 2.546–49), Euripides (*Ion* 265–74), and *Erechtheus* frag. 370, 59–62 Kannicht. On other versions of the birth of Erichthonius/Erechtheus, with the impact that this birth in a nurturing earth has on the representation of the status of the autochthonous Athenian citizen, see Parker (1987: 193–99) and the bibliographical references given in Calame (2009a [2000]: 136–46).

has been manipulated by Euphemus, but the lack of care taken by the son of Poseidon causes the divine clod to fall short of its original destination. Should we be surprised when Apollonius of Rhodes, seconded by a commentator on Pindar, tells us that Euphemus has precisely the ability to synthesize, through his gift of walking on the ocean waters, the categories of sea and land? Conversely, does he not reach Lake Triton by a land route and yet on a boat? This capacity to confound semantic categories is inscribed even in the genealogy of the Taenarian king. His mother, Europa, is in fact the daughter of Tityus, a Giant born from Earth.[32] Doubtless these qualities can make of Euphemus the king of a port city attached to the continent, but not the founder of an essentially continental colony.

Reclaimed by a descendant of Euphemus, the Libyan clod could not have fallen into better hands. Not only has the union of which this bastard is the offspring taken place on an island but, in addition, the Lemnian woman, the Taenarian king's bride during his stay, has killed her legitimate husband. However, before establishing themselves at Thera, the descendants of Euphemus and the murderess "mingle" with the Lacedemonians, as in a sexual union (line 257). And the emigration to Thera would, for its part, have as its frame the colonial enterprise led by Theras the Lacedemonian, the eponymous hero of the island.

I will limit myself to filling in the Pindaric allusions by specifying that Theras, Cadmean by origin and consequently from Thebes, comes from a continental city, even though he lives as a foreigner in Lacedemonia. He is in fact the maternal uncle of Eurysthenes and Procles, the Heraclids who carry on in Sparta the autochthonous dynasty that founds the two dynasties exercising political power over the city. Like the descendants of Euphemus, Theras is an outsider in relation to the political legitimacy of Lacedemonia. But on the island of Calliste, which his arrival transforms into Thera, he recovers his own.[33]

---

32. Apollonius of Rhodes 1.182–84, in his catalogue of the Argonauts, attributes to Euphemus the same ancestry as Pindar does. See also Pausanias 5.17.9, who indicates that, on the chest of Cypselus, Euphemus was presented as the winner of the chariot race in the games for Pelias. It is true that the Hesiodic tradition makes Euphemus into a son of Poseidon and Mecionice, the daughter of Eurotas (Hesiod frag. 253 Merkelbach-West as cited by the scholion ad 4.36c 102.16–9 and developed by the scholion ad 4.15b 99–103).

33. Herodotus 4.147, in a text analyzed in Calame (2011a: 200–41). On the sanctuary of Poseidon and Athena founded by Cadmus at Thera, see Theocrestus of Cyrene (and not Theophrastus) *FrGHist* 761 frag. 3. On other, analogous insular foundations attributed to Cadmus, see Vian (1963: 60–64).

6. THE TRIAD OF FOUNDING GODS

Back, now, to *Pythian* IV. As senders of human actions, the gods in the Pindaric version of Cyrene's colonization play precisely the decisive role one would expect. The foundation phase, which manipulates even the ground of the colony, is placed entirely under the control of Poseidon: This is a "terrestrial" Poseidon, let us call him (to avoid the overused term "chthonian"), whose action is indispensable for creating and stabilizing the foundations of any city. Even at Thera, the above-mentioned worship is offered to Poseidon *Gaieokhos,* "who holds the earth." The sons of the earth god are then naturally the first kings of those cities newly established on firm ground.[34] But on islands and in the colonies, the primordial act of demiurgic foundation accomplished under the auspices of Poseidon remains without effect if it is not followed by an immigration of men coming from the continent, as guided by Apollo. Even the site of Delphi does not escape this scenario. Chthonian Gaia and Poseidon are the ones who utter oracles before Apollo takes the prophetic function back from these primordial divinities. The avowed aim of this divine succession is nothing less than civilization (*hēmerotēs*).[35]

After Poseidon the founder and Apollo the colonizer, we have yet to deal with the third sender of Greek civilizing action, as narrated by Pindar, on the Libyan continent: Zeus. Every phase of this action is favored by the presence, albeit discreet, of Zeus, the father of the Olympian gods, who marks, by an auspicious (*aision,* line 23) clash of thunder, the gift of Libyan earth by one son of Poseidon to another. After its diversion through Thera, this terrestrial root will emerge from the ground that already serves as a foundation for the worship of Zeus Ammon. Beneath the gaze of Zeus's eagles, protectors of the *omphalos* of Delphi, Battus receives from Apollo the oracle enlisting him in the colonizing effort (line 4).[36] Zeus alone is capable of ensuring the fertility of Libyan soil so as to make it the "rich sanctuary" that is consecrated to him (line 56).

This belonging of Libya to Zeus is not expressed merely in the worship of Ammon but also, in legend, by the ancestry of Libya, the granddaughter by Epaphus (line 14) of the son of Cronus, ancestor of the Danaeans, and by

---

34. Poseidon as divinity of the ground, particularly of its continental bowels, and as god of the sea depths (see Burkert 1977: 217–19).

35. Musaeus frag. 2 B 11 Diels-Kranz cited by Pausanias 10.5.6 and 24.4 as well as Ephorus *FrGHist* 70 frag. 150 and 31b. See Sourvinou-Inwood (1987), which lists the various versions of the succession from Ge to Apollo at Delphi while showing the inadequacy of historicist analysis.

36. On the intervention conjugated in the fourth *Pythian* of Zeus and Apollo in relation with Metis and Themis, see Giannini (1979: 42, 49–53).

the characteristic climate of the region around Cyrene, where black clouds gather to fecundate the ground (line 56).[37] Zeus's presence in Libya is required as much because he is the imposer of order over the terrestrial surface as it is because he is the keeper of the fecundating water from "on high." The god of the heights thus orchestrates his action with that of the god of the depths to constitute, through their separation, the terrestrial surface, the world that nurtures mankind.[38] But under the control of Poseidon and Zeus, the African continent still exists merely as the land of Libya. Only with the foundation of Cyrene under the auspices of Apollo will it be marked by the seal of civilization (Greek, of course). By simplifying, no doubt in the extreme, we can represent the collaboration of these three divinities in the colonizing act as a distribution of the isotopies and semantic lines that run through the narrative: to Poseidon the mineral, to Zeus the vegetal, and to Apollo the human.

7. SEMANTIC REVERBERATIONS OF THE SONG: PRAGMATICS

The theme of generation/germination takes upon itself, by turns, figures that are organized into isotopies: mineral, vegetal, and human; attachment of masculine political legitimacy to an earth-motherland; complementarity of Poseidon, Zeus, and Apollo; and so on. These lines of semantic development assure the coherence and richness of the Pindaric narrative. Guaranteed by the assimilation of a variety of enunciative voices that carry the narrative, this play of semantic reverberations and reciprocal metaphors recurs in the other two narrative sections of the Fourth *Pythian*: on one hand, the Argonauts' expedition in the middle of the song; on the other, the fate of Damophilus, a contemporary of Arcesilas the Fourth, at the end. Similarly, the quest for the Golden Fleece in order to get back the royal power in Iolcus, on the one hand, under the control of Apollo, Poseidon, and Zeus;[39] for Damophilus, the Cyrenean

---

37. The Libyan cult of Zeus Ammon is already placed in connection with that of Dodona by Herodotus 2.54–6, who attributes to them a common Egyptian origin. According to the scholion ad 4.28 (100.25–31 Wendel), all Libyan earth was consecrated to Zeus (Malkin 1994: 158–68).

38. On the organizing and fertilizing functions of Zeus, see Burkert (1977: 200–203). The tradition also includes elsewhere, in relation to the fecundity of the ground, a Zeus Chthonius (Hesiod, *Works* 465; see 379, 474, 488).

39. The subtle play of echoes that refer the Pindaric version of the quest of the Golden Fleece back to the foundation legend of Cyrene has been highlighted by Segal (1986: 72–85, 92–93). Segal insists essentially on the passage, across the interchange between sea and land, from instability to the establishment of civic roots. But he does not see that the principal protagonist of the foundation legend of Cyrene is neither Euphemus nor Battus, but the miraculous clod.

exiled to Thebes, on the other hand, the hope of recovering his "house," that is to say, the neighborhood of the spring of Apollo at Cyrene with its joys of the banquet and poetry amid citizens living in harmony (*hēsukhia*, line 296).[40]

In short, it is always the same passage that is in question, circular yet transformational, from a state in which civilization is merely latent to a state of realized civility through an intermediate stage in which the protagonist grapples with primordial forces that, once dominated, give rise to culture. The terrestrial germ of Libya becomes a Greek city after having sunk beneath the ocean waves: Jason, a king in strength, will reign over Iolcus after having imposed tillage, yoke, and marriage on the untamed forces—geological, theriomorphic, and anthropomorphic—of a fringe territory; Damophilus will return to the activities of civilization and political community of men after purging his presumption by undergoing the primordial punishment of Atlas. However, in a reversal that belongs exclusively to Pindar, Damophilus's Titanesque sojourn in Thebes is transformed in extremis into an initiation into poetry in the vicinity of a welcoming and inspirational spring (line 299).[41]

Subtly, the poet inserts into the domain of civilization the place of his composition even while taking up once again the poetic itinerary that opens the poem. By way of Thebes, this leads from Delphi to Cyrene, where the poem is performed as choral song or as citharodic delivery. The song thus ends as it began: at the ritual banquet understood as the location of poetic inspiration. This most skillful movement of recuperation belongs to the constraints that the occasion imposes on the Pindaric narrative of Cyrene's founding.

We thus find in the Pindaric narrative of the creation of Cyrene and Cyrenaica all the traits that characterize the products of the symbolic process. Starting from a more or less locatable historical event and action—the Greek colonization of Cyrene—the narrative borrows figures of different orders from the "natural" world (mineral, vegetal, animal) to inscribe them in a narrative program of anthropomorphic actions. These figures are grouped around certain focalizing themes: autochthony as a manifestation of the generation of a cultured land; herding as a stage in the process of civilization; matrimonial union in reference to the institution of civic order. Organized through the complex syntactic and temporal articulation of the narrative with its ramifications and

---

40. Parallelism glimpsed by Segal (1986: 84–85, 160–61); on the cosmogonic echoes of the same episode, see 103–5, 144. On the *metis* ("cunning intelligence") that Pindar exercises with regard to Damophilus, see Giannini (1979: 60–62); for the problematic mention of that Cyrenean aristocrat at the end of the song, see Gentili et al. (1995: 107–9, 505–10).

41. Those who interpret the circularity of this course as a simple return overlook the transformative aspect; such is the case even with Segal (1986: 89–93). See, however, the fine study by Felson Rubin (1999).

its tension, these figures are distributed along the linear sequence of narrative actions: They form isotopies, those semantic lines and levels of expression that the play of metaphor puts into reciprocal relations, assuring the semantic and poetic coherence of the song. Hence these symbolic products that transfigure reality in the direction of fiction while at the same time manifesting themselves in the most diverse poetic and discursive forms and for different situations of ritual, institutional, and cultural performance. It is in a specific historical and cultural context that the narrative poem makes sense and fulfills the conditions of its pragmatics through a poetical form corresponding to a sung and ritual performance, reactivating the cultural memory of the city to which it is addressed: cultural and institutional pragmatics of a complex narrative, polyphonic, and semantic creation through a song in performance.

WORKS CITED

Athanassaki, Lucia. 2003. "Transformations of Colonial Disruption into Narrative Continuity in Pindar's Epinician Odes." *Harvard Studies in Classical Philology* 101: 93–108.

Baroni, Raphaël. 2007. *La tension narrative: suspense, curiosité et surprise*. Paris: Seuil.

Benveniste, Emile. 1971. [1959]. "Relationships of Person in the Verb." In *Problems in General Linguistics*, translated by Mary E. Meek, 195–215. Coral Gables, FL: Miami University Press.

———. 1974. [1970]. "L'appareil formel de l'énonciation." In *Problèmes de linguistique générale*, II, 79–88. Paris: Gallimard.

Burkert, Walter. 1977. *Griechische Religion der archaischen und klassischen Epoche*. Stuttgart: Kohlhammer.

Calame, Claude. 1974. "Réflexions sur les genres littéraires en Grèce archaïque." *Quaderni Urbinati di Cultura Classica* 17: 113–28.

———. 1995. [1986]. *The Craft of Poetic Speech in Ancient Greece*. Translated by Janice Orion. Ithaca, NY: Cornell University Press.

———. 2004. "Deictic Ambiguity and Auto-Referentiality: Some Examples from Greek Poetics." *Arethusa* 37: 415–43.

———. 2007. "Greek Myth and Greek Religion." In *The Cambridge Companion to Greek Mythology*, edited by Roger D. Woodard, 259–85. Cambridge: Cambridge University Press.

———. 2008. "Les fonctions généalogiques: Acousilaos d'Argos et les débuts de l'historiographie grecque." *Europe* 945/946: 87–108.

———. 2009a. [2000]. *Greek Mythology: Poetics, Pragmatics and Fiction*. Translated by Janet Lloyd. Cambridge: Cambridge University Press.

———. 2009b. [2006]. *Poetic and Performative Memory in Ancient Greece: Heroic Reference and Ritual Gestures in Time and Space*. Translated by Janet Lloyd. Cambridge, MA: Harvard University Press.

———. 2009c. "Referential Fiction and Poetic Ritual: Towards a Pragmatics of Myth (Sappho 17 and Bacchylides 13)." *Trends in Classics* 1: 1–17.

———. 2011a. *Mythe et histoire dans l'Antiquité grecque. La création symbolique d'une colonie*. 2nd ed. Paris: Les Belles Lettres.

———. 2011b. "Myth and Performance on the Athenian Stage: Praxithea, Erechtheus, Their Daughters, and the Etiology of Autochthony." *Classical Philology* 106: 1–19.

———. 2015. *Qu'est-ce que la mythologie grecque?* Paris: Gallimard.

———. 2019 [1998]. "Greek Lyric Poetry, a Non-Existent Genre?" In *Oxford Readings in Greek Lyric Poetry,* edited by I. Rutherford, 33–60. Oxford: Oxford University Press.

Carey, Christopher. 1981. *A Commentary on Five Odes of Pindar: Pythian 2, Pythian 9, Nemean 1, Nemean 7, Isthmian 8.* Salem, MA: Arno Press.

Casewitz, Michel. 1985. *Le vocabulaire de la colonisation en grec ancien. Etude lexicologique: les familles de* κτίζω *et de* οἰχέω-οἰχίζω. Paris: Klincksieck.

Chamoux, François. 1952. *Cyrène sous la monarchie des Battiades.* Paris: de Boccard.

Currie, Bruno. 2005. *Pindar and the Cult of Heroes.* Oxford: Oxford University Press.

Detienne, Marcel, and Jean-Pierre Vernant. 1974. *Les ruses de l'intelligence. La mètis des Grecs.* Paris: Flammarion.

Felson Rubin, Nancy. 1999. "Vicarious Transport: Fictive Deixis in Pindar's *Pythian Fourth*." *Harvard Studies in Classical Philology* 99: 1–31.

Fowler, Robert L. 2006. "Herodotus and His Prose Predecessors." In *The Cambridge Companion to Herodotus,* edited by Carolyn Dewald and John Marincola, 29–45. Cambridge: Cambridge University Press.

Gaboriau, Marc. 1974. "Classification des récits chantés: La littérature orale des populations hindoues de l'Himalaya Central." *Poétique* 19: 313–32.

Gentili, Bruno. 1984. *Poesia e pubblico nella Grecia antica da Omero al V secolo.* Rome: Laterza. Translated as *Poetry and Its Public in Ancient Greece,* translated by A. Thomas Cole. Baltimore: The Johns Hopkins University Press, 1988.

Gentili, Bruno, Paola Angeli Bernardini, Ettore Cingano, and Pietro Giannini. 1995. *Pindaro. Le Pitiche.* Milano: Mondadori.

Giannini, Pietro. 1979. "Interpretazione della *Pitica* 4 di Pindaro." *Quaderni Urbinati du Cultura Classica* 31: 35–63.

Gianotti, Gian Franco. 1975. *Per una poetica pindarica.* Torino: Paravia.

Greimas, Algirdas J., and Joseph Courtés. 1982. [1979]. *Semiotics and Language: An Analytical Dictionary.* Translated by Larry Crist et al. Bloomington: Indiana University Press.

———. 1986. *Sémiotique: Dictionnaire raisonné de la théorie du langage.* Vol. 2. Paris: Hachette.

Grethlein, Jonas, and Antonios Rengakos, eds. 2009. *Narratology and Interpretation: The Content of Narrative Form in Ancient Literature.* Berlin: Walter de Gruyter.

Hansen, William F. 1977. "Odysseus' Last Journey." *Quaderni Urbinati di Cultura Classica* 24: 27–48.

Hurst, André. 1983. "Temps du récit chez Pindare (Pyth. 4) et chez Bacchylide (11)." *Museum Helveticum* 40: 154–68.

———. 1985. "Aspects du temps chez Pindare." In *Pindare. Entretiens sur l'Antiquité classique* 31: 155–97. Vandœuvres: Fondation Hardt.

Lasserre, François. 1976. "L'historiographie grecque à l'époque archaïque." *Quaderni di Storia* 4: 113–42.

Malkin, Irad. 1994. *Myth and Territory in the Spartan Mediterranean.* Cambridge: Cambridge University Press.

Parker, Robert. 1987. "Myths of Early Athens." In *Interpretations in Greek Mythology,* edited by Jan Bremmer, 187–214. London: Croom Helm.

Race, William H. 1997. *Pindar: Olympian Odes, Pythian Odes.* Cambridge, MA: Harvard University Press.

Rastier, François. 1987. *Sémantique interpretative.* Paris: Presses universitaires de France.

Ricoeur, Paul. 1988. [1985]. *Time and Narrative.* Vol. 3. Translated by Kathleen Blamey and David Pellauer. Chicago: The University of Chicago Press.

Rosivach, V. J. 1987. "Autochthony and the Athenians." *Classical Quarterly* 81: 294–306.

Segal, Charles. 1986. *Pindar's Mythmaking: The Fourth Pythian Ode*. Princeton, NJ: Princeton University Press.

Sourvinou-Inwood, Christiane. 1987. "Myth as History: The Previous Owners of the Delphic Oracle." In *Interpretations in Greek Mythology*, edited by Jan Bremmer, 215–41. London: Croom Helm.

Sternberg, Meir. 1987. *The Poetics of Biblical Narrative: Ideological Literature and the Drama of Reading*. Bloomington: Indiana University Press.

Vernant, Jean-Pierre. 1974. *Mythe et société en Grèce ancienne*. Paris: Maspero.

Vian, Francis. 1963. *Les origines de Thèbes. Cadmos et les Spartes*. Paris: Klincksieck.

CHAPTER 10

Policing Literary Theory

Toward a Collaborative Ethics of Research?

FRANÇOISE LAVOCAT

The leading role of so-called French Theory in literary theory and in the humanities generally during the 1970s is well known (see Bergonzi 1990; Docherty 1990; Lotringer and Cohen 2001; Cusset 2008 [2003]; Fish 2008; Lejeune, Mignon, and Pirenne 2013). The phenomenon is not only French, however, and not even only American, even though American campuses have played a decisive role in the invention and development of French Theory. Indeed, the phenomenon was to become influential worldwide. Needless to say, divergent lines of thought took hold with regard to French Theory and were widely debated.[1] In due time, the intellectual trend initiated by Barthes,[2] Foucault, Derrida, and Deleuze, among others, came to be largely hegemonic. This reign was violent both intellectually and institutionally. Violence[3] was

---

1. Literary theories borrowed from the hermeneutical tradition and from analytical philosophy were opponents to French Theory, despite a number of links between these theories and French Theory. The misunderstanding between Derrida and Gadamer is well known (see Grondin 2006: 97–108), as is the opposition of analytical philosophers to French Theory at large (e.g., Descombes 1979, 1983; Bouveresse 1999). For a refutation of Barthes by literary theorists from the perspective of the semantics of fiction and narratology, see Bremond and Pavel (1998).

2. In her biography of Roland Barthes, Samoyault (2015: 314–18) stresses the violence of his statements, particularly in *Mythologies* (2012 [1957]). According to Samoyault, Barthes was not always aware of the violence of his writings and did not anticipate its consequences (2015: 318).

3. For a few thoughts on the inherent violence of language due to its relation to the body, its materiality, and its performativity (exploited in particular in witchcraft) and because

first expressed in the most famous proposals of French Theory: denunciation of the "fascism of language"[4] (Barthes 1978: 14 ff.), contempt for fiction and its pleasures (Barthes [2012] 1957[5] and Sollers [2006] 1968), "deconstruction" of the text, negation of the possibility of meaning and interpretation (Derrida 2001), and so on. The violence of these statements was not only metaphorical. It deliberately relied upon counterintuitive claims and also had strong political implications. The violence of the contents and attitudes was intensified by another kind of violence that came from the hegemony of these theses and the institutional leadership of many of their followers. In this way, the "policing" carried on by French Theory is only one example of the abuses inherent in the dominant position of any intellectual trend. This example, however, is especially relevant for two reasons: because of the particular positioning of the group (and this despite individual differences), and because this hegemony, a few decades later (around 1990–2000), vanished and was replaced by a new trend, perhaps a new form of violence, imposed by the managerial transformation of academic life on an international scale. I will argue that the decline of French Theory together with, more broadly, that of literary theory[6] and the transformation of academic standards are probably linked.

However, the situation does not simply come to a halt with the decline of French Theory. Also to be taken into account is the rapid development and growth, at roughly the same time, of narratology under the aura of the "narrative turn." This phenomenon, dating from the early 1990s, has spread to numerous disciplines (see Kindt 2009: 40), and it now raises at least two fundamental questions: Is narratology to be considered an alternative to French Theory and a model for literary theory?

In this chapter, "policing literary theory" will be understood in several ways, but in two ways in particular. First, during the apex of its reign (and

---

it appears primarily in the assignment of social roles, see Lecercle (1990: 220–63). Significantly, the author lays claim to the "the strong continental flavor" of his position against the philosophy of language of the English-speaking world and "the followers of Wittgenstein" whose aim is to "preserve the possibility of communication and referential use to save language for science" (267). The view contested by Lecercle is precisely the one I wish to defend.

4. Against this view, see Merlin-Kajman (2003).

5. *The Pleasure of the Text* (Barthes [1975] 1973) is certainly not the pleasure of fiction. In *Mythologies* (2012 [1957]), Barthes, following Brecht, condemns the lure of fiction and identification in general. Sollers develops his critique of spectacle, immersion, and narrative in "Logique de la fiction" (2006 [1968]). For a detailed analysis of Sollers's claims against fiction, see Lavocat (2016a: 137–45).

6. On this matter in particular, and with regard to the situation in the UK, see Davis (1992) The decline of literary theory, including that of formalism, is of course relative; the vitality of Russian formalism was recently reasserted at an international conference: "Le formalisme russe cent ans après" (proceedings in *Communications* no. 103, 2018).

even now in its contemporary legacies), French Theory served as a literary theory that policed academic scholarship. I will underscore the historical and political implications of this violence, referring mainly to recent critical French studies devoted to this history (Compagnon 2004 [1998]; Kaufmann 2011; Schaeffer 2011). According to my hypothesis, the violence of French Theory was part of its appeal, but this also contributed to its decline and fall. Second, I will argue that the non-state-centered "policing" of this hegemonic trend was replaced by institutional censorship, largely supported by supranational research policy. An extremely powerful tool for policing academic life has emerged over the past few decades in the form of control procedures, accountability, research norms, language requirements, and so forth. On the whole, this set of circumstances is not favorable for the development of literary theory. However, I will suggest that literary studies, following the example of narratology and in association with comparative literary theory, may well be in a position not only to confront this situation but also to open up avenues toward innovative research.

1. LITERARY THEORISTS AS SERIAL KILLERS

As far as I know, in recent years, only one academic specialist in literary theory, an American living in New York, has made headlines in the French press when she declared that she wanted "to cause harm to texts" (*faire mal aux textes*; Ronell 2009). Warlike rhetoric is a constant feature in the work of Avital Ronell, who is described as an heir of French Theory. In an interview Ronell gave to Vincent Kaufmann, she accumulates bellicose metaphors such as "kidnapping," "hijacking," "attack," "guerilla warfare," "rhetorical troop," "border violation," and so on (Kaufmann 2011: 285–90; see Ronell 2010b). Interestingly enough, in a book written in collaboration with the psychoanalyst Anne Dufourmentelle entitled *Fighting Theory* (Ronell 2010a [2007]), she defends a conception of "writing as fighting" and at the same time discredits theory. This simultaneous and paradoxical association of subversive theoretical positioning and hostility toward theory is meaningful. One may consider that it epitomizes the impasse of literary theory in the aftermath of the reign of French Theory.

Indeed, Avital Ronell's declaration of literary war echoes old slogans that accompanied the rapturous reception of French Theory in the US several decades ago. "Death of the author" (Barthes 1977 [1968]; Foucault 1979 [1969]), "death of the character": All such clamorous announcements were broadly accepted there and generated a mainstream trend. However, even though fans of French Theory are still numerous today and in some cases remain influential, the fashion has waned. Anyone who has read the Winter 1974 issue of *New Literary History* devoted to "Changing Views of Character" (Cixous and Cohen 1974), containing old and new articles against "character" and "identification" (by Roman Ingarden, Hans Robert Jauss, Hélène Cixous, J. Hillis Miller, and others), would not expect to find, nearly forty years later in the same journal, an issue entitled "Character" propounding the opposite view and aimed at refurbishing a psychological perspective on characters from the standpoint of the cognitive sciences (Felski 2011).

In fact, as early as 1992 Sean Burke's *The Death and Return of the Author: Criticism and Subjectivity in Barthes, Foucault and Derrida* had already summed up this literary theory palinode. The same idea of backlash is expressed by the titles of several books calling for the resurrection of the author.[7] This repeated attempt to repair the previous iconoclastic damage reminds one in some ways of the attitude of human tribes who alternate between the destruction and restoration of idols (see Latour 2009).

2. RISE AND FALL OF "LITERARY THEORY"

Over the past fifteen years, many explanations have been put forth as to what happened to "literary theory," or more precisely to what is known in the US as "French Theory," a trend that sprung up between 1960 and 1980, first in France and later in the US, chiefly around the Tel Quel group and the Yale School of criticism. It is noteworthy that simply calling the intellectual production of and around the Tel Quel group "literary theory" or "French Theory" still represents an implicit homage, even on the part of its ambivalent critics such as Antoine Compagnon (2004 [1998]) or Vincent Kaufmann (2011), since they thus discard any other possible theoretical development, at least in France. On this view, French literary studies would be doomed to endlessly rehashing the admission of their own collapse.[8]

The mere aging of a generation or the reorientation of a single individual are in no way enough to account for the demise of this movement.[9] It looks much more like a cruel bonfire of vanities. Indeed, all the postulates and

---

7. For a narratologically friendly assessment of the return of the author, see Jannidis (1999). See also Irwin (2002). The idea of the "death and resurrection of the author" has become so widespread since the beginning of the century that it gave rise to a course taught by Antoine Compagnon in 2002, "Qu'est-ce qu'un auteur?"

8. Kaufmann prefers the expression "mouvance théorico-réflexive" (reflexive–theoretical current; 2011: 13).

9. Dosse highlights the link between the "Gulag effect," when French intellectuals discovered Solzhenitsyn's work, and the decline of structuralism (1997 [1991–1992]: vol. 2, 269–75).

radical watchwords proclaimed at that time in a trenchant manner, rapidly and broadly shared until they became a new doxa taught even in secondary schools, were in the end overthrown. As is well known, the famous "death of the author," along with "the death of the character" and extreme opposition to notions of reference, fiction, history, and interpretation, were to be cancelled out by the corresponding resurrections and rehabilitations of the same concepts to service, often by the same authors who had murdered and abolished them in the first place.[10]

There is no dearth of evidence to account for these sharp swings of the pendulum marking the rise and fall of "literary theory" between the 1970s and the 1990s: the adeptness of its actors, collective psychology, and the cultural upheavals and political context at the end of the twentieth century are variously invoked.[11] But several commentators stress that the fall of "theory" was a consequence of its own violence. Antoine Compagnon (2004 [1998]), who considers that "vis polemica" is built into literary theory, characterizes the movement around the Tel Quel group by its hostility to doxa. According to him, it is "common sense" (as claimed by the subtitle of his book) that naturally won in the end, due to the inevitable relaxing of oppositional defiance. In some ways, we may argue that critics such as Compagnon are trying to "police literary theory" in the French sense of the word *policer*, the equivalent, in English, of "to civilize": regulating and canonizing literary theory, smoothing its hard edges.

On the other hand, the violence of literary theory in the 1970s cannot be understood without seeing how the political context was brought to bear on it (see Matonti 2005; Kaufmann 2011). To put it simply, the original closeness to Marxism of most members of the group, the synergy of the theoretical movement with the May 1968 revolt (let us remember that Barthes's manifesto on "the death of the author" was published at the end of the same year) had no equivalent in other Western countries. The political context gave its impetus and sharp edge to the oppositional dimension of theory. This explains why many of the proposals and the vocabulary of the Tel Quel group have come to

---

10. On the versatile metamorphoses of Barthes in his theoretical choices, see Bremond and Pavel (1998: 18).

11. In the English translation of his influential and controversial book on French Theory, François Cusset writes, "Isn't it simply too late to still be speaking about French Theory *today*? The word *today*, in that sense, conjures up a mix of collective panic and historical changes ... an utterly confused, postcommunist, postcolonial age of global civil war *and* absolute entertainment. ... In such an unsettling present, one wonders if there is anything left to expect from the weird textual American object known as theory, born between the two wars or in the crazy 1970s" (2008 [2003]: xi). In the years since then, these upheavals have in no way abated. A number of reviews of Cusset's book have shed an interesting light on this debate. See, for example, Fall (2005); Elden (2005).

appear as obsolete. To mention a few random examples, there was the stress placed on "text production," the "communism" of writing, the hated bourgeoisie, the challenge to patriarchy and divine authority in the form of the demolition of the author's intention, itself equated with private property, and so on. Such phraseology reflects how the flagrant erosion of the French Communist Party, gathering speed between the 1981 French presidential election and the fall of the Berlin Wall in 1989, coincided with the decline of literary theory. Many intellectuals, students, and teachers of literature had to face a double disappointment during that decade as they saw both their political beliefs and their theoretical choices, often experienced as an existential and moral commitment, coming simultaneously under attack. That collective overturn was motivated by two facts: The theory-cum-political struggle against the bourgeois foe, until then usually and traditionally thought of along the model of class struggle, was lost. But above all, that fight soon found itself at odds with the technological revolution, the commodification of tertiary education, and the internationalization of the academic sphere along with the imposition of managerial rules on it. From this point of view, the theoretical trend of the 1970s seems to belong to another world.

The very specifically French political context of the 1970s and '80s is not therefore the only cause of the violence of literary theory. Without elaborating on this point at length, I would like to propose that the violence of literary theory in those years is a feature of any iconoclastic trend, as Vincent Kaufmann shows very convincingly. Compagnon, in passing, calls this movement "protestant." The will to forcefully free the reader from the pleasure of the text, from his supposed leisurely passivity when immersed in fiction and his alienating identification with the character, is indeed similar to the gesture of smashing idols in order to free the faithful from their fascination with images. The literary theory of the 1970s is also, more broadly, an aspect of what Paul Ricoeur (1970 [1965]: 32) described as the "hermeneutics of suspicion," a phenomenon that prevailed throughout the twentieth century. It is in the name of this tradition, tightly bound to psychoanalysis as well as to deconstructionism, that the reader, at once a theorist and a detective, is called on to track down and break the codes lurking about beneath the misleading transparency of texts. This is another aspect of policing—in this case, positioning the reader, reeducated by theory, vis-à-vis the text.

It did not matter much if the texts were shattered to pieces in the process, as Barthes did in disassembling Balzac's "Sarrazine" in his book S/Z (1974 [1970]).[12] A similar effect was produced by deconstructionism, the theoretical background inspiring Avital Ronell's call "to cause harm to texts."

---

12. For an in-depth critique of Barthes's study, see Bremond and Pavel (1998).

The question, then, is this: Did the following years witness a victory of "common sense"? The indictment of the earlier period went on relentlessly in the 1990s and, more forcefully, during the first decade of this century. The structuralist trend, especially Genette's technical vocabulary adopted in a simplified version by French secondary education, is often blamed for desiccating literary studies. Tzvetan Todorov (2007) and Vincent Jouve (2010), among others, adopted this argument against any technical and specialized vocabulary for literary theory. Even worse, according to William Marx (2004), the dogma of self-reference and the autonomy of the work wound up killing literature by severing its vital links with the world. I would like to insist, though, that these two charges are questionable. It is far from proven that a somewhat specialized lexicon discourages students. My own teaching experience runs counter to this critique: Students are never reluctant to use a specialized vocabulary so long as it serves the purpose of description, classification, or explanation. Moreover, it is doubtful that a passing theoretical fever killed literature: It is more likely that the status of literature has been progressively eroded by competition from other media, born out of the digital revolution, and by the preference new generations have shown for activities other than reading.[13]

The upshot of it is that if that episode in the history of theory, during the 1970s, was detrimental to something, it was mainly to literary theory itself.

The manner in which we interpret the fate of literary theory, as developed by the Tel Quel generation, continues even today to weigh on how we go about evaluating the very possibility of literary theory at large, both for its cultural and its epistemological relevance. Following the decline of French Theory, there would appear to be few paths remaining open for any way forward.

One consequence of this situation has been to look at what happened as a mere swing of the pendulum back the other way—the revenge of common sense, we might say. The argument goes that the majority of the learned community has reverted to its proper place and ceased to dabble in idle speculation. Antoine Compagnon (2004 [1998]: 6) notes that since the study of literature, contrary to other disciplines such as formal logic, has been unable to rid itself of ordinary language, literary studies have reemerged with all the established ideas and methods. Literary theory, though often accused of sterile formalism, has failed to achieve any real formalization. Indeed, there have been a few attempts of this kind (notably by Greimas and his followers), but they have not been audible beyond a limited circle (the same can be said of

---

13. On this point, I rally to the hypothesis of Kauffmann (2011), who further sees in the "reflexive-theoretical current" the swan song of a culture oriented toward literature and the book.

the rare efforts to import formal logic or the neurosciences to literary studies). As already noted, the elements of narratological terminology made available for use by high school students are now widely denounced. We are therefore faced with a rather paradoxical and confusing situation: Some people complain that the literary theory of the 1970s failed to constitute a science (it had the ambition to do so but not the means to succeed), while at the same time they display great reluctance toward any technical, objectifying approach to literature. There even exists a measure of consensus about the intrinsic impossibility of such an endeavor. This position is related to the contemporary vogue of neo-skepticism, but it is probably also a nostalgia manifested, conversely, by a powerful return of literary history (at least according to Vincent Kaufmann). This nostalgia for scientific knowledge and the long shadow of structural theory, though now dismissed by many, may partly account as well for the relative lack of success garnered in France by gender, postcolonial, and cultural studies, except in foreign languages departments.

The "return to square one" thesis, erroneous in my opinion, makes good fodder for radically doubting the validity of *any* approach to literary facts with an objective purpose, echoing the present distrust of any kind of theorization.

3. THE RESEARCH POLICE

The decline of literary theory, according to voices coming from very different backgrounds, has multiple causes, one of them being the legacy of French Theory. In my view, the general context of transformation of academic life and research standards is also partly responsible for this situation.

I will first stress the most questionable aspects of this phenomenon before going on to suggest how literary theorists might possibly turn it to their advantage.

The managerial model for academia is a recent and global development. I do not intend to sketch a history of this situation, which is well known. Suffice it to say that in 2003 the first Academic Ranking of World Universities (ARWU, also called the Shanghai ranking) was published and began to be used by national governments and administrations as a powerful tool to convince the public of the necessity of a radically neoliberal reform of university and academic life. With the managerial turn there came a slew of practices such as evaluation, accountability, branding, financial self-sufficiency, team spirit, and so on. Particularities can of course be seen in different countries. For instance, only in France are researchers required to belong a research center at their own university. Even though one may be the sole representative of a discipline at a particular university (e.g., a musicologist, an archeologist), this person will be expected to participate in research projects involving literary studies, cinema, or mathematics. Never in modern times in democratic countries have the research police been more intrusive and constraining![14]

This context is not favorable for research in the humanities, and for literary theory in particular, because project culture, structures, and institutional reforms are designed mainly with the hard sciences in mind, especially the applied sciences. Academic positions are now explicitly reserved for people who are able to turn out large-scale projects and publish the results in a limited time. Successful researchers must be trained managers. This leaves little room for research, especially in literary theory. The situation is further complicated by the fact that assessments are carried out by peers sitting on interdisciplinary and international committees who may come from totally different backgrounds and have little or no expertise in the research they are called on to assess. Furthermore, research results must be published in English, a serious handicap in many cases, particularly for non-native speakers of English. No wonder, then, that one of the most popular topics in literary studies today, particularly in comparative literature, is translation, a symptom of the lack of comprehension between scholars of widely differing scientific and geographical backgrounds who work together.

It can be safely assumed that the development of French Theory would not have been possible in this institutional context. It seems that we have swapped the non-state-centered terrorism of a hegemonic theory for an institutional policing that poses a threat to originality, abstract and critical thinking, refutation, and specialization in literary studies.

4. NARRATOLOGY AND LITERARY THEORY: PARALLEL PATHS?

Despite everything, I would argue that this situation is not entirely negative, especially for brands of literary theory that are not lacking in scientific ambition, such as narratology and theories of fiction. When narratology, not unlike comparative literature in this regard, ventures into a variety of cultural areas spanning several epochs, it necessarily becomes a collaborative undertaking.

Against this backdrop, evaluation, accountability, collaboration, international standards, and interdisciplinarity may, despite whatever difficulties they may pose, open the way toward a renewal of literary knowledge—a challenge

---

14. See Zarka (2009b) and *Cités* no. 37 (Zarka 2009a), which are devoted to this question.

that French Theory and its offshoots failed to meet, at least in any durable way. Overemphasis should not be placed on clean breaks and discontinuities or on heralding the demise of concepts, entities, and disciplines that may one day be revived, sometimes in a set of circumstances that yield innovative findings. In this way, the present situation can be seen as a call for scholars not to barricade themselves in scattered fortresses of knowledge, a phenomenon that Tony Becher and Paul Trowler (2001) have described as "academic tribes." In contrast to the views held by some, Jean-Marie Schaeffer (2011) considers that the reorganization of the academic sphere imposed by the governments of France and of other European countries serves as an antidote to academic compartmentalization, and that this encourages the search for new forms of consensus within and between the disciplines as far as standards and methods of evaluation are concerned. Despite, or possibly because of, the provocative optimism of this point of view, Schaeffer may well have put forth a valid position.

A more collaborative view of knowledge, inspired by the shared set of postulates found in narratological research, is indeed desirable in literary studies. Authors and characters, to take two striking examples, have not returned from their brief sojourn among the dead unchanged, either for theoreticians of narrative or for historians of literature. Thanks to the burgeoning interdisciplinary dialogue with the cognitive sciences (e.g., Schaeffer 2010 [1999]; Korthals Altes 2014; Carraciolo 2014; Zunshine 2015; Lavocat 2014, 2016b; Gefen 2016; Pelletier 2016) and to research on empathy (e.g., Keen 2010 [2007]; Gefen and Vouilloux 2013) and fictionality as well as to closer attention paid to transgeneric and transmedial forms of narration (to mention only a few of the topics largely sidestepped by French Theory), the research landscape not only of narratology but of narrative studies generally has undergone profound mutations. From this perspective, it is altogether false and counterproductive to state (as Kaufmann does) that academic research and teaching in the supposedly post-theoretical era have reverted to literary history, a nostalgic but outdated homecoming. Literary history itself has grown richer thanks in part to the study of its own history, as witnessed in a collection of essays edited by Compagnon and Debaene (2009). Today, it is no longer possible to turn to literary history as a fail-safe foil against literary theory. On the contrary, reconciling history and theory offers numerous ways to break the deadlock caused by the balkanization of literary studies.

Given the major institutional reforms described above, on the one hand, and the turn away from literary theory as it was practiced under the influence of French Theory, on the other, narratology as it has evolved over the past twenty-five years or so offers a unique opportunity for meeting the challenges facing literary studies today, and it serves as an example of how collaborative research in this field might proceed in the current research environment. International in scope, narratology benefits from work carried on in research centers in numerous countries while transborder associations such as the International Society for the Study of Narrative, the European Narratology Network (founded in 2009), or the Paris Center for Narrative Matters (founded in 2014) focus on a broad variety of narrative objects in a resolutely transdisciplinary spirit, bringing together scholars from differing horizons and creating multiple frameworks for synergies and innovation. Moreover, broadly available publications such as the *Handbook of Narratology* (Hühn, Meister, Pier, and Schmid 2014 [2009])[15] provide a compendium of reference-friendly entries devoted to the generally acknowledged narratological concepts as well as to emergent phenomena including corporate storytelling, narration in various media, narrativity in computer games, and so forth. At the same time, the rise of postclassical narratology since the turn of the century has no particular allegiance to poststructuralism or deconstructionism, having, for the most part, staked out a program distinct from that of the heirs of French Theory. On the whole, this development reflects the rise of the "narrative turn" in the social sciences and humanities, a recognition of the fact that narration extends into fields well beyond that of literary studies (see Meuter 2014 [2009]; Roussin 2017). Together, postclassical narratology and the narrative turn have succeeded in expanding the scope of narrative concerns and in creating an atmosphere favorable for collaborative interdisciplinary research, despite the fact that these various endeavors offer a panoply of theories, methodologies, and objects of research that are not always conducive to consensus.

This situation, while overall favorable, nonetheless results in the tendency to expand narrative phenomena beyond the limits of what Gérard Genette once described as the "frontiers of narrative." It is not always easy to say where narratology stops and other forms of narrative study take over as the different types of double-entry narratologies proliferate, extending from rhetorical narratology or unnatural narratology to postcolonial narratology, and so on, as well as to meta-theoretical forms of reflection that seem to stretch the very limits of the theoretical study of narrative. The accomplishments of narratology must thus be measured against the risks of the field being overextended and diluted into considerations that draw it away from its central concerns. While the expansionism of narratology, as pointed out by Tom Kindt (2009), does come up against a problem insofar as everything is not narrative (fiction, for example, does not boil down to narrativity), it is beyond doubt that

---

15. Also available online as the *living handbook of narratology* at http://www.lhn.uni-hamburg.de/.

the success of narratology can be attributed largely to its opening up to other fields of inquiry and to its many disciplinary hybridizations (and this despite Tom Kindt's argument). Literary theory, without being swallowed up by narratology, can draw inspiration from the way that narratology has developed. This is already the case as far as theories of fiction and comparative literary studies are concerned.

In France, few scholars over the past decades have claimed the title of narratologist. The reasons for this are various. One is that structural narratology (mainly that of Genette) was codified for the purposes of secondary education starting in the 1980s, leaving a bitter taste in the mouths of many young students. Another is that postclassical narratology has never truly taken hold in French-speaking countries, with the consequence that narratology continues to be associated with structuralism, showing limited awareness of its more recent developments. As a general rule, narratologically oriented theorists working in these countries have continued along the lines of discourse analysis that got underway in France during the 1970s rather than follow the Tel Quel–inspired "text theory" propounded by Roland Barthes and his followers, an explicit renunciation of the "scientism" associated with narratology (see Pier 2011 and Pier's contribution to this volume).[16] Also to be taken into account is the widespread influence of Paul Ricoeur's phenomenological philosophy, notably his three-volume *Time and Narrative,* the second volume (1985 [1984]) of which examines structural narratology (particularly Greimas and Genette), effectively configuring narratological analysis within a hermeneutic perspective.[17] Researchers who follow this approach tend to part ways with narratology, although Ricoeur's mark can be seen in publications by Raphaël Baroni (e.g., 2009), Jean-Michel Adam (e.g., 2011: 67–75), and Claude Calame (e.g., 2017), to mention only a few of the more narratologically oriented authors.

One of the particularities in the field of poststructural literary theory in France has been the development of research on fictionality along lines that differ somewhat from those of the rhetorical school of narratology, initiated by Wayne C. Booth and followed up by James Phelan (2005, 2007) and Richard Walsh (2007), among others. It was Jean-Marie Schaeffer and Thomas Pavel who stirred up interest in theories of fiction and immersion from a cog-

---

16. A case in point is Claude Calame, who combines the semio-narrative model of Greimassian semiotics with enunciative pragmatics in an ethnopoetic analysis of ancient Greek narrative (see his contribution to this volume). For a critique of the classical/postclassical paradigm, see Calame (2017: 350–56).

17. Ricoeur's notion of emplotment (*mise en intrigue*) has been widely adopted in Francophone scholarship. Hayden White's approach to emplotment is less well known in French-speaking countries.

nitive perspective (Schaeffer 2010 [1999]) and in universes of belief and possible worlds in their relations with ethical concerns (Pavel 1986). Even though narratology has proven quite receptive to these questions, they do not, per se, have a great deal to do with narrative analysis. In fact, along these lines of reasoning, the distinction between fiction and narrative is one of the essential premises. It should also be noted that none of these authors (with the exception of Thomas Pavel, who teaches in the US) have had an influence on American research comparable to what they have enjoyed in France.

An important trend in French research, under the influence of Ricoeur, Schaeffer, and Pavel (none of whom lay claim to being narratologists), can be observed in a keen interest in theories of fiction, a domain that postclassical narratology has staked out as one of its territories.[18] The originality of the work undertaken in France and in other French-speaking countries lies in the attempt to link theories of fiction to a historical and comparatist perspective, as illustrated, for example, in publications by Teresa Chevrolet (2007), Anne Duprat (2009), Frédérique Aït-Touati (2011 [2008]), and Guiomar Hautcoeur (2018).[19] Closely related to these questions are those of "transfictionality" (Saint-Gelais 2011) and fictionality in role games (Caïra 2007) and in board games such as chess (Caïra 2011).[20]

It is the case that literary theory in France and in other French-speaking countries has not spawned the array of interests and approaches gathered under the vast umbrella of postclassical narratology.[21] What characterizes French-speaking researchers working closest to narratology today is a particular configuration bringing together theories of fiction, history, hermeneutics,[22] the cognitive sciences, and comparative studies against the backdrop of a certain scientific ambition inherited from structuralism. Through this conception of literary theory as a form of knowledge, French research does nonetheless bear affinities with narratology, both classical and in its renovated forms, thanks in particular to its openness to interdisciplinarity and transmediality.

---

18. See for example Nielsen, Phelan, and Walsh (2015).

19. Also to be mentioned (among others) are the authors brought together in publications such as *Usages et théories de la fiction* (Lavocat 2004), *La théorie littéraire des mondes possibles* (Lavocat 2010), and *Fiction et cultures* (Lavocat and Duprat 2010).

20. See also Caïra's contribution to this volume.

21. A recent exception is Raphaël Baroni (2017), who adopts a number of premises from postclassical narratology. See also his contribution to this volume.

22. Attempts to map out the interface between narratology and the theory of interpretation (without any particular allegiance to Ricoeur) can be found mostly outside France. In addition to Kindt and Müller (2003) are Petterson (2009) and especially Korthals Altes (2014).

5. THE EXAMPLE OF NARRATOLOGY: TOWARD A MORE COLLABORATIVE AND SHAREABLE LITERARY THEORY

We need to draw a few lessons from the vicissitudes and the glory and fall of the literary theory of the 1970s if we want to avoid rehashing them in what could only be an apparently new guise. We should work toward building and passing on a kind of literary knowledge that would refrain from being mainly polemical. Which does not mean that debate is to be barred!

In my view, and in order to participate in knowledge shared by a broad international and interdisciplinary community, literary theory may wish to take stock of the following principles. It is not my intention to police literary theory, nor do I have the means to do so. My proposals belong to the normative level.

Literary theory can benefit from cutting its ties to political struggle. The political overdetermination of questions related to character, author, and fiction, for example, tend to deviate toward biased research. Although the politicization of theory may well encourage a temporary surge of interest, it threatens research with early obsolescence due to its focus on narrow and fleeting social and cultural issues.

Second, I believe that metaphorical transfer into the metalanguage employed by literary theory (see Bouveresse 1999) can be moderated. The metaphorical transfer of concepts borrowed from other disciplines (such as catastrophe theory and other Schrödinger's cats) has damaged the credibility of literary theory and hampered it in its dialogue with other fields of knowledge. Literary theory has undeniably lost influence in the concert of (rival) disciplines: One only need witness the meager place left to literary studies in research tenders and large national and international pluridisciplinary projects. Outraged self-defense reactions after the "Sokal affair" (see Jeanneret 1998; Cusset 2008 [2003]) did nothing to placate attacks, only aggravating the collective blindness of literary specialists.[23] If we concede that inter- or transdisciplinarity is a factor of renewal of disciplines (which can admittedly be debated; see Moutier, Passeron, and Revel 2006), including literary theory,

---

23. After successfully submitting to a prestigious American journal a fake article parodying the style of "French Theory," Alan Sokal and Jean Bricmont published a book in 1997 entitled *Impostures intellectuelles* in which they belittled the most distinctive theses and stylistic features in French Theory. The book stirred up an impassioned and lively debate, especially in France, mainly to defend French authors and denounce the narrow scientism (according to their detractors) espoused by Sokal and Bricmont. Significantly, Cusset (2008 [2003]) titled the introduction of his book "The Sokal Affair" ("L'effet Sokal"). This was an old controversy, but it illustrates perfectly the decline (despite the number and the virulence of its defenders) of "French Theory."

then it would be best to rid our language about literature of its more idiomatic elements and go for a metalanguage that can be shared, a language that abides by scientific standards. On this matter, it is undeniable that classical narratology succeeded in providing conceptual frameworks and a terminology that have proved pertinent and fruitful for narrative analysis. However, these matters remain subject to debate and revision, as can be seen in discussions over the metaphorical use in literary studies of such concepts as "voice" (Patron 2009), "game" (Aarseth 1997), and "transport" and "immersion" (Lavocat 2016b). It is sometimes due to the startling innovations brought about by the introduction of other disciplines (artificial intelligence, the complexity sciences, or ludology, for example) or taken over from a different epoch or civilization that misleading expedients in the form of metaphorical usages of terminology appear.

Last, literary theory—and narratology—would profit from being more comparative in three different areas: historical research, theoretical studies in non-Western narrative, and intermediality. The tendency to simplify literary phenomena of earlier centuries was one of the weaknesses of literary theory during the 1970s. Narratology, however, has sought to provide an antidote to this shortcoming by taking greater account of the historical dimension of narrative (as witnessed by Claude Calame's work on ancient Greek literature or by Monika Fludernik's analyses of medieval narrative, to mention only two examples). Similarly, one of the reasons for the decline of literary theory was its almost complete disregard for non-Western literatures. This situation has shown clear signs of changing, however, as can be seen in the development of narratology in China (see Luo's 2017 overview of this question; on the reception of postclassical narratology in China, see Shang 2019). Another weak point of literary theory was its largely text-centered perspective. Research in narratology has taken important steps toward rectifying this shortcoming through its contributions to transmediality and intermediality. Marie-Laure Ryan, to take one example, has made a major contribution in this area by distinguishing between "old" media and "new" (or computer-based) media (Ryan 2006). Such studies have opened the way to the development of a "media-conscious narratology," starting with Ryan (2004) and continuing up to Ryan and Thon (2014) and beyond. Among a growing body of francophone research in this area are a recent narratological study of comic strips (Boillat, Borel, Oesterlé, and Revaz 2016) and Raphaël Baroni and Marc Marti's 2014 work on video games and interactivity as well as Olivier Caïra's (2007, 2011) research on games and video games. Also to be noted in this connection is metalepsis, an inherently paradoxical phenomenon that spans the various media, highlighting the sometimes startling effects of their interaction (see Genette 2004;

Pier and Schaeffer 2005; Kukkonen and Klimek 2011), and that at the same time lies at the crossroads of narratology and theories of fiction (see Lavocat 2016a: 473–520).

It is through developments of these kinds that narratology can avoid becoming, in turn, the police of literary theory. Interdisciplinarity, transmediality, comparative studies, hermeneutic and meta-hermeneutic reasoning—such topics make it possible to resist the fossilization of postulates transformed into dogmas as a side effect of the prestige of the authorities that have formulated them and passed them on to others. It is the opening up of inquiry offered by these lines of research that can serve to offset the impoverishment of narratology by reducing it to a collection of mechanically used tools cut off from any form of interpretation.

6. CONCLUSION

Did literary theory die with the movement of the 1970s? If we only mean by "literary theory" a weapon used in combat, if its sole purpose is to "describe and defend literature in its autonomy and specificity" (Kaufmann 2011: 13) without taking into account any other media than the text, if it is only a body of doctrines (anti-realism, self-reference, iconoclasm), then we cannot but answer in the affirmative. Nevertheless, vast fields of knowledge open to expert inquiry and theorization have appeared thanks to the triply comparative reconfiguration called for by our times and briefly outlined above. We may call "theory" the elaboration of comparatistic concepts with a truly general explanatory scope bearing on cultural artefacts (their nature, their history, their uses), tempered with a strong reflexive dimension. There can be no theory without a meta-theory, without questioning the premises, conditions, and aims of theory. On this score, there is no denying that one of the strong points of narratology is precisely its capacity for meta-theoretical reflection.[24]

However, I concede that my appeal for a more collaborative practice is unlikely to meet with unanimous approval, and this for several reasons. The first has to do with achieving objectivity and reaffirming the possibility and necessity of devising a truly nonliterary metalanguage. Second, some will judge that "policing literary theory" (in the sense of civilizing it), silencing its "vis polemica," would make its charm and interest vanish. And finally, a liter-

---

24. A case in point is Liesbeth Korthals Altes's *Ethos and Narrative Interpretation* (2014). For Tom Kindt (2009), the reflexive tendency of narratology is one of its deficiencies. I would argue rather that this meta-theoretical dimension is indeed a sign of its capacity for transformation and development.

ary theory adapted to bland global standards is precisely the direction that institutional management of research is pushing scholars to take. I am aware of the ambivalence of the current evolution, imposed by the internationalization of academic standards and the imperative of applying managerial rules to research. At the same time, I am acutely aware that literary theory may suffer a severe setback as a result of overzealous attempts at uniformization.

These objections notwithstanding, and in order to carve out a space for survival and longevity, I believe that scholars must transform literary studies and literary theory into a discipline whose contents can be shared, transmitted, and accumulated, a discipline with which other disciplines and cultural areas will find it both possible and desirable to engage in dialogue. The renaissance of narratology in its various guises offers an exemplary opening in favor of such a dialogue.

WORKS CITED

Aarseth, Espen J. 1997. *Cybertext: Perspectives on Ergotic Literature*. Baltimore: The Johns Hopkins University Press.

Adam, Jean-Michel. 2011. *Genres de récits. Narrativité et généricité des récits*. Louvain-la-Neuve: Harmattan-Académia.

Aït-Touati, Frédérique. 2011. [2008]. *Fiction of the Cosmos, Science and Literature in the Seventeenth Century*. Translated by Susan Emmanuel. Chicago: The Chicago University Press.

Baroni, Raphaël. 2009. *L'Œuvre du temps*. Paris: Seuil.

———. 2017. *Les Rouages de l'intrigue*. Geneva: Slatkine.

Baroni, Raphaël, and Marc Marti, eds. 2014. "Les bifurcations du récit interactif: contintuité ou rupture?" *Cahiers de Narratologie*, 27. https://journals.openedition.org/narratologie/6996.

Barthes, Roland. 1974. [1970]. *S/Z*. Translated by Richard Miller. New York: Hill and Wang.

———. 1975. [1973]. *The Pleasure of the Text*. Translated by Richard Miller. New York: Hill and Wang.

———. 1977. [1968]. "The Death of the Author." In *Image Music Text*, translated by Richard Miller, 142–48. London: Fontana.

———. 1978. *Leçon inaugurale de la Chaire de sémiologie littéraire du Collège de France prononcée le 7 janvier 1977*. Paris: Seuil.

———. 2012. [1957]. *Mythologies*. Selected and translated from the French by Richard Howard and Annette Lavers. New York: Hill and Wang.

Becher, Tony, and Paul Trowler. 2001. [1989]. *Academic Tribes: Intellectual Enquiry and the Cultures of Discipline*. Buckingham: Open University Press.

Bergonzi, Carlo. 1990. *Exploding English, Criticism, Theory, Culture*. Oxford: Oxford University Press.

Boillat, Alain, Marine Borel, Raphaël Oesterlé, and Françoise Revaz. 2016. *Case, strip, action! Les feuilletons en bandes dessinées dans les magazines pour jeunesse (1946–1959)*. CH-Gollion: Infolio.

Bouveresse, Jacques. 1999. *Prodiges et vertiges de l'analogie. De l'abus des belles-lettres dans la pensée*. Paris: Raisons d'agir éditions.

Bremond, Claude, and Thomas Pavel. 1998. *De Barthes à Balzac. Fictions d'une critique, critiques d'une fiction*. Paris: Albin Michel.

Burke, Sean. 1992. *The Death and Return of the Author: Criticism and Subjectivity in Barthes, Foucault and Derrida*. Edinburgh: Edinburgh University Press.

Caïra, Olivier. 2007. *Jeux de rôle. Les forges de la fiction*. Paris: CNRS Éditions.

———. 2011. *Définir la fiction. Du roman au jeux d'échecs*. Paris: Éditions EHESS.

Calame, Claude. 2017. "From Structural Narratology to Enunciative Pragmatics: Greek Poetic Forms between Mythical Narrative and Ritual Act." In *Emerging Vectors of Narratology*, edited by Per Krogh Hansen, John Pier, Philippe Roussin, and Wolf Schmid, 335–59. Berlin: De Gruyter.

Caracciolo, Marco. 2014. *The Experientiality of Narrative: An Enactivist Approach*. Berlin: De Gruyter.

Chevrolet, Teresa. 2007. *L'Idée de fable. Théories de la fiction poétique à la Renaissance*. Geneva: Droz.

Cixous, Hélène, and Keith Cohen, eds. 1974. "Changing Views of Character." Special issue, *New Literary History* 5, no. 2.

Compagnon, Antoine. 2002. "Introduction: mort et résurrection de l'auteur." In "Théorie de la littérature: qu'est-ce qu'un auteur?" *Fabula. La recherche en littérature*. http://www.fabula.org/compagnon/auteur1.php.

———. 2004. [1998]. *Literature, Theory, and Common Sense*. Translated by Carol Cosman. Princeton, NJ: Princeton University Press.

Compagnon, Antoine, and Vincent Debaene, eds. 2009. "Literary Histories of Literature." *Romanic Review* 100, no. 1/2.

Cusset, François. 2008. [2003]. *French Theory: How Foucault, Derrida, Deleuze & Co Transformed Intellectual Life in the United States*. Translated by Jeff Ford. Minneapolis: University of Minnesota Press.

Davis, Colin. 1992. "Synthèse perdue et condition postmoderne: situation de la théorie littéraire en Grande-Bretagne." *Littérature* 87: 88–94.

Derrida, Jacques. 2001. "Deconstructions: The Im-Possible." In *French Theory in America*, edited by Sylvère Lotringer and Sande Cohen, 13–21. New York: Routledge.

Descombes, Vincent. 1979. *Le même et l'autre. Quarante-cinq ans de philosophie française (1933–1978)*. Paris: Minuit.

———. 1983. *Grammaire des objets en tous genres*. Paris: Minuit.

Docherty, Thomas. 1990. *After Theory: Postmodernism/Postmarxism*. London: Routledge.

Dosse, François. 1997. [1991–1992]. *History of Structuralism*. 2 volumes. Translated by Deborah Glassman. Minneapolis: University of Minnesota Press.

Duprat, Anne. 2009. *Vraisemblances. Poétiques et théorie de la fiction, du Cinquecento à Jean Chapelain, 1500–1670*. Paris: Honoré Champion.

Elden, Stuart. 2005. "Review of François Cusset, *French Theory: Foucault, Derrida, Deleuze & Cie et les mutations de la vie intellectuelle aux États-Unis* (Paris: La Découverte, 2003)." *International Journal of Baudrillard Studies* 2, no. 1 (January). http://www2.ubishops.ca/baudrillardstudies/vol2_1/elden.htm.

Fall, Juliet J. 2005. "Review of François Cusset, *French Theory: Foucault, Derrida, Deleuze & Cie et les mutations de la vie intellectuelle aux États-Unis* (Paris: La Découverte, 2003)." *Foucault Studies* 2, no. 1: 154–58.

Felski, Rita, ed. 2011. "Character." Special issue, *New Literary History* 42, no. 2.

Fish, Stanley. 2008. "French Theory in America." *New York Times*, April 6, 2008. http://opinionator.blogs.nytimes.com/2008/04/06/french-theory-in-america/.

Foucault, Michel. 1979. [1969]. "What Is an Author?" In *Textual Strategies: Perspectives in Post-Structuralist Criticism,* edited by J. V. Harari, 141–60. Ithaca, NY: Cornell University Press.

Gefen, Alexandre. 2016. "La fiction est-elle un instrument d'adaptation? L'interprétation des textes littéraires pour la psychologie évolutionniste en question." In *Interprétation littéraire et sciences cognitives,* edited by Françoise Lavocat, 138–68. Paris: Hermann.

Gefen, Alexandre, and Bernard Vouilloux, eds. 2013. *Empathie et esthétique.* Paris: Hermann.

Genette, Gérard. 2004. *Métalepse. De la figure à la fiction.* Paris: Seuil.

Grondin, Jean. 2006. *L'herméneutique.* Paris: Presses universitaires de France.

Hautcœur, Guiomar. 2018. *Roman et secret. Essai sur la lecture à l'époque modern.* Paris: Garnier.

Hühn, Peter, Jan Christoph Meister, John Pier, and Wolf Schmid, eds. 2014. [2009]. *Handbook of Narratology.* 2 volumes. 2nd ed. Berlin: De Gruyter.

Irwin, William, ed. 2002. *The Death and Resurrection of the Author.* New York: Greenwood Press.

Jannidis, Fotis, ed. 1999. *Rückkehr des Autors: Zur Erinnerung eines umstrittenen Begriffs.* Tübingen: Niemeyer.

Jeanneret, Yves. 1998. *L'affaire Sokal ou la querelle des impostures.* Paris: Presses universitaires de France.

Jouve, Vincent. 2010. *Pourquoi étudier la littérature?* Paris: Armand Colin.

Kaufmann, Vincent. 2011. *La faute à Mallarmé. L'aventure de la théorie littéraire.* Paris: Seuil.

Keen, Suzanne. 2010. [2007]. *Empathy and the Novel.* 2nd ed. New York: Palgrave.

Kindt, Tom. 2009. "Narratological Expansionism and Its Discontents." In *Narratology the Age of Cross-Disciplinary Narrative Research,* edited by Sandra Heinen and Roy Sommer, 35–47. Berlin: Walter de Gruyter.

Kindt, Tom, and Hans-Harald Müller. 2003. "Narrative Theory and/or/as Theory of Interpretation." In *What is Narratology? Questions and Answers Regarding the Status of a Theory,* edited by Tom Kindt and Hans-Harald Muller, 205–19. Berlin: Walter de Gruyter.

Korthals Altes, Liesbeth. 2014. *Ethos and Narrative Interpretation: The Negotiation of Values in Fiction.* Lincoln: University of Nebraska Press.

Kukkonen, Karin, and Sonja Klimek, eds. 2011. *Metalepsis in Popular Culture.* Berlin: De Gruyter.

Latour, Bruno. 2009. *Sur le culte des dieux faitiches. Suivi de Iconoclash.* (Les Empêcheurs de penser en rond). Paris: La Découverte.

Lavocat, Françoise, ed. 2004. *Usages et théories de la fiction. Le débat contemporain à l'épreuve des textes anciens (xvie-xviiie siècles).* Rennes: Presses universitaires de Rennes.

———, ed. 2010. *La Théorie littéraire des mondes possibles.* Paris: CNRS Éditions.

———. 2014. "Fact, Fiction, Cognition." *Neohelicon* 41, no. 2: 350–70.

———. 2016a. *Fait et fiction. Pour une frontière.* Paris: Seuil.

———, ed. 2016b. *Interprétation littéraire et sciences cognitives.* Paris: Hermann.

Lavocat, Françoise, and Anne Duprat, eds. 2010. *Fiction et cultures.* Paris: Lucie éditions.

Lecercle, Jean-Jacques. 1990. *The Violence of Language.* New York: Routledge.

Lejeune, Anaël, Olivier Mignon, and Raphaël Pirenne, eds. 2013. *French Theory and American Art.* Brussels: Sternberg Press.

Lotringer, Sylvère, and Sande Cohen, eds. 2001. *French Theory in America.* New York: Routledge.

Luo, Huaiyu. 2017. "Comparison of Chinese-Western Narrative Poetics: State of the Art." In *Emerging Vectors of Narratology,* edited by Per Krogh Hansen, John Pier, Philippe Roussin, and Wolf Schmid, 361–79. Berlin: De Gruyter.

Marx, William. 2004. *L'Adieu à la Littérature.* Paris: Minuit.

Matonti, Frédérique. 2005. "La politisation du structuralisme. Une crise dans la théorie." *Raisons politiques* 2, no. 1: 49–71.

Merlin-Kajman, Hélène. 2003. *La Langue est-elle fasciste? Langue, pouvoir, enseignement*, Paris: Seuil.

Meuter, Norbert. 2014. [2009]. "Narration in Various Disciplines." In *Handbook of Narratology*, edited by Peter Hühn, Jan-Christoph Meister, John Pier, and Wolf Schmid, vol. 1: 447–67. Berlin: De Gruyter.

Moutier, Jean, Jean-Claude Passeron, and Jacques Revel, eds. 2006. *Qu'est-ce qu'une discipline?* Paris: La Découverte.

Nielsen, Henrik Skov, James Phelan, and Richard Walsh. 2015. "Ten Theses about Fictionality." *Narrative* 23, no. 1: 31–73.

Patron, Sylvie. 2009. *Le Narrateur. Introduction à la théorie narrative*. Paris: Armand Colin.

Pavel, Thomas. 1986. *Fictional Worlds*. Cambridge, MA: Harvard University Press.

Pelletier, Jérôme. 2016. "Quand l'émotion rencontre la fiction." In *Interprétation littéraire et sciences cognitives*. Edited by Françoise Lavocat, 106–37. Paris: Hermann.

Petterson, Bo. 2009. "Narratology and Hermeneutics." In *Narratology the Age of Cross-Disciplinary Narrative Research*, edited by Sandra Heinen and Roy Sommer, 11–35. Berlin: Walter de Gruyter.

Phelan, James. 2005. *Living to Tell about It: A Rhetoric and Ethics of Character Narration*. Ithaca, NY: Cornell University Press.

——. 2007. *Experiencing Fiction: Judgments, Progressions, and the Rhetorical Theory of Narrative*. Columbus: The Ohio State University Press.

Pier, John. 2011. "Is There a French Postclassical Narratology?" In *Current Trends in Narratology*, edited by Greta Olson, 336–67. Berlin: De Gruyter.

Pier, John, and Jean-Marie Schaeffer, eds. 2005. *Métalepses. Entorses au pacte de la représentation*. Paris: Éditions de l'EHESS.

Ricoeur, Paul. 1970. [1965]. *Freud and Philosophy: An Essay on Interpretation*. Translated by Denis Savage. New Haven, CT: Yale University Press.

——. 1985. [1984]. *Time and Narrative*. Vol. 2. Translated by Kathleen McLaughlin and David Pellauer. Chicago: The University of Chicago Press.

Ronell, Avital. 2009. "Je veux faire mal aux textes." *Le Monde des Livres*, April 6, 2009.

——. 2010a. [2007]. *Fighting Theory: Avital Ronell in Conversation with Anne Dufourmantelle*. Translated by Catherine Porter. Urbana: University of Illinois Press.

——. 2010b. *Lignes de front*. Translated by Daniel Loayza. Paris: Stock.

Transatlantica. Revue d'Etudes Américaines 1. https://transatlantica.revues.org/579.

Roussin, Philippe. 2017. "What Is Your Narrative? Lessons from the Narrative Turn." In *Emerging Vectors of Narratology*, edited by Per Krogh Hansen, John Pier, Philippe Roussin, and Wolf Schmid, 383–404. Berlin: De Gruyter.

Ryan, Marie-Laure, ed. 2004. *Narrative across Media: The Languages of Storytelling*. Lincoln: University of Nebraska Press.

——. 2006. *Avatars of Story*. Minneapolis: University of Minnesota Press.

Ryan, Marie-Laure, and Jan-Noël Thon, eds. 2014. *Storyworlds across Media: Toward a Media-Conscious Narratology*. Lincoln: University of Nebraska Press.

Saint-Gelais, Richard. 2011. *Fictions transfuges. La transfictionnalité et ses enjeux*. Paris: Seuil.

Samoyault, Tiphaine. 2015. *Roland Barthes*. Paris: Seuil.

Schaeffer, Jean-Marie. 2010. [1999]. *Why Fiction?* Translated by Dorrit Cohn. Lincoln: University of Nebraska Press.

——. 2011. *Petite écologie des études littéraires. Pourquoi et comment étudier la littérature?* Paris: Éditions Thierry Marchaise.

Shang. Biwu. 2019. "Postclassical Narratology in China: Receptions and Variations." In *Word and Text* Vol. IX: 47–64. http://jlsl.upg-ploiesti.ro/site_engleza/documente/documente/Arhiva/Word_and_text_2019/02%20Shang.pdf.

Sokal, Alan, and Jean Bricmont. 1998. [1997]. *Fashionable Nonsense: Postmodern Intellectuals' Abuse of Science*. New York: Picador.

Sollers, Philippe. 2006. [1968]. "Logique de la fiction." In *Logique de la fiction et autres textes*, edited by Philippe Forrest, 15–53. Nantes: C. Defaut.

Todorov, Tzvetan. 2007. *La Littérature en péril*. Paris: Flammarion.

Walsh, Richard. 2007. *The Rhetoric of Fictionality: Narrative Theory and the Idea of Fiction*. Columbus: The Ohio State University Press.

Zarka, Yves Charles, ed. 2009a. *Cités* no. 37. *L'Idéologie de l'évaluation. La grande imposture*.

———. 2009b. "Éditorial. Qu'est-ce que tyranniser le savoir?" *Cités* no. 37: 3–6.

Zunshine, Lisa, ed. 2015. *The Oxford Handbook of Cognitive Literary Studies*. Oxford: Oxford University Press.

CONTRIBUTORS

RAPHAËL BARONI is a professor at the University of Lausanne. He is a co-founder of the Network of the French-Speaking Narratologists (RéNaF); the Group for the Study of Comics (GrEBD); and the Pole for Transmedial Narratology (NaTrans), based at the Faculty of Arts at the University of Lausanne. He is the author of *La tension narrative* (Seuil, 2007), *L'œuvre du temps* (Seuil, 2009), and *Les rouages de l'intrigue* (Slatkine, 2017). He is a co-editor of several anthologies and journal issues, among them *Narrative Sequence in Contemporary Narratology* (The Ohio State University Press, 2016) and *Introduction à l'étude des cultures numériques* (Armand Colin, 2020).

DENIS BERTRAND is professor emeritus at the University of Paris 8-Vincennes-Saint-Denis and at the Nouveau Collège d'Études Politiques (Paris 8-Paris Nanterre). He is a member of the Scientific Council of the City of Paris, former president of the Association Française de Sémiotique, and co-director of the Séminaire de Sémiotique de Paris. His work explores the fields of literature, social discourse, media, and politics. He regularly appears in the media (Public Sénat, France 5). He has published several books, including *Précis de sémiotique littéraire* (Nathan, 2000); written numerous articles on the relationship between semiotics, literary theory, and rhetoric; and edited several collective works, including *Régimes sémiotiques de la temporalité* (PUF, 2006), *La transversalité du sens* (PUV, 2007), *Croyance, crédit, créance* (Hermann, 2012), *La négation, le négatif, la négativité* (Actes sémiotiques, 2014), *Sens et médiation* (AFS, 2015), *La parole aux animaux* (Fabula, 2017), and *Greimas aujourd'hui: l'avenir de la structure* (AFS, 2019).

OLIVIER CAÏRA is an assistant professor of sociology at the IUT d'Evry (France) and a game designer. He codirects the seminar "Recherches contemporaines en narratologie" at the Centre de recherches sur les arts et le langage (CNRS/EHESS) in Paris. A specialist in the history of self-regulation in Hollywood and in the ethnography of tabletop role-playing games, he has published *Hollywood face à la censure* (CNRS, 2005), *Jeux de rôle: les forges de la fiction* (CNRS, 2007), and *Définir la fiction. Du roman au jeu d'échecs* (EHESS, 2011). His latest book, *Le Cerveau comme machine* (Georg, 2019), is a study on the representation of extreme intelligence in fiction (cinema and television).

CLAUDE CALAME is a director of studies at the École des Hautes Études en Sciences Sociales in Paris and a member of the Centre AnHiMA (Anthropologie et Histoire des Mondes Antiques). Formerly, he was a professor of Greek language and literature at the University of Lausanne. He has taught at the Universities of Urbino and Siena in Italy as well as at Yale University. In English translation he has published *The Craft of Poetic Speech in Ancient Greece* (Cornell, 1995), *The Poetics of Eros in Ancient Greece* (Princeton, 1999), *Myth and History in Ancient Greece: The Symbolic Creation of a Colony* (Princeton, 2003), *Masks of Authority: Fiction and Pragmatics in Ancient Greek Poetics* (Cornell, 2005), *Poetic and Performative Memory in Ancient Greece* (Harvard, 2009), *Greek Mythology: Poetics, Pragmatics and Fiction* (Cambridge, 2009), and most recently in French *La tragédie chorale. Poésie grecque et rituel musical* (Les Belles Lettres, 2018).

BENOÎT HENNAUT is currently the director of the National School for Visual Arts of La Cambre in Brussels. He trained as a philologist and holds a joint doctorate from the Université Libre de Bruxelles and the École des Hautes Études en Sciences Sociales in Paris. His dissertation, published as *Théâtre et récit, l'impossible rupture* (Garnier, 2016), is a study of narrativity in postdramatic theater from 1975 to 2004. He has also published "Building Stories around Contemporary Performing Arts: The Case of Romeo Castelluci's *Tragedia Endogonidia*" (in *Beyond Classical Narration: Unnatural and Transmedial Narrative and Narratology*, edited by Jan Alber and Per Krogh Hansen, De Gruyter, 2014). More recently, he has worked on the relationships between theater and politics in South America, particularly in Argentina ("Possibilités d'un théâtre politique contemporain. Étude de la réinvention politique et sociale dans le champ du théâtre argentin indépendant post 1983," *Cahiers du CAP*, vol. 4, 2017, and "Noticias Argentina," *Alternatives théâtrales*, no. 137, 2019). Since 2006, Benoît Hennaut has combined his academic career with professional involvement in theater, dance, and the visual arts in several major institutions in France and Belgium.

FRANÇOISE LAVOCAT is a professor and the chair of comparative literature at the Université Sorbonne Nouvelle—Paris 3. She is a former fellow at the Wissenschaftkolleg zu Berlin (2014–2015) and is currently a member of the Institut Universitaire de France (2015–2020). She specializes in theories of fiction (fact and fiction, possible worlds, character), early modern literature, and narratives of catastrophes. She is president of the International Society for Fiction and Fictionality Studies (https://fiction.hypotheses.org). Her publications include *Arcadies malheureuses, aux origines du roman moderne* (Champion, 1997) and *La Syrinx au bûcher, Pan et les satyres à la renaissance et à l'âge baroque* (Droz, 2005). She has edited *Usages et théories de la fiction, la théorie contemporaine à l'épreuve des textes anciens* (Presses Universitaires de Rennes, 2004) and *La La théorie littéraire des mondes possibles* (CNRS, 2010) and has co-edited *Fiction et cultures* (SFLGC, 2010). Her most recent book is *Fait et fiction: pour une frontière* (Seuil, 2016).

SYLVIE PATRON is a *maîtresse de conférences habilitée à diriger des recherches* (lecturer and research supervisor), director of the Paris Centre for Narrative Matters at the Université de Paris, and president of the International Society for the Study of Narrative. A specialist in the history and epistemology of literary theory, she is the author of several books, including *Le narrateur. Introduction à la théorie narrative* (Armand Colin, 2009), reprinted as *Le narrateur. Un problème de théorie narrative* (Lambert-Lucas, 2016), and *La mort du narrateur et autres essais* (Lambert-Lucas, 2015), translated as *The Death of the Narrator and Other Essays* (WVT, 2019). She has also edited three anthologies in the field: *Théorie, analyse, interprétation des récits/Theory, Analysis, Interpretation of Narratives* (Lang, 2011), *Introduction à la narratologie post-classique. Les nouvelles directions de la recherche sur le récit* (Septentrion, 2018), and *Small Stories: un nouveau paradigme pour les recherches sur le récit* (Hermann, 2020). A fourth edited volume, titled *Optional-Narrator Theory: Principles, Perspectives, Proposals*, is forthcoming (University of Nebraska Press).

JOHN PIER is professor emeritus of English at the University of Tours and a statutory member of the Centre de recherches sur les arts et le langage (CNRS/EHESS) in Paris, where he co-directs the seminar "Recherches contemporaines en narratologie." A co-founder of the European Narratology Network and past president of the ENN Steering Committee, his numerous articles and book chapters on narrative theory and literary semiotics have appeared in publications in France and abroad. He is also co-editor of the book series Narratologia at De Gruyter and serves on the editorial board of a number of journals. Among the more than fifteen volumes he has edited or co-edited are *The Dynamics of Narrative Form* (Walter de Gruyter, 2004), *Métalepses. Entorses au pacte de la représentation* (EHESS, 2005), *Théorie du récit. L'apport de la recherche allemande* (Septentrion, 2007), *Theorizing Narrativity* (Walter de Gruyter, 2008), *Narratologies contemporaines* (EAC, 2010), *L'effacement selon Nabokov. Lolita versus The Original of Laura* (Université de Tours, 2014), *Handbook of Narratology* (1st ed., 2009; 2nd ed., De Gruyter, 2014), *Emerging Vectors of Narratology* (De Gruyter, 2017), *Jan Mukařovský. Ecrits 1928–1946* (EAC, 2018), and *Le formalisme russe cent ans après*, in *Communications* no. 103 (2018).

FRANÇOISE REVAZ is professor emeritus of French linguistics at the University of Freiburg in Switzerland. A narratologist, she is the author of numerous publications devoted to narrative including *Les Textes d'action* (Kliencksieck, 1997) and *Introduction à la narratologie. Action et narration* (De Boeck, 2009). With Raphaël Baroni, she co-edited *Narrative Sequence in Contemporary Narratology* (The Ohio State University Press, 2016). Her work currently bears on segmentation into units (chapters and episodes) in comics and in serial novels. Her latest book is a collective work on the analysis of serials in comics published in periodicals during the

1950s titled *Case, Strip, Action!* (Infolio, 2016). This publication was awarded the Papiers Nickelés SoBD prize at the Paris Salon de la BD in Paris in 2017 as the best work on comics and graphic heritage.

RICHARD SAINT-GELAIS is a professor in the Department of Literature, Theatre and Cinema at the Université Laval, where his research and teaching focus on literary theory, twentieth-century literature, and paraliterature. Since his work on the Nouveau Roman, Saint-Gelais has examined the relationship between science fiction and modern fiction. More recently, he has explored the concept of transfictionality. He is a member of the Centre de recherche internuniversitaire sur la littérature et la culture québécoises (CRILCQ) and the author of *Châteaux de pages, la fiction au risque de sa lecture* (Hurtubise HMH, 1994), *L'empire du pseudo: modernités de la science-fiction* (Nota Bene, 1999), and *Fictions transfuges. La transfictionnalité et ses enjeux* (Seuil, 2011). His most recent contributions in English can be found in *Counterfactual Thinking—Counterfactual Writing* (edited by Dorothee Birke, Michael Butter, and Tilmann Köppe, De Gruyter, 2011) and in *Archeology, Anthropology, and Interstellar Communication* (Vakoch ed., NASA, 2014).

INDEX

Aarseth, Espen J., 157

academia, neoliberal reform of, 208–9, 210

Academic Ranking of World Universities (ARWU), 208

academic scholarship: managerial model and expectations for, 209; policing of, 202–3, 206, 208–9

actants and actantial identity: in poetic forms, 178, 179; in semiotic theory, 138, 140–41, 141n2, 143–44; in theater, 73, 79

Adam, Jean-Michel, 25, 27, 106, 112n2, 114n4, 115, 212; *Genres de récits*, 92, 114

aesthetics, of Nouveau Roman, 22

Altes, Liesbeth Korthals, *Ethos and Narrative Interpretation*, 216n24

American University of Paris, 137

analepsis, 21, 94, 177

L'analyse du discours dans les études littéraires (Amossy and Maingueneau), 113

Aquino, John T., 164

Aristotle, 28, 97; *Poetics*, 96, 159

Athenian autochthony, double myth of, 192–93

"Atome 21–93," 95

auctorial genres, 126, 127, 128–29, 132

Audet, René, 78n14

Auroux, Sylvain, 47, 48–49

authorial intrusions, 55

authors: "death and resurrection" of, 204, 204n7, 205; and distinction from narrator, 64–65; narrators as, 61–64. *See also* paratexts

autochthony: Athenian double myth of, 192–93; in Pindar's Fourth *Pythian Ode*, 193–94, 193n30

Bakhtin, Mikhail, 121–22

Banfield, Ann, 32–35, 44–45, 49, 50

Barbauld, Anna Laetitia, 46

Barkey, Grace Ellen, 80

Baroni, Raphaël: influence of Ricoeur on, 212; *La Tension narrative*, 11; and narrative tension, 4; overview of narrative theory, 2, 2n2; and postclassical narratology, 213n21; research of, 215

Barthes, Roland: author as narrator in, 36; critique of intellectual trend of, 201–2, 201n2; and developments in narrative theory, 22; hermeneutic code of, 27;

228 • INDEX

"Introduction à l'analyse structurale des récits," 18–19, 92, 114; *Mythologies,* 202n5; narrativity and immanence, 45, 138; narratologists' object of inquiry, 117n7; and other media in narratology, 2n1; *The Pleasure of the Text,* 202n5; and plot dynamics, 16, 17; *S/Z,* 19–20, 21, 206; and structuralism, 114n4

Bateson, Gregory, "A Theory of Play and Fantasy," 162–63

Becher, Tony, 210

Beetle in the Anthill, 66

Belgian television (RTBF) on Flanders' secession, 166

Benedetti, Mario, "Cinco años de vida," 43

Benveniste, Émile: "L'appareil formel de l'énonciation," 118; definition of enunciation, 122; "Les niveaux de l'analyse linguistique," 118; Ryan's description of work by, 32; "Sémiologie de la langue," 119; theory of enunciation of, 115, 118–21, 124, 140, 179; and time, 173n2; and translinguistics, 114n4

bibliographies, theater and narrative in, 71

Blair Witch Project, The, 166

Boillat, Alain, 96

Booth, Wayne C., 212

Bordron, Jean-François, 143

Bordwell, David, 77

Bourdieu, Pierre, *Les Règles de l'art,* 23

Brandt, Per Aage, 142

Brecht, Bertold, 85; *The Caucasian Chalk Circle,* 80

Bremond, Claude, 2n1, 22; *Logique du récit,* 20–21

Bricmont, Jean, *Impostures intellectuelles* (with Sokal), 214n23

Brigode, François de, 166

Bronckart, Jean-Paul, 25–26, 27

Brooks, Peter, 17

Bruce, Leo, *Case with No Conclusion,* 63

Burke, Sean, *The Death and Return of the Author,* 204

Cadigan, Pat, *Fools,* 59–60, 59n6

Cahiers de narratologie, 9

Caïra, Olivier, 215

Calame, Claude: and historical dimensions of research, 215; influence of Ricoeur on, 212; and scientism of narratology, 212n16; use of enunciative criteria for analysis, 179n14

Canadian Broadcast Standards Council, 166

canonic narrative schema: in *Don Quixote,* 149–50, 152; in Pindar's Pythian *Fourth,* 181–82, 183–87; in plots, 177; in poetic discourse, 177

cardinal functions, 18–19, 25

Castle (ABC), 64n13

Centre de recherches sur les arts et le langage (Cral), 9

Centre de recherche sur les médiations (CREM), 9

Centre National de Recherche Scientifique (CNRS), 9

Cervantes, Miguel de, *Don Quixote*: as critical text for narratologists, 140, 149; fictitious publication context in, 61–62; narrative enunciation and illusions in, 150–52; narrative schema in, 149–50, 152

Charaudeau, Patrick, *Dictionnaire d'analyse du discours* (with Maingueneau), 111

Chatman, Seymour, 72, 73, 74; "The Literary Narrator," 72

Chekhov, Anton: *The Three Sisters,* 84, 85, 85n24. See also Wooster Group

China, narratology in, 215

Chomsky, Noam, 117–18

classical narratology: expectation of French language skill in, 24; and pan-narrator theories, 5; pragmatics in, 22. See also structural narratology

cognitivism, 14, 17n9, 24

Cohn, Dorrit, 81, 157, 161

comic strip narratives: and authors' freedom, 6; autonomy of episodes in, 103; beginnings and endings in, 99, 99n5, 104–5; canonic narrative structure of, 107, 107n12; mini-plots in, 104; semantic unity in, 100, 100n6; study of, 215; suture markers in, 101–2, 104n8; temporality in, 94–96

commensurability in narrative theory, 48

commentaries, explicit, 39, 42

Communications, transdisciplinarity in volume 8 of, 2

Compagnon, Antoine: course by, 204n7; criticism of Tel Quel group, 204, 205; on French Theory movement, 206; and ordinary language in study of literature, 207; and study of literary history, 210

conflict, 15

constructivism, 16, 147

contextualism, 120

Coquet, Jean-Claude, 139, 144; *La quête du sens*, 143

Courtés, Joseph, 136n1. *See also under* Greimas, Algirdas Julien

Culler, Jonathan, 117–18

curiosity, 19, 20n12, 21

Currie, Gregory, 37–39, 44, 46, 49

Cusset, François, 205n11

Cyrene. *See* Greece, ancient; Pindar's Fourth Pythian Ode

Dannenberg, Hilary, 13

Debaene, Vincent, 210

deconstructionism, 202, 206, 211

dedications, 58

Defoe, Daniel, *A Journal of the Plague Year*, 131

Deleuze, Gilles: on contracts and institutions, 167; critique of intellectual trend of, 201–2

Deleuze, Gilles, and Félix Guattari: on concepts and planes of immanence, 146–48, 152; *Qu'est-ce que la philosophie?* (*What Is Philosophy?*), 139–40, 145–47

Deodato, Ruggero, *Cannibal Holocaust*, 166, 169

Derrida, Jacques, 201–2. *See also* deconstructionism

detective novels, 61, 61n9, 62, 63

digital media, 7

digital narratives, 4n5

Dine, S. S. Van, Philo Vance mysteries, 66

Dionne, Ugo, 95, 103; *La voie aux chapitres*, 57

Dire Straits, *Money for Nothing*, 166

discourse: argumentation model of, 137; narrative model of, 137–38; narrativity as organizing principle of, 140. *See also* self-constituting discourses

discourse analysis: emergence of, 6; in France, 212. *See also* French discourse analysis

Dos Passos, John, *U. S. A*, 131

Doubrovsky, Serge, *Pourquoi la nouvelle critique*, 113

Doyle, Arthur Conan: *Memories and Adventures*, 105; Sherlock Holmes series, 61, 62–63, 64–65

Dufourmentelle, Anne, *Fighting Theory* (with Ronell), 203

Eco, Umberto, 105–6

Ecole des Hautes Etudes en Sciences Sociales (EHESS), 9

Elam, Keir, 71

Elsinck, Henk, 60; *Murder by Fax*, 60

emplotment, 13, 25, 212n16; in media sagas, 101

English narratologists: and cognitivist essays, 24; continued research in the 1960s and 1970s, 1; and convergence with French research, 2; functionalist paradigms of, 11–12, 16–17; and successful novels, 23

Enunciate: in Barthes, 114–15; description of, 179; understanding through semiotics of, 144; use of term, 114n5

enunciation: in discourse analysis, 132; mediating role of, 118–24; positioning of, 125; relationship with narrative poems, 179; and scene of enunciation, 127–30; theory of, 112, 112n2, 114–15, 118–24, 140, 179, 179n14. *See also* Pindar's Fourth *Pythian Ode*

epigraphs, 57–58, 57n4

errors in narrative, 56, 64–65, 66

European Narratology Network, 211

events and eventfulness, 6, 21, 24, 24n13, 78, 78nn13–14, 97

experientiality, 75, 75n6

extradiegetic narrators, 39, 46, 84n23, 130

fabula: independence of narrative planning from, 26; and narrative discourse, 77; and plots, 12–13; as representation in reader's mind, 15; in Russian formalism, 116

Fayol, Michel, 24, 26

feuilleton, 93, 107n13

fiction: claims against, 202, 202n5; compared to documentary communication, 160–62; criticism of the pleasure of, 206; defining, 162–64, 168–70; expanded field of, 160 fig. 1; fictionality, 212–13; fictitious *versus* fictional, 60n7, 65; framing of, 64, 67, 164–66; illocutions attributed to author, 37–38; mimetic and axiomatic, 159; and mode of communication, 159; as narrative, 157; nonmimetic and simulation games, 158–60; problematic fictionality, 156–58; role of author in, 49; sociological issues in framing of, 167–68; theory of, 155–56, 157, 212–13

fictional world, access to, 36–37

Field, Andrew, 67

Fillion, Nathan, 64n13

film genre: narrators in, 72–73; serial forms of, 93

Fish, Stanley, 55

Flaubert, Gustave, *Madame Bovary*, 65–66

Fludernik, Monika: and experientiality, 75nn6–7; and historical dimensions of research, 215; natural narratology of, 14; and playscripts, 77; *Towards a 'Natural' Narratology*, 75–76

focalization, 71, 87, 87n26

Fontanille, Jacques, 23, 139; *Pratiques sémiotiques*, 145. *See also under* Greimas, Algirdas Julien

formalism, critiques of, 17

Foucault, Michel: *L'archéologie du savoir*, 127n17; critique of intellectual trend of, 201–2

framing and frame theory: and defining fiction, 162–64; for documentary and simulation games, 162–64; importance of, 8; sociological problems with framing instructions, 167–68; top-down and bottom-up fictional framing, 164–66

France: literary research in, 212–13; narratologists in, 212; reorganization of academia in, 208–9, 210. *See also* French discourse analysis; French narratology; French structuralist theory; French Theory

Frasca, Gonzalo, 159–60

French discourse analysis: approaches to, 114; Bakhtin and, 121–24; Benveniste and, 118–21; centrality of genre to, 125; as context-oriented, 112, 120, 132; description of, 111–12; emergence of, 112–13; as framework for narratology, 24; *langue versus parole* in, 116–18, 119; mediating role of enunciation in, 118–24; modes of genericity in, 130–31; priority to text and discourse in, 115–16, 119–20, 132; and scenes of enunciation, 127–30; self-constituting discourses and, 126–27; speech genres in, 124–26. *See also* structuralism

French narratology: and formalism, 11; language of scholarly work in, 24; objectivist *versus* functionalist perspectives, 11–16; and postclassical narratology, 2, 3; resurgence of interest in, 2, 137; shift to author-reader interaction, 11; and structuralism, 1–2; and tension in canonized literature, 28; websites, research centers, and seminars on, 9

French structuralist theory: functional conceptions in, 16–22; functionalism in plot dynamics in, 18; narrative discourse in, 77

French Theory: decline of, 204; hegemonic position of, 201–2; and literary knowledge, 210; opposition to, 201n1; parody of, 214n23; policing of scholarship by, 202, 203; political context of, 205–6, 205n11

Frye, Northrop, 118

functionalist approaches. *See* Sternberg, Meir

functionalist paradigms: cognitivism and, 24; compared with objectivist paradigms, 12–16; in French structuralist theory, 16–22; incorporation of objectivist paradigms with, 23; minimization of, 22–23; in textual linguistics and discourse analysis, 24–27

games: board, quest, and video games, 157; framing and frame theory for, 162–64; with logical-mathematical "engine," 156, 215; nonmimetic and simulation games in fiction, 158–60, 169

Gass, William, *Willie Masters' Lonesome Wife*, 59n6

Gaudreault, André, 73

Gaut, Berys, 35, 36

generic scenes, 128, 129, 130

genericity: impact on textuality, 107, 107n11; modes of, 130–31; routine and auctorial, 126, 127, 128–29, 132. *See also* discourse analysis; speech genres; suspended narrative

Genette, Gérard: attribution of epigraphs, 57n4; autodiegetic narrators, 81; Barthes as reference for, 45; and covert errors in narrative theory, 46; definition of narrative metalepsis, 84n23; and developments in narrative theory, 17, 22, 211; *Discours du récit*, 54; intentionality, 77n12; interpretation of paralipsis, 21; narrative model of, 49, 50; and narrative planning, 26; narrativity and immanence in, 138; narrator's existence in theater, 72; *Nouveau discours du récit*, 110; *Seuils*, 54; technical vocabulary of, 207; and work of Ricoeur, 2. See also immanence

Gervais, Bertrand, 24, 24n14

global scenes, 128, 129, 130

Goffman, Erving, *Frame Analysis*, 162, 164, 167

Greece, ancient: development of Cyrene, 172–74, 172n1, 179; Greek poetry in, 179n14; myths and legendary history in, 8; myths and legendary history of, 172, 174, 175–76; poetic forms in, 175n5, 176; way of telling history in, 173–74. See also Pindar; Pindar's Fourth *Pythian Ode*

Greimas, Algirdas Julien: actants and actors in theory of, 178; approach to discourse analysis of, 114; *Dictionary* (*Sémiotique. Dictionnaire raisonné de la théorie du langage*) (with Courtés), 138, 140–41, 143, 146; on discourse and narrativity, 142; *Du Sens II*, 139, 141; and Ricoeur's work, 2; *Sémantique structurale*, 146; and semio-narrative system, 177; semiotics theory of, 23; *Sémiotique des passions* (with Fontanille), 146

Grivel, Charles, 22; *Production de l'intérêt romanesque*, 21

Hamburger, Käte: and horizon of retrospection, 44, 45; no narrator theory of, 32, 34; and pan-narrator theory, 34; theory of fiction of, 161, 162; and theory on first-person novels, 49

Handbook of Narratology (Hühn, Meister, Pier, and Schmid), 211

Harris, Zellig S., 114

Harry Reid example, analysis of, 12–13, 19, 21

Hauthal, Janine, 85

Herman, David, 14, 17, 78–79, 117n7, 120–21

hermeneutics: Barthes and hermeneutic codes, 16, 20–22, 27; and current research, 213, 216; and dramatic performance, 83; and French Theory, 201n1; and Ricoeur, 2, 206, 212, 213

heterodiegetic narrators, 39, 41, 42, 46, 63

Hildesheimer, Wolfgang: *Marbot. Eine Biografie*, 128; *Sir Andrew Marbot*, 156–57, 169

Histoire des théories linguistiques Laboratory, 47

historic-legendary traditions, 175

historical research on concepts in narrative theory: narrative model in, 48–50; on principles, 47–48

Hollywood, 164–65

Holmesology, 62–63, 64–65

homodiegetic narrators, 46, 66

horizon of retrospection in narrative theory, 43–45

Houellebecq, Michel, 142

Hühn, Peter, 78n13

humanities research and neoliberal reforms, 209

ideological values in literary theories, 22

immanence: in approach to structural analysis, 113; and context, 7; *Don Quixote*'s regimes of, 149–52, 153; in early narratological work, 138; in fiction, 45; Genette's work in, 54; key concept of, 141, 141n3; and narrativity, 7; plane of, 139–40; principle of, 139–40, 143, 143n4; from principle to planes of, 144–48; regimes of, 7, 147–49, 152–53; and structures of narrativity, 139, 143–44, 148–49; as theoretical and methodological requirement, 153

intentionality, 14, 24, 77, 77n12, 78

International Society for the Study of Narrative, 211

interpretation: and context, 117; and cultural history, 164; and deconstruction, 202; and framing, 164, 165, 173, 178; functional, 19, 21, 26; and interface with narratology, 213; multiplicity of, 56; narrators and boundaries of, 86; in optional narrator-theory, 40, 42; uncertainty of, 65. See also paratexts

intradiegetic narrators, 46

isotopy, 114, 178

Jahn, Manfred, 74, 76
Japanese theater, 84, 85n24
Jouve, Vincent, 207

Kafka, Franz, *Amerika*, 55–56, 56n3, 66
Kania, Andrew, 35–37, 40–42, 46, 49, 50
Kaufmann, Vincent, 204, 204n8, 206, 207n13
Kelleter, Frank, *The Media of Serial Narrative*, 92n1
Kellogg, Robert, 36
Kindt, Tom, 211–12, 216n24
Kirsch, Adam, 56, 66
Köppe, Tilmann, and Jan Stühring, 35–42, 44, 46, 49–50
Kuroda, S.-Y., 32–35, 44–45, 49, 50

Laboratoire Interdisciplinaire Récits Cultures Sociétés (LIRCES), 9
Laermans, Rudi, 83
Larivaille, Paul, 27
Lauwers, Jan: background of, 80; *Le Désir*, 81, 81n18; dramaturgic choices of, 70; *Images of Affection*, 81–82, 83, 86, 87; *Integral Version*, 81; Shakespearean works of, 86; *Snakesong Trilogy*, 81, 83, 86–87; use of meta-theatrical narrators, 85
LeCompte, Elizabeth, 70, 80, 84, 85. *See also* Wooster Group
Lévi-Strauss, Claude, "The Structure of Myth," 110
linguistics: immanence as foundation of, 143; theories, history of, 32, 47–48. *See also* text linguistics
literary history, expansion of, 210
literary theory: decline of, 202, 202n6; effect of neoliberal reforms to academia on, 208–9; formalization of, 207–8; narratology as model for, 8–9, 212; principles toward collaboration and shareability in, 214–16; and promise for, 216–17; rise and fall of, 204–7; uniform standards for research in, 217; warlike rhetoric of theorists, 203–4; weaknesses of, 215
Little Nemo in Slumberland, 96
Lotman, Yuri, 78n13

Maigret novels, 66
Maingueneau, Dominique: *Contexte de l'oeuvre littéraire*, 112n2; *Dictionnaire d'analyse du discours* (with Charaudeau), 111; enunciation and scenography, 129; modes of genericity identified by, 131; *Pragmatique pour le discours littéraire*, 112n2; self-constituting discourses, 126, 127, 127n17; on speech genres, 124–26; on structuralism, 113; on text and context, 120
Mann, Klaus, 56n3
Margolin, Uri, 37, 42, 44, 47; "Necessarily a Narrator or Narrator if Necessary," 34
Marx, William, 207
Maziarczyk, Grzegorz, 59n6
media, and status of literature, 207, 207n13
media sagas: beginnings and endings of, 98; closure of episodes in, 103; description of, 6; recurrent elements in, 99–100; and suspended narratives, 93; suture markers in, 101
mega-narrators, 73
memoirs, and concept of narrator, 45–46
Merleau-Ponty, Maurice, 142
metalanguage, 121
metalepsis: in *Don Quixote*, 62; and frame theory, 169; narrative, 84n23, 86, 215–16; as paradoxical phenomenon, 215; and paratexts' influence on narrative, 96; in postdramatic performance, 62
metalingvistika, 121
meta-novels, 151, 152
mimetic representation: and aesthetic tension, 28; fiction and, 7, 159; and nonmimetic forms of narratives, 7
Moirand, Sophie, 100
Monfort, Bruno, 106
Morsillo, Sandrine, 166
Murder by Fax, 66
Murdoch, Iris, *The Red and the Green*, 161
Murray, Janet, 157
myth as invented concept, 174–75

Nabokov, Vladimir, *Pale Fire*, 66–67, 67n16
narrative interest: book on, 21; functionalist approaches to, 13; hermeneutic and pro-

airetic codes' function in, 20, 20n12; and interplay between temporal sequence and teleology of narrative, 15–16; in literary didactics, 28n18; suspense and curiosity, 19 (*see also* narrative tension); waning interest in, 22–23

Narrative Matters (conference), 137

narrative tension: in all literatures, 27–28; Bronckart's view on, 25–26; and instabilities, 20n12; and plots, 178; suspense and, 24n13, 24n14. *See also* Baroni, Raphaël

narrative theory: factors affecting, 2–3; history of concepts in, 47–50

narrative turn: development of, 2, 8, 202, 211; and postclassical narratology, 110

narratives: autonomy of, 55; macropropositions in, 13; in media besides literature, 2n1, 3–4; multilevel temporality of, 94

narrativity: Greimas and, 136; and narrative interests, 13; objectivist *versus* constructive paradigms in, 16; relationship with narrative discourse, 78; and semiotic conception of meaning, 139; shift from strict narratology to, 139, 140–42; Sternberg's definition of, 14; as tool in analyzing narrative discourse, 78–79, 78n14

narratology: affinities of French research with, 213; application to theater, 71–72; capacity for meta-theoretical reflection, 216, 216n24, 217; challenges in, 3–4, 4n5; collaborative and transdisciplinary approaches in, 210–11; conceptual frameworks and terminology of, 215; effect of interpretation on narratives, 65; history of concept of narrators, 45–47; learning from sociology of fictional framing, 169; rapid development of, 202; relationship with paratextual studies, 67; and renewal of literary knowledge, 209–10; rhetorical school of, 1, 3, 22, 212–13; risks of overextension of field of, 211; as a self-critical discipline, 4; terminological issues in, 116. *See also* academia, neoliberal reform of; classical narratology; discourse analysis; fiction; immanence; literary theory; narrativity; paratexts; Pindar's Fourth *Pythian Ode*; postclassical narratology; structural narratology; suspended narrative; theater

narrators: presenter figure in theater and film, 72; in the role of author of the book, 61–64; in theatrical narratives and performances, 71, 72–73, 73n3, 76n11, 82, 87; as theatrical stylistic devices, 80–87; types of, 80–81

Needcompany, 70, 80, 86

New Literary History, changing attitudes in, 204

Nielsen, Henrik Skov, 33

Nietzschean typology of illusion, 148

no-narrator theory, 32–33, 35. *See also* optional-narrator theory

Nouvelle critique, 112–13

novels: that question narrative illusions of their narrative, 151; twofold dimension of, 54

Nünning, Ansgar, 117n9

objectivist paradigms, compared to functionalist paradigms, 12–16, 23

optional-narrator theory and theorists: adoption of term, 33; on analytic argument for pan-narrative theory, 35–36; on argument from mediation for pan-narrative theory, 39–40; on blocked inference argument for pan-narrative theory, 37–38; on distinction of fiction argument for pan-narrative theory, 38–39; and errors concerning history of concept of narrator, 45–47; existence of narrators in first-person fiction, 50; first and second generations of, 5; historical perspectives in work of, 43–47, 50; need for further analysis, 42; on ontological gap argument for pan-narrator theory, 36–37; positive arguments for, 40–43. *See also* pan-narrator theory

O'Sullivan, Sean, 105n9

Oura, Yasusuke, 168

pan-narrator theory: analytic argument for, 35–36; argument from mediation for, 39; blocked inference argument for, 37–38; challenges to, 31, 33–35, 49; critique of, 5; description of, 33; distinction of fiction argument for, 38–39; narrators in first-person fiction, 50; need for further analysis, 42; ontological gap argument for, 36–37. *See also* optional-narrator theory and theorists

parafictionalization, 65–67

paralipsis, 21

paratexts: effect on narrative of, 56–57, 58, 59, 60; errors in narratives, 64–65; narrators in the role of authors, 61–64; readers of the book in the book, 62; segregation from the narrative, 57–58; as site of negotiation among extratextual agents, 54–55. *See also* meta-novels

paratextual studies, 5, 55, 67

paratopy, 127

Paris Center for Narrative Matters, 9, 211

Pascal, Blaise, *Provinciales*, 131

Passalacqua, Franco, 16

Patron, Sylvie, 44; *Introduction à la narratologie postclassique*, 3

Pavel, Thomas, 71, 212–13

Pavis, Patrice, 74n4

Pelc, Jerzy, 65

performance studies, 74n4

performances: as distinct from scripts, 74, 76n10; as narrative discourse, 75–79, 75n5, 87; problems of narrator's discourse in, 81–82

peritextual fiction, 64

Petitjean, André, "Le récit en questions," 3

Pfister, Manfred, 71

Phelan, James, 15n7, 20n12, 212

Pianzola, Federico, 16

Pier, John, 24, 59n6, 110, 114n4, 116

Pindar: isotopies from poems of, 178; *Pythian Odes*, 173; theory of enunciation applied to, 179–81; use of melic verse, 176

Pindar's Fourth *Pythian Ode*: autochthony in, 192–94; isotopies and gendered metaphors regarding Cyrene in, 189–92, 190n25, 191nn26–28, 196, 198; narrative divergences and tensions in, 185–88; narrative reorientation in, 185–86; overview of narrative development of, 197–98; from performance to story and back in, 180, 188; semantic development in, 188–89, 196; temporal, spatial, and schematic analysis of, 180–89; triad of gods in founding and civilizing Cyrene in, 195–96, 195nn34–35, 196nn37–38

Plato, *Republic*, 159

plot: Adam on narrative tension and sequence in, 25; canonic narrative schema in, 177; completeness and closure in, 15; complication in, 27; dynamics of, 18, 18n11, 27–28; and events, 78n13; narrative sequence in, 11, 17, 17n9, 25, 27; and narrative tension, 178; objectivist *versus* functionalist perspectives on, 12–13, 13n3; as outdated concept, 22–23; *versus* progression of a narrative, 15n7; reconceptualization of, 23–24; and terminological issues, 116. *See also* narrative tension

poetic discourse: canonic narrative schema in, 177; cultural representation in, 178–79, 198; narrative development in, 177; syntactic and semantic dimensions of, 177–78; and twofold dimension of texts, 54. *See also* Pindar's Fourth *Pythian Ode*

point of view, 71

Pôle de Narratologie Transmédiale (NaTrans), 9

Polkinghorne, Donald, *Narrative Knowing and the Human Sciences*, 137–38

postclassical narratology: association with structuralism, 212; as context-oriented, 110; and discourse analysis, 24; and francophone narratology, 2; interest among French speakers in, 3; and pan-narrator theories, 5; research in, 1; rise of, 211; and theories of fiction, 213; varieties of, 117n9

postdramatic theater: dramatic potential of narrative in, 88; narrative discourse in, 71, 73–79, 83, 87. *See also* Lauwers, Jan; LeCompte, Elizabeth; narrators; Needcompany; theater; Wooster Group

poststructuralism, 211, 212–13

Poulet, Georges, *Les Chemins actuels de la critique*, 113

pragmatics: Bakhtin and, 121; in classical narratology, 22; conceptions of, 176–77; and discourse analysis, 112; emphasis on, 11. *See also* functionalist paradigms

Prince, Gerald, 117

proairetic codes, 27

prolepsis, 94, 177

Propp, Vladimir, 17, 18, 27, 141, 150

Proust, Marcel, 113; *Á la Recherche du temps perdu*, 22; *Contre Sainte-Beuve*, 112

Race, William H., 180

Rasputin and the Empress trial, 164–65

readers: and completeness of suspended narratives, 96; expectations of, 12, 13; and interactions with authors, 11; and limits of the fictional frame, 64–65; and narrativization of texts, 12, 14; and need for resolution, 15; parafictionalization by, 65–67; paratexts and horizon of expectations, 55; paratextual experience of the narrative, 57, 59; reeducation of, 206; relationship with discourse, 5, 11, 15, 26, 27; and suspended narratives, 102, 104, 105–6

reality, principle of, 144, 177

Réseau des Narratologues Francophones (RéNaF), 9

Revaz, Françoise, 215

Ricardou, Jean, 22; *Les lieux-dits*, 58; *La Prise de Constantinople*, 58, 66

Richard, Jean-Pierre, 113

Richardson, Brian, 80–81, 81nn16–17

Richardson, Samuel, *Pamela*, 129–30, 130n22, 131

Ricoeur, Paul: and hermeneutics of suspicion, 206; influence on Gervais's work, 24; notion of emplotment, 212n16; on structural analysis of narrative, 114n5, 212; *Temps et récit*, 138, 212; and theories of fiction, 213; and time, 173n2; use of work by Greimas and Genette, 2

Robbe-Grillet, Alain, 22

Romanticism, 112–13, 124n13

Ronell, Avital, 206; *Fighting Theory* (with Dufourmentelle), 203

Rulfo, Juan, *Pedro Páramo*, 43

Russian formalism, 17, 116, 202n6

Ryan, Marie-Laure: and "non-narrator theory," 32, 33; and panfictionality, 156; stages of narrativity of, 78–79; study of fictionality by, 157, 163; and transcending nature of narrative, 2n1, 215

Sabry, Randa, 57

Saint-Gelais, Richard, 157

Salmon, Christian, *Storytelling*, 2, 2n3, 137

Samoyault, Tiphaine, 201n2

Saussure, Ferdinand de: Benveniste's departure from work of, 119; formulation of *langue* and *parole* of, 117, 117nn7–9, 123, 132; sense through difference, 141n3

scenes of enunciation: in discourse analysis, 132; scenography, 128–31, 128n20; types of, 127–28, 129

Schaeffer, Jean-Marie: and intentionality, 77n12; on reorganization of academia, 210; study of fictionality by, 157, 162, 212–13; and successful narratives, 96

Schechner, Richard, 74n4, 76n10; Performance Group of, 80

schema theory, 17n9

Schmid, Wolf, 78n13

Schmidt, Paul, 84

Scholes, Robert, 36

science fiction novels, 58–59

Scrutton, Lord Justice, 165

Searle, John R., 49, 64, 77n12, 162, 163; "The Logical Status of Fictional Discourse," 161

Segal, Charles, 188

Segal, Eyal, 13

segmentation, 57

segmentation of narratives: and influence on narratives, 5, 57–58; method of distributionalism, 114; numbered and titled chapters, 103. *See also* suspended narrative

self-constituting discourses, 126–27, 129, 131, 132

semantic and syntactic analysis: role of pragmatics in, 178–79; and semantic unity, 99–100

semio-narrative approaches to narrative, 176–80

semiotics: and current research, 138–39; first didactic presentation of, 136n1; Fresca's conception of, 159–60; growth of discipline of, 141; interdefinition of concepts in, 146; modality in, 141, 142; of narrative structures, 140; and narrativity, 7; narrativity in, 136–37, 142; pragmatic environs of, 143, 143n4; principle of reality in, 144. *See also* immanence

sentences: Saussure's description of, 117. *See also* Bakhtin, Mikhail; Benveniste, Émile; discourse analysis serial novels, 93

serial *versus* series, 105–6, 105n9

Shen, Dan, 11

Simenon, Georges, Maigret novels of, 63–64

simiotics, 159–60

Sokal, Alan, 214; *Impostures intellectuelles* (with Bricmont), 214n23

Sollers, Philippe, "Logique de la fiction," 202n5

speech genres: and addressivity, 122; and ancient rhetoric, 124n13; characteristics of, 123; and enunciation, 127–28, 132; refinements to category of, 125

Spitzer, Leo, *Stilstudien*, 112

Stanzel, Franz Karl, 72

Starobinski, Jean, 113

Stegner, Page, 67

Sternberg, Meir, 13–14, 15, 17

Stoker, Bram, *Dracula*, 37

story: story/discourse paradigm, 77, 115–16, 123; and storyworlds, 12, 14–15, 17. *See also* narrative tension; plot

storytelling, 27, 137

storytelling narrators, 41

structural narratology: and codification in secondary education, 212; in France, 110–11; French discourse analysis and, 112; and *langue*, 117n9; transdisciplinarity in, 2. *See also* classical narratology

structuralism: age of, 112; analysis beyond the sentence, 114n5; and growth of discourse analysis, 113; in linguistics, 117n8; nostalgia for, 208; technical vocabulary of, 207

Strugatsky, Arkady and Boris, *Beetle in the Anthill*, 57–58, 58n5

Stühring, Jan. *See* Köppe, Tilmann, and Jan Stühring

Sue, Eugène, *Le Morneau-Diable ou l'Aventurier*, 93

suspended narrative: autonomy of episodes in, 101–2; boundary lines in, 98–99; coherence of episodes in, 101–5; description of, 6; distinctions between "serial" and "series," 105–6, 105n9, 106n10; fragmented unity in, 96–97; interest in, 92n1; multilevel temporality in, 94–96; overview of, 93–94; semantic unity in, 99–100; suture markers and cotextuality in, 100–101; as transmedial genre, 105n10, 106–7

suspense, 19, 20n12, 21, 24

Swiss National Scientific Research Fund, 93

"Tarzan" (*Vaillant*), 103–4

Tel Quel group, 204, 205, 207

television shows, 93, 105n10, 107n13, 131

text linguistics: and discourse analysis, 112, 112n2, 132; narratology and, 119; and structural analysis, 114n5; text-structure and text-products in, 114–15, 119; theories of enunciation and utterance as complementary to, 123. *See also* discourse analysis; utterance, theory of

theater: and distinctions between texts and performances, 74, 74n4; enactment and performance as narrative discourse in, 75–79; existence of narrators in, 74–75; narrative function in, 6, 73, 76–77, 76n11, 77, 79, 84; narrators as meta-theatrical tools in, 84–87; narrators as organizers and commentators in, 83–85; as object of narratological study, 71–73; onstage narrators in, 80–83; spectators of as narratees, 76–77, 85, 88; weakening of narrators in, 86–87

theater scripts, 74, 75, 76

thematic criticism, 113

Thomson-Jones, Katherine, 35, 36, 37, 39

thrillers, 60

Thucydides, 175–76

Todorov, Tzvetan: "Les catégories du récit littéraire," 116; on detective novels, 61n9; and developments in narrative theory, 22; narrativity and immanence in, 138; on *sjuzhet* and plot, 18n11; on suspense and curiosity, 19; on technical vocabulary for literary theory, 207; translation of "Thematics," 18

Tomashevsky, Boris, 19, 26; "Thematics," 18

transdisciplinarity, 214–15

translinguistics, 114, 114n4, 119, 123, 132

transmedial and transgeneric forms of narration, 210, 215

transtextual cotextuality, 101

Trowler, Paul, 210

true art, 23

type A models. *See* objectivist paradigms

type B models. *See* functionalist paradigms
typography, 58–60

Ubersfeld, Anne, 74n4
University of Paris Diderot, 137
utterance, theory of, 122, 123, 132. *See also* enunciation, theory of

Valk, Kate, 82, 83–85, 85n24, 86
Vanhaesebrouck, Karel, 75n5
video game industry, 165
violence of language, 201–2, 201–2n3

Walsh, Richard: and blocked inference argument, 37–38; challenge to pan-narrator theory of, 34–35, 38–39; and co-presence, 44; and fictional narrators, 42, 44–46, 49, 212; view of relationship between discourse and *fabula*, 77

War of the Worlds, The, 166
Weinrich, Harald, 98
Welles, Orson, adaptation of *The War of the Worlds*, 166
White, Hayden, 212n16
Williams, Tennessee, *The Glass Menagerie*, 80
Wilson, George, 37, 40, 44
Wolf, Werner, 78–79
Wooster Group, 70, 80, 81–82; *Brace Up!*, 83–85, 85n24; *Frank Dell's the Temptation of Saint Antony*, 82, 82n21; *To You the Birdie! (Phèdre)*, 84–85

Yale School of criticism, 204

Zilberberg, Claude, 23
Zola, Émile, 124–25

THEORY AND INTERPRETATION OF NARRATIVE

JAMES PHELAN, PETER J. RABINOWITZ, AND KATRA BYRAM, SERIES EDITORS

Because the series editors believe that the most significant work in narrative studies today contributes both to our knowledge of specific narratives and to our understanding of narrative in general, studies in the series typically offer interpretations of individual narratives and address significant theoretical issues underlying those interpretations. The series does not privilege one critical perspective but is open to work from any strong theoretical position.

Contemporary French and Francophone Narratology edited by John Pier

We-Narratives: Collective Storytelling in Contemporary Fiction by Natalya Bekhta

Debating Rhetorical Narratology: On the Synthetic, Mimetic, and Thematic Aspects of Narrative by Matthew Clark and James Phelan

Environment and Narrative: New Directions in Econarratology edited by Erin James and Eric Morel

Unnatural Narratology: Extensions, Revisions, and Challenges edited by Jan Alber and Brian Richardson

A Poetics of Plot for the Twenty-First Century: Theorizing Unruly Narratives by Brian Richardson

Playing at Narratology: Digital Media as Narrative Theory by Daniel Punday

Making Conversation in Modernist Fiction by Elizabeth Alsop

Narratology and Ideology: Negotiating Context, Form, and Theory in Postcolonial Narratives edited by Divya Dwivedi, Henrik Skov Nielsen, and Richard Walsh

Novelization: From Film to Novel by Jan Baetens

Reading Conrad by J. Hillis Miller, Edited by John G. Peters and Jakob Lothe

Narrative, Race, and Ethnicity in the United States edited by James J. Donahue, Jennifer Ann Ho, and Shaun Morgan

Somebody Telling Somebody Else: A Rhetorical Poetics of Narrative by James Phelan

Media of Serial Narrative edited by Frank Kelleter

Suture and Narrative: Deep Intersubjectivity in Fiction and Film by George Butte

The Writer in the Well: On Misreading and Rewriting Literature by Gary Weissman

Narrating Space / Spatializing Narrative: Where Narrative Theory and Geography Meet by Marie-Laure Ryan, Kenneth Foote, and Maoz Azaryahu

Narrative Sequence in Contemporary Narratology edited by Raphaël Baroni and Françoise Revaz

The Submerged Plot and the Mother's Pleasure from Jane Austen to Arundhati Roy by Kelly A. Marsh

Narrative Theory Unbound: Queer and Feminist Interventions edited by Robyn Warhol and Susan S. Lanser

Unnatural Narrative: Theory, History, and Practice by Brian Richardson

Ethics and the Dynamic Observer Narrator: Reckoning with Past and Present in German Literature by Katra A. Byram

Narrative Paths: African Travel in Modern Fiction and Nonfiction by Kai Mikkonen

The Reader as Peeping Tom: Nonreciprocal Gazing in Narrative Fiction and Film by Jeremy Hawthorn

Thomas Hardy's Brains: Psychology, Neurology, and Hardy's Imagination by Suzanne Keen

The Return of the Omniscient Narrator: Authorship and Authority in Twenty-First Century Fiction by Paul Dawson

Feminist Narrative Ethics: Tacit Persuasion in Modernist Form by Katherine Saunders Nash

Real Mysteries: Narrative and the Unknowable by H. Porter Abbott

A Poetics of Unnatural Narrative edited by Jan Alber, Henrik Skov Nielsen, and Brian Richardson

Narrative Discourse: Authors and Narrators in Literature, Film, and Art by Patrick Colm Hogan

An Aesthetics of Narrative Performance: Transnational Theater, Literature, and Film in Contemporary Germany by Claudia Breger

Literary Identification from Charlotte Brontë to Tsitsi Dangarembga by Laura Green

Narrative Theory: Core Concepts and Critical Debates by David Herman, James Phelan and Peter J. Rabinowitz, Brian Richardson, and Robyn Warhol

After Testimony: The Ethics and Aesthetics of Holocaust Narrative for the Future edited by Jakob Lothe, Susan Rubin Suleiman, and James Phelan

The Vitality of Allegory: Figural Narrative in Modern and Contemporary Fiction by Gary Johnson

Narrative Middles: Navigating the Nineteenth-Century British Novel edited by Caroline Levine and Mario Ortiz-Robles

Fact, Fiction, and Form: Selected Essays by Ralph W. Rader edited by James Phelan and David H. Richter

The Real, the True, and the Told: Postmodern Historical Narrative and the Ethics of Representation by Eric L. Berlatsky

Franz Kafka: Narration, Rhetoric, and Reading edited by Jakob Lothe, Beatrice Sandberg, and Ronald Speirs

Social Minds in the Novel by Alan Palmer

Narrative Structures and the Language of the Self by Matthew Clark

Imagining Minds: The Neuro-Aesthetics of Austen, Eliot, and Hardy by Kay Young

Postclassical Narratology: Approaches and Analyses edited by Jan Alber and Monika Fludernik

Techniques for Living: Fiction and Theory in the Work of Christine Brooke-Rose by Karen R. Lawrence

Towards the Ethics of Form in Fiction: Narratives of Cultural Remission by Leona Toker

Tabloid, Inc.: Crimes, Newspapers, Narratives by V. Penelope Pelizzon and Nancy M. West

Narrative Means, Lyric Ends: Temporality in the Nineteenth-Century British Long Poem by Monique R. Morgan

Understanding Nationalism: On Narrative, Cognitive Science, and Identity by Patrick Colm Hogan

Joseph Conrad: Voice, Sequence, History, Genre edited by Jakob Lothe, Jeremy Hawthorn, James Phelan

The Rhetoric of Fictionality: Narrative Theory and the Idea of Fiction by Richard Walsh

Experiencing Fiction: Judgments, Progressions, and the Rhetorical Theory of Narrative by James Phelan

Unnatural Voices: Extreme Narration in Modern and Contemporary Fiction by Brian Richardson

Narrative Causalities by Emma Kafalenos

Why We Read Fiction: Theory of Mind and the Novel by Lisa Zunshine

I Know That You Know That I Know: Narrating Subjects from Moll Flanders *to* Marnie by George Butte

Bloodscripts: Writing the Violent Subject by Elana Gomel

Surprised by Shame: Dostoevsky's Liars and Narrative Exposure by Deborah A. Martinsen

Having a Good Cry: Effeminate Feelings and Pop-Culture Forms by Robyn R. Warhol

Politics, Persuasion, and Pragmatism: A Rhetoric of Feminist Utopian Fiction by Ellen Peel

Telling Tales: Gender and Narrative Form in Victorian Literature and Culture by Elizabeth Langland

Narrative Dynamics: Essays on Time, Plot, Closure, and Frames edited by Brian Richardson

Breaking the Frame: Metalepsis and the Construction of the Subject by Debra Malina

Invisible Author: Last Essays by Christine Brooke-Rose

Ordinary Pleasures: Couples, Conversation, and Comedy by Kay Young

Narratologies: New Perspectives on Narrative Analysis edited by David Herman

Before Reading: Narrative Conventions and the Politics of Interpretation by Peter J. Rabinowitz

Matters of Fact: Reading Nonfiction over the Edge by Daniel W. Lehman

The Progress of Romance: Literary Historiography and the Gothic Novel by David H. Richter

A Glance Beyond Doubt: Narration, Representation, Subjectivity by Shlomith Rimmon-Kenan

Narrative as Rhetoric: Technique, Audiences, Ethics, Ideology by James Phelan

Misreading Jane Eyre: *A Postformalist Paradigm* by Jerome Beaty

Psychological Politics of the American Dream: The Commodification of Subjectivity in Twentieth-Century American Literature by Lois Tyson

Understanding Narrative edited by James Phelan and Peter J. Rabinowitz

Framing Anna Karenina: Tolstoy, the Woman Question, and the Victorian Novel by Amy Mandelker

Gendered Interventions: Narrative Discourse in the Victorian Novel by Robyn R. Warhol

Reading People, Reading Plots: Character, Progression, and the Interpretation of Narrative by James Phelan

www.ingramcontent.com/pod-product-compliance
Lightning Source LLC
Chambersburg PA
CBHW030110010526
44116CB00005B/178